F

PR(
VIOLE

DATE DUE

ILL HC17			
63034463			
3/51/10			
MAY 0 3 2013			

Demco, Inc. 38-293

Fourth Edition

PROFILING VIOLENT CRIMES

An Investigative Tool

Ronald M. Holmes
University of Louisville

■ ■ ■ ■ ■ ■

Stephen T. Holmes
University of Central Florida

SAGE

Los Angeles • London • New Delhi • Singapore • Washington DC

For information:

SAGE Publications, Inc.
2455 Teller Road
Thousand Oaks,
   California 91320
E-mail: order@sagepub.com

SAGE Publications India Pvt. Ltd.
B 1/I 1 Mohan Cooperative
   Industrial Area
Mathura Road, New Delhi 110 044
India

SAGE Publications Ltd.
1 Oliver's Yard
55 City Road
London EC1Y 1SP
United Kingdom

SAGE Publications Asia-Pacific
   Pte. Ltd.
33 Pekin Street #02-01
Far East Square
Singapore 048763

Printed in the United States of America

Library of Congress Cataloging-in-Publication Data

Holmes, Ronald M.
Profiling violent crimes: An investigative tool/Ronald M. Holmes, Stephen T. Holmes. — 4th ed.
     p. cm.
Includes bibliographical references and index.
ISBN 978-1-4129-5997-1 (cloth)
ISBN 978-1-4129-5998-8 (pbk.)
   1. Criminal investigation—Psychological aspects. 2. Criminal behavior—Research—Methodology. 3. Criminal methods—Research—Methodology— Case studies. I. Holmes, Stephen T. II. Title.

HV8073.5.H65 2009
364.3—dc22   2008023611

Printed on acid-free paper

09   10   11   12   10 9 8 7 6 5 4 3 2

Acquiring Editor:	Jerry Westby
Editorial Assistant:	Eve Oettinger
Production Editor:	Sarah K. Quesenberry
Copy Editor:	Tony Moore
Proofreader:	Sally Jaskold
Indexer:	Jeanne Busemeyer
Typesetter:	C&M Digitals (P) Ltd.
Cover Designer:	Gail Buschman
Marketing Manager:	Christy Guilbault

Brief Contents

Detailed Contents

Preface

In the last quarter of a century, "psychological profiling" has become a household term. Everyone, it seems, wants to be a profiler. In the classes we teach, students will come up after class and want our advice in the best way to reach their career goals of becoming profilers. Patiently, we hope, we tell them there are several ways. First one could become a federal agent with one of the several agencies that utilize such skills. Another way is to become a police officer, obtain the skills through various assignments and education, and then move into the homicide unit. Or, one could become an academic, align oneself with a police department, and sooner or later, maybe, get the opportunity to profile a case. Most students want to become a profiler immediately, like Harry Potter waving his magic wand inculcating the skills and transferring them into future Robert Resslers. Fortunately, neither Harry, his friends Ron and Hermione, nor even Professor Dumbledore can make this happen. But one can only wish.

Profiling has continued to be popular in the mass media. As stated in the previous editions, the mass media in earlier times has featured characters such as Charlie Chan, Boston Blackie, and, of course, the greatest profiler of all fiction, Sherlock Holmes. The many works of Sir Arthur Conan Doyle illustrated Holmes's many successful profiles and the way he had formed his profiles. The attention to detail is the key. In the TV series *Psych* the main character purports to have special mental powers that help him see the details that others miss.

Usually the profiler is the "law and order" character. Clarice Starling of *Silence of the Lambs* or Will Graham of *Red Dragon*, both written by Thomas Harris, are protagonists. Both are fictional characters with superb skills as profilers. Perhaps the best profiler in Harris's books is the serial killer himself, Hannibal Lecter, profiling from a prison in Oregon. He is the expert because he has been there. He states that the crimes of these violent men (including himself) can only be understood by placing oneself in their fantasies. These fantasies have been explained to us, and some are in the book, so read with care and place yourself in this position when attempting to understand them.

During the past several years, we have profiled more than 600 homicides and rape cases, almost all of which were submitted by police agencies. Although this may appear to be a shift in the faith of these officers in the abilities of the profilers, it must be said that these same agencies seek help from astrologers, psychics, and others who enjoy a similarly dubious reputation with many in the general public and criminal justice system.

Despite the imperfect and sometimes shoddy reputation of many profilers in the business today, we have and will continue to combine the knowledge of both social and forensic sciences. Although no profile is entirely accurate, we have done surprisingly well given the limited information contained in many of the case files that we have worked on. This is not to say we are special; rather, it simply means that by relying on common sense and having a keen sense of perception and an understanding of aberrant behavior, we have been successful. This is not a skill that we have developed on our own. There have been many people who have shed light on what to look for and what to focus on. These people have included many police officers, homicide officers, fellow academics, and many offenders in prison convicted of a plethora of violent offenses. Our interviews have probably taught us more about the ability of getting inside of the perpetrators' heads than any other source. After all, as rational people (although some would argue with that characterization), it is difficult to understand the actions and behaviors of the irrational, unless explained in lay terms and first-hand accounts.

We would also like readers of this fourth edition of this volume to note that throughout the text we often use the term "psychological profiling"; however, what we mean is sociopsychological profiling. Because *sociopsychological* is rather a large and unwieldy term, we often refer to it as psychological profiling, and the reader should keep that in mind. We attach the prefix *socio* because what a thorough profile offers is more than a personality sketch. A thorough profile includes sociodemographic data, which are not usually part of the classic definition of psychological profiling. Age, race, gender, occupation, education, and other factors make up the social core variables addressed in the profiling process.

Since the first edition of this book, much has changed in psychological profiling, and in this edition we have added some materials. We have included a new chapter on Santeria and the occult. With the influx of many into the United States who practice Santeria and Palo Mayombe, crimes resulting from a few practitioners may be easier to understand when one is versed in the faith, dogma, and icons of these faiths. We have deleted the JonBenet Ramsey case and have inserted another case, the unsolved Lizzie Borden murder case. This should be an interesting chapter and can be supplemented with a wealth of information easily accessible on the Internet. We have decided to leave the chapter on Jack the Ripper in this fourth edition, as it is a classic unresolved serial murder. We leave it up to the reader to explore the facts, look at the evidence, and form one's own opinion on who killed Mr. and Mrs. Borden, and who really was Jack the Ripper.

No book is written without the input of others. We have thanked them below and in previous editions, but we are especially indebted to those who have labored in the investigation of the cases we discuss and others that we draw on for our own knowledge.

Chris Anderson, Concorde College

Delores Craig-Moreland, Wichita State University

Stan Crowder, Kennesaw State University

Christopher Hale, Southern Connecticut State University

Chandrika Kelso, National University

Keith F. Killacky, Lewis University

Jo Ann Short, Northern Virginia Community College, Annandale Campus

Without these people and cases, our insight into the field of psychological profiling would be certainly limited.

Ronald M. Holmes
Stephen T. Holmes

1

Psychological Profiling

An Introduction

❖　❖　❖

Historically, crime and criminals have galvanized the attention of law-abiding citizens. Whatever the reason, be it the romance of a Capone or a Dillinger, or the utter lack of any understanding of how or why criminals can do what they do, books, TV, and movies flood the market with police and crime. Russell Vorpagel (1998), an ex-FBI agent, speaks of his own contributions to the development of psychological profiling in the early years with the FBI. In his book, *Profiles in Murder: An FBI Legend Dissects Killers and Their Crimes,* he claims that he along with Ressler, Douglas, and others were pioneers in the process of crime scene analysis. Further, Vorpagel states that he was instrumental in helping Detective Ray Biondi in Sacramento, California, with the Richard Trenton Chase murder case. Unfortunately, Vorpagel was not able to profile Chase's suicide by pills while Chase was in Vacaville prison.

Robert Ressler, another retired FBI agent, speaks of the same Richard Chase case in his book co-authored with Tom Shachtman, *Whoever Fights Monsters* (1992), but with only one line devoted to the help of Vorpagel in developing a separate profile, amazingly similar to Ressler's own: "The fact that Chase so precisely fit the profile that I had drawn up in conjunction with Russ Vorpagel was gratifying to me . . ." (p. 9). Ressler continues to mention other serial killers, such as Ted Bundy, John Wayne Gacy, David Berkowitz, Edmund Kemper, Peter Sutcliffe, Jeffrey Dahmer, and mass killer Richard Speck. Unfortunately there is no mention of an interviewing methodology used in the meetings. Ressler has published another book with Shachtman entitled *I Have Lived in the Monster: Inside the Minds of the World's Most Notorious Serial Killers* (1997). In this book, interesting stories abound that relate to Ressler's work with many serial killers during his career in the FBI.

Not to be outdone, John Douglas and his co-author Mark Olshaker wrote *Mind Hunter: Inside the FBI's Elite Serial Crime Unit* (1995). In this book, Douglas lays claim to a friendship with Thomas Harris, the author of *Red Dragon* (1981), *The Silence of the Lambs* (1988), and *Hannibal* (1999). He takes the reader along the steps in his work in several major cases and the effects that the profiling work has on mind and health. The book jacket claims that he is the model for Jack Crawford in Harris's book *The Silence of the Lambs,* a claim, however, that Harris denies (T. Harris, personal interview, June 20, 2000). The book jacket also says that Douglas has interviewed dozens of serial killers and assassins—Richard Speck, Charles Manson, and James Earl Ray among them. He has published two other books, *The Cases That Haunt Us: From Jack the Ripper to JonBenet Ramsey, the FBI's Legendary Mindhunter Sheds*

Light on the Mysteries That Won't Go Away (Douglas & Olshaker, 2000) and *The Anatomy of Motive: The FBI's Legendary Mindhunter Explores the Key to Understanding and Catching Violent Criminals* (Douglas & Olshaker, 1999). Douglas and his co-author lead the reader through several celebrated unsolved homicides. One is the JonBenet Ramsey case, in which Douglas offers reasons for his belief that JonBenet's parents were not involved in the murder of the young beauty queen. He reacts with some vigor to the criticisms of his own professionalism and reacts to the criticism aimed at him by his former colleagues in the FBI. Douglas also offers a profile of his own on the infamous Jack the Ripper case. Both books address Douglas's law enforcement career and his involvement with serial murderers.

The Evil That Men Do: FBI Profiler Roy Hazelwood's Journey Into the Minds of Sexual Predators is another book written by a retired FBI profiler, Roy Hazelwood, along with Stephen Michaud (2001). Hazelwood was known as a profiler of sexual predators, especially rapists. In this publication, the reader is once again privy to the special talents of the FBI agents and the manner in which they were of aid to police departments across the world in the successful resolution of their cases.

As profilers, we have met many people involved in the field. Some of these encounters have been pleasant and some not. As a general rule, we have found that those who don't advertise their rates in their Web pages are the most reputable. Colleagues like Eric Hickey, Steve Egger, and a few more enjoy favorable reputations in the criminal justice system.

Regardless, there is a tremendous amount of interest in the field of profiling. But we must remember that it is only one tool and by itself has never solved a murder case, despite the statements made by some.

Profilers are often also seen on TV. These shows illustrate the work of a profiler and how neatly the whole crime is resolved in a one-hour program. But unlike a vintage *Dragnet* episode, criminals are not always brought to justice. Every killer is not peacefully arrested with nothing more than an MO or a quick confirmation of the identity of the perpetrator. This MO (method of operation or modus operandi) holds to a basic principle: Each perpetrator commits his crime in a certain manner. Therefore, each time a person commits a crime, he will do it in the same or at least similar fashion. This is a prodigious step in logic, and one that has been validated by tradition and common sense, both, however, less-than-reliable sources of knowledge.

For the homicide investigator, where the motives of normal killings are absent, a psychological profile may be the investigative tool essential to a successful resolution of the case (Douglas & Burgess, 1986; Douglas, Burgess, Burgess, & Ressler 1993; Palmiotto, 1994; Sears, 1991). How accurate are the profiles? This will obviously depend on the expertise of the persons involved in such an assessment. Kocsis, Orwin, and Hayes (2000) reported that profilers appear to have higher skills when compared to other groups. They claim the most accurate groups are, in order of accuracy: professional profilers, psychologists, students, police officers, and self-declared psychics. That psychologists ranked second in the study suggests that psychologists are better at this endeavor than police officers, perhaps because of their understanding of human behavior. The researchers also reported that psychics are the least reliable of the groups. They apparently depend more on the stereotypes of murderers than a true understanding of the mind and mentality of a killer. The research also suggests that police probably would do better at profiling if they were educated in the principles of the process (Peterson, 1997).

Thus profiling, or criminal investigation assessment, is an *educated* attempt to provide investigative agencies with specific information as to the type of individual who committed a certain crime (Geberth, 1981).

Of course, profiles are not suitable in all cases, even in some murder cases (Holmes & Holmes, 1992, 2000). They are usually more efficacious in cases where the unknown perpetrator has displayed indications of psychopathology (Geberth, 2006; Holmes & Holmes, 2000). Crimes most appropriate for psychological profiling are those where discernable patterns are able to be deciphered from the crime scene or where the fantasy/motive of the perpetrator is readily apparent. Table 1.1 suggests a few of these appropriate crimes; however, this list is not exhaustive, and any of these specifically mentioned crimes may not present enough evidence to develop a useful profile.

It is important to come to a general understanding of the type of person who would commit an offense such as a lust murder or spree killing. Inherent within the premise of the validity and reliability of a profile is that the person who commits these crimes has a personality that reflects pathology. In some cases the crimes may be thoroughly planned and executed, as in many of the recent school shooting cases (e.g., Virginia Tech and Northern Illinois). In other crimes, chaos, the lack of planning, mutilations, and other elements reflected in the crime scene are also usually reflective of his/her personality. Therefore, the crime scene itself reflects pathology.

Table 1.1   Crimes Most Suitable for the Development of an Offender
Profile

Suggested Crimes for Profiling
Sadistic sexual assaults
Sexual homicide
Postmortem cases of abuse and humiliation
Motiveless fire settings
Lust and mutilation murders
Rape
Occult and ritualistic crimes
Child sexual abuse including pedophilia
Bank robberies
Anonymous obscene communications

THE SHOOTINGS AT NORTHERN ILLINOIS UNIVERSITY

In February 2008, 27-year-old Steven Kazmierczak, a former graduate student majoring in sociology at Northern Illinois University, entered a lecture hall and shot 21 students and then killed himself. Four females and one male student were killed. The killer carried his weapons in a guitar case. Kazmierczak, well liked by other students and the professors at the university, was reported to have recently stopped taking medication for depression.

There are no known reasons for his action; however, he did have a history of mental problems, and he had been admitted to a psychiatric setting after high school, but he stayed only a short time. He enlisted in the army in 2001 but was discharged 6 months later for unspecified reasons. One possible motive could be that he broke up with his girlfriend a few days previous to the mass murder. Students put up six white crosses on campus in front of the Holmes Student Center; one had no name: Kazmierczak's.

As we will mention later in this text, each offender will leave part of him- or herself at the crime scene. Additionally, we have discovered in the crimes we have profiled for various police departments across the world, now over 600, that offenders commit their crimes in certain manners. If it is a serial crime, the crimes are similar—not always identical, but similar. It is the responsibility of the profiler to offer insight from the physical evidence of the pathology exhibited in the crime scene (Michaud, 1986).

Also worthy of note is the fact the crime profiles are usually completed after the fact. While the police and other public health officials often know that people are not right and are capable of very heinous violence, there is no simple way that we or any psychologist or psychiatrist can predict the future behavior of these offenders. Hence, even the development of a psychological profile of the two most recent school shooters before their murderous events would not have been of much use to police or other officials before they went on their homicidal sprees.

Of course, a good criminal investigative assessment will also depend to some extent on the working relationship between the police agency desiring a profile and the profiler. This should be self-evident, but nonetheless it is important to state and understand. One reason for this is that if the police agency has no faith in the process or the profiler, information may not be included that is vital to the profile itself. This omission can be simply negligence or it could be intentional; hopefully, it is usually unintentional.

THE VIRGINIA TECH SCHOOL SHOOTINGS

On April 16, 2007, 23-year-old Seung Hui Cho killed two students at West Ambler Johnson resident hall and then returned to his dorm room and changed his clothes. He then mailed a package to NBC News in New York containing an 1,800-word diatribe, pictures of himself, and various video clips. He then marched across campus to Norris Hall and chained the three exit doors shut from the inside. In the next 11 minutes, the shooter killed 30 more students and himself, firing between 150 and 200 rounds.

All told, Cho killed 32 students and himself, making this episode one of the most deadly school shooting incidents in the history of the United States.

❖ INDUCTIVE VERSUS DEDUCTIVE PROFILING

There are two different postures to adopt to develop a profile. One is the inductive approach, and the other is the deductive approach. At first glance they seem to be mutually exclusive, but on a closer examination they share some commonalities.

Inductive Criminal Investigative Assessments

The inductive approach to profiling rests with a simple premise, an assumption that if certain crimes committed by different people are similar, then the offenders must also share some type of common personality traits. The information gathered comes from past crimes, past known offenders, and other sources of information, including the media.

There are obvious advantages to this type of profile. It is quick, inexpensive, and there is no need to blend the academic disciplines of sociology, psychology, criminology, and psychiatry. Thus the profiler does not necessarily need any special skill or knowledge of the field of human behavior. For example, this type of profiler would not need to know the work of some of the early pioneers in the field of psychology, such as Sigmund Freud (1856–1939), William James (1842–1910), John Watson (1878–1958), and B. F. Skinner (1904–1990). Their valuable work in human behavior could be ignored, as what happens in the inductive approach is that an assessment of one crime is offered simply from similar crime scenes.

Deductive Criminal Investigative Assessments

This method is slightly different. From a thorough analysis of the crime scene and the evidence left at that scene, the profiler is able to construct a mental picture of the unknown offender. As profilers, we know from experience that one of the most vital elements in the analysis of a crime is victimology. Despite a profiler's request that a police agency disclose all known information about the victim, this is the one element that typically lacks adequate information. The more one knows about the victim, the more one knows about the offender. Thus from this perspective the profile is drawn from the physical and nonphysical (love, hate, rage, fear, etc.) evidence.

The profile drawn from this perspective is agonizingly slow. Much care is taken in the examination of forensic reports, victimology, etc., and the report will take much longer to develop using only this approach. Looking at the crime scene evidence is imperative. This is one problem we have with the profile done for the Ramsey family on the murder of their young daughter, JonBenet. The crime scene was destroyed by the time the profiler was able to develop an assessment. It would have been important to know, for example, the exact positioning of the hands, the manner in which the garrote was found, and the position of the body in relationship to the opening of the door to that small room. There are other questions that needed to be addressed, and the answers could have only been obtained from the examination of the physical evidence present at the scene. The physical evidence will also be an indicator of the nonphysical evidence.

For example, in a southern state an elderly White female was beaten to death in her home. The killer had been in the home when she arrived from a night out with two companions. As she undressed in her unlit bedroom, the killer came upon her from the back and hit her over the head and bludgeoned her to death. From the crime scene it was apparent that the killer had been there for some time, perhaps awaiting her return from an evening of entertainment on the town. He had a bottle of wine sitting in the hallway, and it was uncorked. This victim was an exceptionally clean housekeeper and would not have left that container of spirits in the hallway. The killer felt comfortable enough to drink some of the wine, and he also apparently knew where the bottle had been kept in the pantry. Before she came home, he went into the bedroom and placed pictures in frames of the victim's nieces and nephews facedown in the bedroom.

From the description of this crime scene it is easy to see there is a combination of inductive and deductive reasoning. Knowing something of the academic disciplines of psychology, sociology, criminology, and psychiatry, a clear picture of the mind and mentality of the unknown killer is revealed. Also, we can gather some information from similar cases, when oftentimes the victim is killed by a relative—elderly female, no sexual assault, the picture frames detail—and these other similar cases can educate us to the possible identity of the killer.

Ideally, then, we can use both methods to develop a psychological profile. It is important to use both methods simply because there are benefits to both. One may be quicker to develop, while the other takes more time but can evaluate the unknown offender from a perspective that is different from the other offenders who have committed similar crimes. There are items to bring to the assessment from both the deductive approach and the inductive approach. With the deductive approach, for example, one assumption is that any crime is accompanied by a fantasy. Certainly in looking at the forensic evidence at a similar crime scene, with persons arrested for a similar crime, in the deductive method a profiler can "interpret" the crime scene and examine the fantasy present in the crime scene itself.

While inductive profiling may not be as reliable as the deductive method, there is no reason to ignore the possible benefits derived from the utilization of this method, and combining the benefits of both is truly the correct response.

❖ GOALS IN PROFILING

There is some confusion when the topics of goals and objectives are discussed. Simply stated, goals are broad general statements of what is to be accomplished. Objectives are specific, measurable statements to be accomplished by a given time (Craig, 1980, p. 24). Goals are usually statements individuals or organizations offer to direct their efforts toward some reward. Obviously, these efforts take varied forms. It may be a certain number of units manufactured by a truck plant per time period, or a number of violent personal crimes cleared by arrests. Objectives are the means to be used to satisfy the goals of the organizations, and objectives must be measurable.

Goals in profiling are not distinctly unique. They exist to aid the criminal justice system in its battle against crime. As such, there are three major goals.

Goal 1: To Provide the Criminal Justice System With a Social and Psychological Assessment of the Offender

The purpose of this goal is very simple. It should provide basic and sound information concerning the social and psychological core variables of the offender's personality. This assessment should include race, age range, employment, religion, marital status, education, and so on.

This psychological packet will focus the investigation. Instead of dealing with a wide range of possible perpetrators, the profile will reduce the scope of the investigation. This will have a direct effect on the number of days and weeks spent on the case by positioning the police toward a successful resolution.

A profile contains information that alerts the law enforcement professional to the possible psychological traits present in a crime scene. It can predict future possible attacks as well as probable sites of attacks.

Case Study

Recently a profile was completed for a police department in a southern city where in the course of 4 months four young women were murdered, with their throats cut. None of the four women was sexually molested, but there were several commonalities.

The profile offered information as to the age, education, residence, and a predicted period of time when the perpetrator would strike again. The profile was accurate even to the day that the next attack would occur. The police department, with confidence in the profiling packet, redoubled their efforts with the positive benefit of the apprehension of the attacker on the night predicted.

Goal 2: To Provide the Criminal Justice System With a Psychological Evaluation of Belongings Found in the Possession of the Offender

This particular goal is very important to investigators when they have a prime suspect. It may be that all of the physical evidence, witness reports, and all pertinent information point toward one suspect. The psychological profile may suggest items the offenders may have in their possession: souvenirs, photos, pornography, and so on. These items will serve as a reminder of the violent episode. In the case of a serial pedophile, we are familiar with pedophiles' child pornography collection. By analyzing the collection, the profiler can offer the police interrogator with a plan to interview the alleged offender as to choice of victim, seduction or capturing strategies, and other pertinent information gleaned from the collateral evidence found in the possession of the charged offender. This same statement can be said of other types of offenders undergoing interrogation—offenders such as arsonists, serial killers, and rapists.

Case Study

Jerry Brudos was a serial killer who was sent to the Oregon State Penitentiary for the brutal and sadistic killing of young women in the late 1960s. He died in prison only recently. Brudos had a shoe fetish, and he had stolen a pair of high-heeled black shoes during the course of a robbery and rape. He often wore the shoes around his home and demanded his wife to do the same. One victim, a young National Merit scholar, was forced to wear the shoes even as he hung her from the rafter in his garage. In addition, Brudos was involved in triolism, a sexual behavior in which sexual gratification is gained by seeing oneself and/or others in sexual scenes. Combining his transvestism with triolism, Brudos took pictures of himself wearing the high-heeled shoes, panties, bra, and stockings. He also took pictures of his wife nude and photographed three of his four victims. One victim was already dead when he photographed her (Stack, 1983).

If profiling had been popular and used by the Salem Police Department, such a profile might have alerted the police to the possibility of finding souvenirs or trophies in the possession of Brudos. This physical evidence, if listed on a search warrant, could have been invaluable material to be used in his trial. It might have also alerted police to the possibility of film that might display nude females or other suspicious pictures coming through local businesses for development. As it did transpire, Brudos convinced his wife that she could pose for him in the nude because big labs process too much film to look at every picture. They look at the first or the last and that's all (Stack, 1983, p. 33). Brudos apparently used this same subjective rationale when he photographed his victims.

Goal 3: To Provide Interviewing Suggestions and Strategies

Once a subject is apprehended, a profile packet should contain information regarding proper and effective methods of interviewing and interrogation. This can be crucial.

The profile packet should contain information regarding different personalities and effective strategies in soliciting information from a diverse group of offenders. Not all people react to questioning in the same fashion. For one type of offender, one strategy may be effective, but it is a drastic mistake to assume all offenders will respond to the same interviewing strategy. For example, not all serial murderers kill for the same reason, and not all respond to the same type of interviewing strategy. Violent personal offenders also vary with their motives as well as their responses to interrogation.

Case Study

In a small Midwestern town, 15-year-old Diana Harris and her boyfriend were shot. Their bodies were found in his car parked in a lonely lovers' lane area. She died of one shot to the left temple, and her male companion was mortally wounded with a single shot entering under his left armpit. One additional bullet was fired through the passenger-side window. No physical evidence other than the bullets was obtained.

The police department investigated this case thoroughly but unsuccessfully. After talking with the mother and stepfather, one detective believed that the stepfather was not telling all he knew. Most people feared Mr. Harris. A football coach, he carried himself in such a manner that defied anyone to doubt his virility, masculinity, or intelligence.

The detective interviewed the stepfather about the case. After questioning him for several hours, the police officer asked him pointedly if he had killed his stepdaughter and her boyfriend.

Breaking into profuse perspiration, the man replied, "Not in my right mind did I kill them. You'll have to prove that I did." Instead of keeping some pressure on the stepfather, a coffee break was taken. After regrouping himself psychologically, Mr. Harris denied any knowledge or responsibility in this case. All progress stopped, and the investigation came to a halt. All strategies used provided no further information.

Finally this police department requested direction in the interrogation of Mr. Harris. Suspecting he demanded to be in control but with a flaw in his personality, a far different strategy was offered. The suspect was taken into an interrogation room where pictures of the crime scene lined the four walls. The suspect was told that the police really wanted to solve the crime of the murder of his stepdaughter. Despite all they had done, they were getting nowhere, and they needed help. The pictures of the crime scene served as constant reminders of what had occurred, not only to his stepdaughter but to the boy as well.

After the suspect believed that he was now in control of the investigation and could offer some helpful suggestions to the police, he became fully engrossed in the case. The more he talked, the more familiar he became with the details of the crime. After more than 8 hours, the man broke down and cried. Then the detective resumed his questioning, and the man confessed to the double homicide.

❖ PROFILING: AN ART, NOT A SCIENCE

Not everyone agrees that psychological profiling is of benefit to law enforcement (Jenkins, 1994). Indeed, not all crimes are suitable for the profiling process.

> While virtually any crime showing mental, emotional, or personality aberration can be analyzed for profiling purposes, certain crimes are particularly appropriate for the process; these crimes include a series of rapes, serial murders, child molesting, ritualistic crimes, threat communications, violence in the workplace, and serial arson. (Hazelwood & Burgess, 1995, p. 12)

Vernon Geberth, a retired homicide commander with the New York Police Department and author of many books dealing with homicide investigations, was in 1994 and still is being misquoted today as saying that he "was not aware of one serial murder case where a profile led to an arrest." In a personal communication with Geberth, he said that the actual quote should be as follows:

> Criminal profiling is an excellent law enforcement tool. However, it is just one of many tools and does not replace good investigative techniques. In fact, I don't know of any profile in and by itself that has resulted in an actual arrest. (V. Geberth, personal communication, February 6, 1995)

While there may be some truth to this criticism, it is reasonable to expect that the profiler's years of education and training will be of value to law enforcement in its attempts to solve heinous and difficult crimes. But again, we agree with Geberth: By itself, a profile does not solve any crime. It is only one forensic tool of many that should be utilized in the investigation of a crime.

There are a few discrete rules to adhere to in the profiling of a difficult criminal case. Of course, educated guesses are made. They are, however, aided by knowledge gained from the profiler's experience in the criminal justice system and from his familiarity with relevant concepts in criminology, sociology, psychology, and psychiatry. In addition, the profiler is aided by an intuitive sense in the profiling process. That is, he develops a feel for the crime. This is the art dimension. Nonprofessional sources of information seldom have the mixture of competencies essential for efficient profiling.

❖ CONCLUSION

There are obvious cases that are more suitable and appropriate for psychological profiling than others. The role of the profiler, then, is to assist the police department in its investigations of the cases in which additional aid is sought for the successful resolution of a case, such as lust murder, rape, and the like. The successful profiler will blend his educational and training background to offer insight into the type of person who would commit the crime currently under investigation. It is, however, more than a simple list of suspected characteristics. The profiler will keep in mind his role in assisting the police by fulfilling fundamental processes in the profiling endeavor. The goals, then, are reached as much through education and training as they are through the acquired art of profiling itself.

❖ REFERENCES

Craig, D. (1980). *Hip pocket guide to planning and evaluation*. Austin, TX: Learning Concepts.

Douglas, J., & Burgess, A. (1986). Criminal profiling: A viable investigative tool against violent crime. *FBI Law Enforcement Bulletin, 55*, 9–13.

Douglas, J. E., Burgess, A. W., Burgess, A. G., & Ressler, R. (1993). *Crime classification manual*. London: Simon & Shuster.

Douglas, J., & Olshaker, M. (1995). *Mind hunter: Inside the FBI's elite serial crime unit*. New York: Scribner.

Douglas, J., & Olshaker, M. (1999). *The anatomy of motive: The FBI's legendary mindhunter explores the key to understanding and catching violent criminals*. New York: Scribner.

Douglas, J., & Olshaker, M. (2000). *The cases that haunt us: From Jack the Ripper to JonBenet Ramsey, the FBI's legendary mindhunter sheds light on the mysteries that won't go away*. New York: Scribner.

Geberth, V. (1981). Psychological profiling. *Law and Order, 29*, 46–49.

Geberth, V. (2006). *Practical homicide investigation* (4th ed.). Boca Raton, FL: CRC Press.

Harris, T. (1981). *Red dragon*. New York: Putnam.

Harris, T. (1988). *The silence of the lambs*. New York: St. Martin's.

Harris, T. (1999). *Hannibal*. New York: Delacorte.

Hazelwood, R., & Burgess, A. (1995). *Practical aspects of rape investigation* (2nd ed.). Baton Rouge, LA: CRC Press.

Hazelwood, R., & Michaud, S. (2001). *The evil that men do: FBI profiler Roy Hazelwood's journey into the minds of sexual predators*. New York: Scribner.

Holmes, R., & Holmes, S. (1992). Understanding mass murder: A starting point. *Federal Probation, 56*, 53–61.

Holmes, R., & Holmes, S. (2000). *Murder in America* (2nd ed.). Thousand Oaks, CA: Sage.

Jenkins, P. (1994). *Using murder: The social construction of serial homicide*. New York: Aldine de Gruyter.

Kocsis, R., Orwin, H., & Hayes, A. (2000). Expertise in psychological profiling: A comparative assessment. *Journal of Interpersonal Violence, 15*(3), 311–331.

Michaud, S. (1986, October 26). The FBI's new psyche squad. *New York Times Magazine*.

Palmiotto, M. (1994). *Criminal investigation*. Chicago: Nelson Hall.

Peterson, M. (1997). Practical analytical techniques: A necessary addition to police education. *Journal of Criminal Justice Education, 8*(1), 19–35.

Ressler, R., & Shachtman, T. (1992). *Whoever fights monsters*. New York: St. Martin's.

Ressler, R., & Shachtman, T. (1997). *I have lived in the monster: Inside the minds of the world's most notorious serial killers*. New York: St. Martin's.

Sears, D. (1991). *To kill again*. Wilmington, DE: Scholarly Resources.

Stack, A. (1983). *The lust killer*. New York: Signet.

Vorpagel, R. (1998). *Profiles in murder: An FBI legend dissects killers and their crimes*. New York: Dell.

2

Profiling in Fantasy and Fact

❖ ❖ ❖

The true crime genre has long been an interest to readers. New crime books represent a steady flow onto the bookshelves of local bookstores. *The Silence of the Lambs, The Diary of Jack the Ripper, Cases That Haunt Us, Hannibal,* and many others provide fuel for the insatiable reading appetites for true and fictional crime readers (Douglas & Olshaker, 2000; Harris, 1999; Harrison & Maybrick, 1994). Obviously this is nothing new. Since the 1880s, Sir Arthur Conan Doyle, G. K. Chesterton, Agatha Christie, Earl Biggers, Lawrence Sanders, Thomas Harris, Caleb Carr, Patricia Cornwell, John Sandford, Michael Connelly, James Patterson, and many others have written novels that have influenced readers' impressions of violent crimes and criminals.

Who are some of these fictional characters that have galvanized our interests in murder and mayhem? Let us examine some of the more popular.

❖ SHERLOCK HOLMES: THE MASTER DETECTIVE

In the late 1800s, actually just before the horrific crimes of Jack the Ripper, a fictional master detective contributed his delving mind to police departments and citizens alike in the solving of particularly puzzling and horrible crimes. Four books were written about Holmes along with scores of short stories. Accompanied by his good friend and associate Dr. Watson, Sherlock Holmes solved case after case, rarely failing. This point is illustrated in Holmes's dialogue with a young wife who, in one story, asks his help:

Wife: He [Major Prendergast] said that you could solve anything.

Holmes: He said too much.

Wife: That you are never beaten.

Holmes: I have been beaten four times—three times by men, and once by a woman.

Wife: But what is that compared with the number of your successes?

Holmes: It is true that I have been generally successful. (Doyle, 1891c, p. 70)

Holmes solved his cases by deduction (note our descriptions of the inductive and the deductive methods described in the previous chapter). He recognized things that others missed. His colleague,

Dr. Watson, was constantly amazed by what Holmes was able to see, many times recognizing the nonphysical evidence as presented through the physical evidence.

Watson says:

> But I was always impressed with a sense of my own stupidity in my dealings with Sherlock Holmes. Here I had heard what he had heard, I had seen what he had seen, and yet in his words it was evident that he saw clearly not only what had happened, but what was about to happen. (Doyle, 1891d, p. 35)

The consummate detective, Holmes took note of evidence that others neglected. On many occasions, he remarked, "Perhaps I have trained myself to see what others overlook" (Doyle, 1891b, p. 42).

Sherlock Holmes maintained that the educated and trained mind of the detective is the most important forensic tool in the resolution of a crime. The master detective investigated his cases with great care, examining each minute detail. In *The Basecombe Valley Mystery* (1891a), for example, Holmes deduced from the manner in which a man has been struck over his left shoulder that the perpetrator was left handed and walked with a limp. When Holmes explains to Watson how he has reached this conclusion, the good doctor is once again astounded by what Holmes has seen and he (Watson) has not.

In *The Man With the Twisted Lip* (1891e), Holmes investigates the case of a missing husband. One clue centers on the manner in which a letter has been addressed:

Holmes:	I perceive that whoever addressed the envelope had to go and inquire as to the address.
Mrs. St. Claire:	How can you tell?
Holmes:	The name, you see, is in perfectly black ink, which has dried itself. The rest is of the grayish color which shows that blotting paper has been used. If it had been written straight off, and then blotted, none would be the deep black shade. This man has written the name and there has then been a pause before he wrote the address, which can only mean that he was not familiar with it. (Doyle, 1891e, p. 89)

Holmes amazes not only Watson but also the missing man's wife with this observation. He notes confidently, perhaps arrogantly, that the letter is only a trifle, "but there is nothing so important as trifles" (p. 89). Is the devil in the details? Certainly Holmes would believe so.

The gift of Sherlock Holmes is his attention to detail. The physical scene, or the crime scene, is more than simply a site of an accumulation of evidence; there is a synergism that arises from the interaction of offender, victim, and scene. A forensic anthropologist may be able to tell the height, weight, and even the race of an offender from a footprint, but a footprint says nothing of the offender's personality. It is imperative for investigators to examine nonphysical evidence because it adds to the quality of the scene. From a profiling point of view, both physical and nonphysical evidence can provide clues to the offender's personality. Holmes had that knack. This was never more visible than when someone would come to his door, and he could tell the person's occupation, education, residence, and past history, all from the wear of his sleeve.

Holmes never reached the point where he could be described as a psychological profiler. This is due to no small part to the influence of the school of criminology that was in vogue at the time. The classical school of criminology, which was quickly followed by the positive school, laid the theoretical groundwork for the assumption that humans are in complete control of their actions. Under positive school thinking, people were thought to become criminals because of their "savage genes" inherited from their "savage ancestors" or other constitutional (or physical) factors (Ferrero-Lombroso, 1911). If the psychodynamic model had been better known and accepted at the time, Sherlock Holmes no doubt would have been more heavily involved in the psychological analysis of the criminals he investigated.

❖ WILL GRAHAM AND *RED DRAGON*

Thomas Harris has written a terrifying novel about a serial murderer that is more than an explanation of the mind of the killer. Terrifying and strange, bizarre yet compelling, *Red Dragon* (1981) examines the psychological and mystical relationship between the killer, Francis Dolarhyde, and his profiler, Will Graham.

As the novel opens, Graham is a retired FBI agent, living in Marathon Island, Florida with his wife and son. Before his retirement, he was involved in a murder investigation so intense that it resulted in his leaving the Bureau. However, a friend and former coworker convinces him to come out of retirement to undertake one last case, the case of the "Red Dragon," a serial killer. Harris takes the reader inside the mind of the profiler as Graham goes to the crime scenes in Atlanta and Birmingham.

In Atlanta, the Leeds family has been killed, both the parents and three children. The children were placed by the killer facing the bed, with their backs to the wall. The parents were found in their own bed. Mr. Leeds was bound and tied to the headboard, and his throat was slashed.

After examining the Leeds home crime scene, Graham returns to his motel room, where he mentally reconstructs the crime. The eyes of the victims were open; Graham thinks, "Were they 'witnesses' to the killings? Were they an audience?" Recalling a lit candle in the bedroom, Graham thinks about how its glimmering light may have served as a visual facilitator of horror. The flickering light would simulate expression in their faces (p. 29). Carrying on a mental conversation with the unknown killer, Graham asks:

Why did you move them [the children] again? Why didn't you leave them that way? There's something you don't want me to know about you. Why, there's something you're ashamed of. Or is it something you can't afford for me to know?

Did you open their eyes?

Mrs. Leeds was lovely, wasn't she? You turned on the light after you cut his throat so Mrs. Leeds could watch him flop, didn't you? It was maddening to have to wear gloves when you touched her, wasn't it? (p. 29)

Totally immersed in the multiple killings of the two families, Graham creates a profile of the killer that helps to narrow the scope of the investigation and provides a structure on which to base an understanding of the killer's personality. With sophisticated police technology, including techniques that are not currently in the repertoire in the real world of forensics, the Red Dragon is eventually brought to justice in a rather unusual way.

No other novel, in our opinion, gives the reader such vivid and realistic insight into the mind of the profiler, despite the retorts of former FBI agents. Although it is a work of fiction, it illustrates well the introspective nature and art of profiling.

Will Graham becomes personally involved in the Red Dragon case. He loses his objectivity. He becomes so intimately involved that he carries on conversations with the unknown and unseen perpetrator as well as with the victims. He believes in the need to go to the crime scene because there still lingers a "shadow" of the crime. Photographs, written reports, witness statements, and the investigation that ensues almost lead to fatal consequences, not only for Graham, but for his wife and son.

Red Dragon provides a fictional introduction to the real world of profiling and to the art involved in the profiler's immersion in a case. In this novel, there is little hard science to the profiling process; Graham proceeds for the most part based on his feelings. And these feelings nearly destroy the person he is.

❖ CLARICE STARLING AND *THE SILENCE OF THE LAMBS*

In Harris's next book, *The Silence of the Lambs* (1988), Will Graham has apparently returned to Marathon Island, just a few miles from Key West. The book opens at the FBI Academy at Quantico. Clarice Starling has been called to the section chief's office. Jack Crawford remembers Starling as a graduate student at the University of Virginia, where he lectured in a criminology seminar. He has called this agent-in-training to aid him by interviewing Dr. Hannibal Lecter, the infamous cannibal and serial killer. A psychiatrist, Lecter has been in prison and antici-pates never being released from confinement.

Clarice and Lecter develop a strange relationship, and he offers her some information about a particular murder case. Meanwhile, the rela-tionship with Jack Crawford deepens, and she learns some concepts and precepts of the profiling process from both. In West Virginia, another murder has occurred in the small town of Potter. This killing has some similarities to other known killings committed by an unknown serial killer.

Standing next to the body, she and Crawford have this conversation:

"What do you see, Starling?"

"Well, she's not a local—her ears are pierced three times each, and she wore glitter polish. She got maybe two weeks or so hair growth on her legs. And see how soft it's grown in. I think she got her legs waxed. Armpits too. Look how she bleached the fuzz on her upper lip. She was pretty careful about herself, but she hasn't been able to take care of it for a while." (p. 76)

With these few statements gleaned from the physical evidence, the scope of the investigation narrows slightly. She is starting to learn her trade as a profiler, which in the next book, *Hannibal*, dissipates with her emerging personal relationship with Dr. Lecter. The notes she takes will help her track down Jame Gumb, aka Buffalo Bill.

In this book, the reader is alerted to the role of physical evidence as it contributes to the psychological profile. Certainly, the FBI would not send an agent-in-training to interview a serial killer as Lecter. This criticism is often aimed at Harris, but in his defense it *is* a work of fiction. Starling is viewed as a neophyte—no real experience in law enforcement, although her deceased father was a former sheriff in West Virginia who was killed in the line of duty. Throughout the book, she learns quickly from two professionals, the section chief and the killer, Dr. Lecter.

❖ ZOE KOEHLER: A FEMALE SERIAL MURDERESS

Lawrence Sanders's 1981 novel *The Third Deadly Sin* is the story of a woman, Zoe Koehler, who has a deep fantasy life that involves the killings of male strangers. Zoe has never really come to terms with her female identity, and there is a hidden part of her personality that no one but her victims has seen. She works in an office during the day, arrives at work daily on time, eats her lunch at her desk, and goes home to an empty apartment. She has felt rejection all of her life: Her father psychologically isolated himself from her in her childhood, and her husband deserted her after only a few years of marriage. The millions of men in her city barely acknowledge her existence.

Zoe's painful menstrual periods announce a metamorphosis in which she changes from a nondescript entity to a killer. She changes from her drab work clothes to seductive clothing, transforming her appearance further with a wig, and travels across town to cocktail lounges at convention sites. She allows herself to be picked up and accompanies her victims to their room, where they anticipate a sexual encounter. In one such incident, after Zoe and her victim go to his room, she says, "I have to make wee-wee and then I'll come back to you. I'll do anything you want. And I mean anything" (p. 34). When she returns to the room, after having removed her clothing, she comes to the bed, where the man waits, carrying a Swiss Army knife beneath her towel. She plunges the knife into the man's neck.

[The victim] made a sound, a gargle, and his heavy body leaped convulsively from the bed. Blood spouted in streams, gobbets, a flood that sprayed the air with a crimson fog. It soaked the bed, dripped onto the floor.

With bloodied, slippery hand, she drove the knife blade again and again into his genitals. No triumph or exultation in her face. Not grinning or yowling, but intent and businesslike. Saying aloud with each stab, "There. There." (p. 34)

Edward X. Delaney, a central figure in several of Sanders's novels, is a retired detective from New York's finest who serves as a special consultant to the police department. Delany, an amateur profiler, assumes an unofficial posture in investigating the "Hotel Ripper Case." He tells his wife that he suspects the killer is a woman:

All I'm trying to do is to put together a profile. Not a psychological profile—those things are usually pure bullshit. I'm trying to give the killer certain personal and emotional characteristics that give us a more accurate picture of the kind of woman she is. (p. 200)

Despite his protests concerning the nature of profiling, Delaney develops a psychological profile of the unknown suspect. He offers a picture of a young woman, 5 feet 5 inches to 5 feet 7 inches tall, "probably a young woman, say in the area of eighteen to forty" (p. 200). How does he come up with this age range? "She's strong enough to rip a man's throat and she's young enough to have menstrual periods" (p. 200). Because the killings occur monthly, 26 days apart, Delany connects the murders with a woman's menstrual cycle. Using practical reasoning, Delany continues: He decides she must be intelligent; she carefully plans each act, washes the evidence away, leaving no fingerprints. In addition, he believes the killer dresses and acts in a conservative fashion and is probably "mousy. Until she breaks out and kills" (p. 328).

Delaney's profile is accurate. It leads the police to narrow the investigation and finally to obtain an arrest warrant for the murderess. They are too late, however; they find her dead alongside her lover.

❖ ALEX CROSS

James Patterson has written a series of fictional crime books featuring Alex Cross, a 6-foot, 3-inch, 200-pound former athlete. He earned his PhD in psychology from Johns Hopkins with a concentration in abnormal and forensic psychology. After graduation, he tried to find a niche in private practice but financially was not able to support himself and his family. He joined the Washington, DC Police Department as a psychologist and then joined the FBI in the Hoover Building in Washington.

Patterson's protagonist is a family man, living with his two sons and daughter and his grandmother, Nana Mama. The children's mother, Maria, was killed in a drive-by shooting several years before. Cross's second wife lives in Seattle with his third son. She has custody of the youngest Cross because of the potential dangers involved with his work.

Cross works on cases using traditional police tactics and maintains relationships with police in DC, as well as special agents with the FBI. But he looks at crimes differently; he blends human behavior with what the physical and nonphysical evidence offers.

In Patterson's *Roses Are Red* (2000), Dr. Alex Cross takes on a new criminal, the "Mastermind." An antagonist, this criminal genius is responsible for bank robberies and murderers. Pairing with a young FBI agent, Cross offers a profile:

> Here's what we know now. A single man committed the Citibank, First Union, First Virginia, and Chase robberies and murders. We know he's selecting crew members that are willing to kill. He's only interested in recruiting killers.
>
> Our profile tells us he's a white male between thirty-five and fifty. He's probably well-educated, with a thorough knowledge of banks and their security systems. He may have worked for a financial institution in the past, or even more than one, and might have a grudge against them. He robs banks for the money, but the murders are probably for revenge.

As the story develops, this mini-profile proves fairly accurate. Although the Mastermind is not apprehended, his identity becomes known to the reader as one of the FBI agents.

Unlike some other profilers, Cross is educated and has practical experience.

❖ DR. LASZLO KREIZLER: *THE ALIENIST* AND *ANGEL OF DARKNESS*

Caleb Carr (1994) has written a fascinating novel about killing and psychological profiling. In *The Alienist*, a profile is developed of an unknown child killer. The character, Dr. Kreizler, is trying to get inside the mind of the serial killer. He and his inner circle of friends brainstorm in their development of a profile.

"I don't understand," I said, "Why would the murderer cut their throats if he'd already strangled them?"

"Blood lust," Marcus answered, very matter-of-factly, as he ate his soup.

"Yes, blood lust," Lucius agreed. "He was probably concerned with keeping his clothes clean so that he wouldn't attract any attention during the escape. He needed to see the blood—or maybe smell it. Some murderers have said it's the smell rather than the sight that satisfies them."(p. 100)

The profile continues. The profiler believes the killer's mother was unloving, rejecting, and uncaring and that the killer has some kind of deformity having to do with the eyes. The profile proves accurate, and the killer is eventually brought to justice.

In Carr's next book, *The Angel of Darkness* (1997), the story is told from the perspective of Kreizler's young protégé. The doctor again offers a profile throughout the book that is changed as his friend, the detective, feeds him with more information. The profile leads the reader to a point where the killer is better understood as a murderous personality.

Although the stories are set in the late 1800s, psychodynamic information becomes a part of the profile, but later developments that have made profiling more than simply an educated "guessing game" are missing from the considerations of Dr. Kreizler. Considering the time and the crimes, though, the profile in fiction is an enlightening and educational experience.

❖ OTHER WORKS OF FICTION AND PSYCHOLOGICAL PROFILING

Some of the most intriguing works of fiction concerning murder, mayhem, and profiling are the works of John Sandford. His *Prey* series are alive with the work of his protagonist, Lucas Davenport, a wealthy detective with the Minneapolis Police Department (Sandford, 1994, 1995, 1997, 1998, 1999, 2000, 2001). Earning his wealth from the development of software, Davenport uses his knowledge of the human condition and the hard science of homicide investigation scenes to offer pictures of the unknown subject. For example, in *Chosen Prey* (2001), Davenport examines the "cemetery" that the unknown serial killer has made. He knows the killer's "Ideal Victim Type" and shares his thoughts with his police investigators. The profile is not a written document but a working mental picture of the type of person they are looking for. *Secret Prey* and *Certain Prey* follow this same basic format. The detective is just as concerned with the physical evidence as well as the nonphysical evidence; they both blend and point to a soon-to-be-caught offender.

Patricia Cornwell has invited us all to join in the fight to eradicate crime through the efforts of Dr. Kay Scarpetta, a medical examiner and attorney in Virginia. In books such as *Postmortem, From Potter's Field*, and *Black Notice,* Scarpetta investigates crimes along with her detective partner, Pete Marino (Cornwell, 1991, 1996, 1999). Looking at the physical evidence at the crime scene, the corpse, or what the evidence suggests, Scarpetta and Marino are able to make profiles of the unknown subjects.

❖ PROFILING IN FACT

In a novel, the successful resolution of a murder is usually neatly reached. Too often, the reader will note, the crime is neatly solved in the last page or two. Unfortunately, profiling does not always yield the same result. Let us examine as illustration four cases: those of Adolf Hitler, George Metesky (the Mad Bomber), Richard Kuklinski, and Dennis Rader (the BTK killer).

Profile of Adolf Hitler

In 1943, the Office of Strategies Services (OSS) sought the help of Dr. Walter C. Langer, a psychiatrist. Dr. Langer, commissioned by Colonel William "Wild Bill" Donovan, was given the task of providing the OSS with a profile of Adolf Hitler. Specifically they wanted to know the following:

> If Hitler is running the show, what kind of person is he? What are his ambitions? . . . We want to know about his psychological make-up—the things that make him tick. In addition, we ought to know what he might do if things begin to go against him. (Langer, 1972, p. 19)

Langer hired three research assistants who were all familiar with the psychodynamic model. The researchers scoured the New York City

Library and their own reading lists and solicited personal interviews with people who had intimate knowledge of Hitler. Langer's goal was to provide the OSS and Donovan with an objective psychological profile of Adolf Hitler that "might serve as a common basis for decisions in the future" (Langer, p. 31). To this end, here is a summary of Langer's (1943) profile:

As the tide of battle turns against Hitler it may be well to consider very briefly the possibilities of his future behavior and the effect that each would have on the German people as well as on ourselves.

1. Hitler may die of natural causes.

This is only a remote possibility since, as far as we know, he is in fairly good health except for his stomach ailment, which is, in all probability, a psychosomatic disturbance. The effect such an event would have on the German people would depend on the nature of the illness which brought about his death. If he would die from whooping cough, mumps, or some other ridiculous disease, it would be a material help in breaking the myth of his supernatural origins.

2. Hitler might seek refuge in a neutral country.

This is extremely unlikely in view of his great concern about his immortality. Nothing would break the myth more effectively than to have the leader run away at the critical moment. Hitler knows this and has frequently condemned the kaiser for his flight to Holland at the close of the last war. Hitler might want to escape as he has escaped from other unpleasant situations, but it seems almost certain that he would restrain himself.

3. Hitler might get killed in battle.

This is a real possibility. When he is convinced that he cannot win, he may lead his troops into battle and expose himself as the fearless and fanatical leader. This would be most undesirable from our point of view because his death would serve as an example to his followers to fight on with fanatical, death-defying determination to the bitter end. This would be what Hitler would want, and he has predicted this eventuality:

We shall not capitulate . . . no, never. We may be destroyed, but if we are, we shall drag a world with us . . . a world in flames. . . . But even if we could not conquer them, we should drag half the world into destruction with us and leave no one to triumph over Germany. There will not be another 1918.

At a certain point he could do more toward the achievement of this goal by dying heroically than he could by living. Furthermore, death of this kind would do more to bind the German people to the Hitler legend and ensure his immortality than any other course he could pursue.

4. Hitler might be assassinated.

Although Hitler is extremely well protected, there is a possibility that someone may assassinate him. Hitler is afraid of this possibility and has expressed the opinion that

> His own friends would one day stab him mortally in the back. . . . And it would be just before the last and greatest victory, at the moment of supreme tension. Once more Hagen would slay Siegfried. Once more Hermann the Liberator would be murdered by his own kinsmen. The eternal destiny of the German nation must be fulfilled yet again, for the last time.

This possibility, too, would be undesirable from our point of view, inasmuch as it would make a martyr of him and strengthen the legend.

It would be even more undesirable if the assassin were a Jew, for this would convince the German people of Hitler's infallibility and strengthen the fanaticism of the German troops and people. Needless to say, it would be followed by the complete extermination of all Jews in Germany and the occupied countries.

5. Hitler may go insane.

Hitler has many characteristics that border on the schizophrenic. It is possible that when faced with defeat his psychological structure may collapse and leave him at the mercy of his unconscious forces. The possibilities of such an outcome diminish as he becomes older, but they should not be entirely excluded. This would not be an undesirable eventuality from our point of view, since it would do much to undermine the Hitler legend in the minds of the German people.

6. German military might revolt and seize him.

This seems unlikely in view of the unique position Hitler holds in the minds of the German people. From all the evidence it would seem that Hitler alone is able to rouse the troops, as well as the people, to greater efforts, and as the road becomes more difficult this should be an important factor. One could imagine, however, that as defeat approaches, Hitler's behavior may become more and more neurotic and reach a point where it would be well for the military to confine him. In this case, however, the German people would probably never know about it.

If they discovered it, it would be a desirable end from our point of view because it would puncture the myth of the loved and invincible leader.

The only other possibility in this connection would be that the German military should decide, in the face of defeat, that it might be wiser to dethrone Hitler and set up a puppet government to sue for peace. This would probably cause great internal strife in Germany. What the ultimate outcome might be would depend largely on the manner in which it was handled and what was done with Hitler. At the present time the possibility seems extremely remote.

7. Hitler may fall into our hands.

This is the most unlikely possibility of all. Knowing his fear of being placed in the role of the vanquished, we can imagine that he would do his utmost to avoid such a fate. From our point of view, it would not be undesirable.

8. Hitler might commit suicide.

This is the most plausible outcome. Not only has he frequently threatened to commit suicide, but from what we know of his psychology it is the most likely possibility. It is probably true that he has an inordinate fear of death, but being a hysteric he could undoubtedly screw himself up into the superman character and perform the deed. In all probability, however, it would not be a simple suicide. He has too much of the dramatic for that, and since immortality is one of his dominant motives we can imagine that he would stage the most dramatic and effective death scene he could possibly think of. He knows how to bind the people to him, and if he cannot have the bond in life he will certainly do his utmost to achieve it in death. He might even engage some other fanatic to do the final killing at his orders.

Hitler has already envisaged a death of this kind, for he has said to Rauschning, "Yes, in the hour of supreme peril I must sacrifice myself for the people." This would be extremely undesirable from our point of view because if it is cleverly done it would establish the Hitler legend so firmly in the minds of the German people that it might take generations to eradicate it.

Whatever else happens, we may be reasonably sure that as Germany suffers successive defeats Hitler will become more and more neurotic. Each defeat will shake his confidence still further and limit his opportunities for proving his own greatness to himself. In consequence he will feel himself more and more vulnerable to attack from his associates and his rages will increase in frequency. He will probably try to compensate for his vulnerability by continually stressing his brutality and ruthlessness.

His public appearances will become less and less for, as we have seen, he is unable to face a critical audience. He will probably seek solace in his Eagle's Nest on the Kehlstein near Berchtsegaden. There among the ice-capped peaks he will wait for his "inner voice" to guide him. Meanwhile, his nightmares will probably increase in frequency and intensity and drive him closer to a nervous collapse. It is not wholly improbable that in the end he might lock himself into this symbolic womb and defy the world to get him.

In any case, his mental condition will continue to deteriorate. He will fight as long as he can with any weapon or technique that can be conjured up to meet the emergency. The course he will follow will almost certainly be the one that seems to him to be the surest road to immortality and at the same time drag the world down in flames. (Langer 1943, pp. 244–248)

Thus, this profile stemmed from a psychodynamic perspective of the Hitler personality and the world as it existed at the time of Hitler's final situation. The psychological profile of Hitler himself included the following elements:

- Hitler's parents influenced him tremendously.
- Hitler's father was cold, distant, and domineering.
- Hitler's mother was judged to be considerate, long suffering, and overly affectionate to Hitler.
- Hitler felt some rejection from the mother's refusal to leave the abusive father and husband to care for and protect young Adolf.

- Because of the influence of his parents, Hitler in his adult years was unable to establish and maintain strong personal relationships with others.

From this perspective, Langer and his associates were able to predict the behavior of Hitler in the possible ending of World War II. A picture emerged of Hitler as believing himself to be infallible and omnipotent. However, the profile indicates that Hitler was a megalomaniac with a fragile psychological foundation. Despite these perceived deep psychological issues, it is clear that Hitler believed that he was the responsible agent for the advancement of Germany as a superpower and once again to the status it so rightly deserved.

Thus Hitler saw himself as an intellectual, a man of the world, and the savior for the German people. He was a patron of the arts, despite the failure in his youth to be admitted to an art school; he was an outstanding legal scholar, despite no formal training; and when he was in his 20s, he grew a Christlike beard and wanted to be a Catholic priest. During World War II, he likened himself to Christ to the German people.

Benefits of the Profile

Langer's profile was intended to offer insights into the personality of Adolf Hitler so that if he was captured at the end of the war, an interrogation strategy would be in place that would help authorities elicit information from him.

To help the OSS plan for several eventualities, the profile offered the above possibilities. Despite its strong Freudian psychoanalytic orientation, Langer's profile proved to be amazingly accurate as far as the scenarios for the war's end were concerned. Hitler did commit suicide in a bunker with Eva Braun. He never married, perhaps because he never found anyone he felt was enough like his mother. Hitler's writings from the time near the end of the war indicate that he appeared to be on the fringe of mental illness. He also left many documents that pointed toward some unusual sexual leanings: coprolagnia and urolagnia (sexual excitement gained from eating feces and drinking urine) and others. Langer's work was not in vain. It proved to be a worthy attempt in using profiling as a tool to understand an aberrant personality.

The Mad Bomber and Dr. Brussel

In the 1950s, New York City was alerted to a series of bombings that paralyzed the city with fear. George Metesky was finally arrested due in some part to the profile developed by a psychiatrist, Dr. Brussel. Living with his two unmarried sisters in a suburb of New York City, Metesky made trips often to Manhattan. One explanation that he used was to attend mass at St. Patrick's Cathedral. Later in the investigation, it was determined that the visits to the city aligned themselves with the bombings.

Dr. Brussel was approached by a detective from the New York City Police Department and asked to develop a profile. The profile included the following:

- The bomber was middle-aged—probably around 50.
- The bomber was neat, meticulous, and skilled at his work. Everything from the carefully constructed bombs, to the neat lettering, to the careful planning of the bombs indicated his neatness.
- The bomber was overly sensitive to criticism.
- The bomber was foreign or spent the majority of his time with foreign people.
- The bomber had at least a high school education but probably no college.
- The bomber was a Slav and probably Roman Catholic.
- The bomber lived in Connecticut, not New York.
- The bomber suffered from an Oedipal complex.

The profile was then published by several newspapers on December 25th, 1956. An employee of Con Edison who happened to read the profile, began looking through the company's employee workers' compensation files and found a file of a man who was injured in a plant accident on September 5, 1931. The file contained several threats that George Metesky had made against the company, and several of the words/phrases matched the letters that had been published by the bomber. The employee called the police and the police went to investigate.

When they went to Metesky's house he went into his bedroom to change his clothes, and when he emerged from his room, he was dressed in a double-breasted suit, the same type of clothing mentioned in the profile: "When you catch him he'll be wearing a double-breasted suit."

This is perhaps the first case of psychological profiling on a local level that gave a sense of professionalism and credence to psychological profiling. The statement regarding the double-breasted suit seemed to legitimize the total effort by Brussel. Additionally, the profile itself was instrumental in the total investigation effort by the law enforcement agency and was successful against a real-world series of criminal activities.

Richard Kuklinski

Convicted murderer and self-professed serial killer, Richard Kuklinski was known as the "Ice Man." Born into a family of an abusive mother and a brutal father, Richard learned very early in life the value of violence. He committed his first killing when he was 14 years of age, beating his victim with a stick. At age 18, he killed another man in a bar who had insulted him. He followed the man to his car, came up to the car, poured gasoline on him, lit the gas, and watched the man die in flames. At age 21, he beat another man to death with a pool stick.

Richard had confessed to more than 100 murders to police and the media. He was only tried for two and was sentenced to two life sentences in 1988. He was called the Ice Man because of the manner in which he stored some bodies in a freezer to hinder deterioration.

"Nothing bothers me, nothing at all."

—Richard Kuklinski

Kuklinski had gained a great deal of notice from the crime syndicate because of his propensity for violence. He allegedly became a hit man for the Gambino crime family. An imposing figure, standing over 6 feet 4 inches and weighing almost 300 pounds, he killed many with poison and some with guns and other weapons.

Kuklinski was raised in a family that produced a psychopath. He had a history of violence to animals at an early age and killed cats. He had one brother who was allegedly killed by his father, and he also had another brother who was convicted of the rape and murder of a 12-year-old girl. Kuklinski married in 1961, and he and his wife, Barbara, had three children. The family stated that they never knew exactly what Kuklinski did for a living. They claim that they believed he was a professional salesman and broker. The family lived well in a nice home in the suburbs. Kuklinski charged thousands of dollars per hit, earning enough money to support his family in an upper-middle-class lifestyle.

The Ice Man was caught in an undercover operation by the New Jersey State Police and was charged with two counts of murder, although the police believed he had killed scores of people on his own and for the mob. His cruelty was legend among the mob, and he killed without remorse. He stated that he felt only badly about one kill—the one when he was 18 and set the man afire in his own car.

What kind of personality did Kuklinski have? Certainly someone in the mental health field would categorize him as psychopathic or sociopathic. His early experiences at the hands of abusive and unloving parents, his history of cruelty to animals, and his lack of emotions, remorse, and sorrow certainly are all symbolic of a psychopathic individual. But is it that simple, one diagnosis of psychopathy? Kuklinski appeared to not trust or love anyone other than family members. He professed his love for Barbara Hendren Kuklinski, his wife of 45 years, and for his children. He stated that he only felt happy and content when he was with his family. No positive emotions were directed outside his home. He had no feelings about the many he killed and left in public places, cut up in pieces in the Gemini Lounge in New Jersey, or left in freezers. He had only feelings for his family. He trusted no one else. Could that be a sign of a paranoid personality? Could he have signs of a psychopath as well as a paranoid personality? We think so.

Richard Kuklinski cases would have been very difficult to profile. He was a "multiple window" killer. Some were left where they died. Others were cut up into pieces and deposited in faraway separate dump sites, and others were left at sites apart from the murder site to be found by others. There have been rudimentary attempts at profiling the Ice Man after the fact. Bruno's *The Iceman: The True Story of a Cold-Blooded Killer* (1993) and Carlo's *The Ice Man: Confessions of a Mafia Contract Killer* (2006) both tried to offer some insight into the mind and mentality of a sadistic and hedonistic serial killer. But there may be no true understanding of this type of killer. Profiling might be of some aid for the investigation of the crime, but the true proven aids would be good old-fashioned investigation skills and, perhaps more important, superior investigative techniques.

Dennis Rader—The BTK Strangler

Dennis Rader, the self-proclaimed BTK (Bind, Torture, Kill) killer, was born in 1945. Born to William and Dorothea Rader, Dennis was the oldest of four brothers. After graduating from high school, he went to college for only a short period of time and then joined the Air Force. He returned home to Park, Kansas, a small town located in the suburbs of Wichita, and married in 1971.

Rader and his wife had two children, and he worked several jobs in the Wichita area, mostly in security firms. He then went back to college and earned his degree in administration of justice in 1979. This was 5 years after he had killed five people. During that same period he was a Boy Scout leader and a board member of his church and served on several community boards, including that of the Humane Society.

Rader often took souvenirs from his victims. The police were reluctant to mention this to the media, but Rader would often send taunting letters to the police mentioning and describing the manner in which he would bind, torture, and kill his victims.

In 2004 Rader started sending a series of communications to the police that led to his arrest. He also sent a floppy disk traced to the Lutheran church where he was a member. Rader was arrested on February 25, 2005. He confessed to 10 counts of murder and received 10 consecutive life terms that requires a minimum of 175 years with no possibility of parole. Since Kansas has no death penalty, this was the maximum penalty.

What would the psychological profile of Dennis Rader be? Of course, there was an abundance of offers made to the police on the type of person who could have committed such murders. The typical profile would have been a married male, someone in his 30s, well educated, living in his own home in the suburbs, with a private place in his own home, has children, and is a respected member of his community. This profile not only fits Rader but also perhaps a couple hundred thousand other men in the area around Wichita.

Other profilers were involved. Robert Ressler, John Douglas, and Roy Hazelwood, all former FBI profilers, offered their thoughts about the identity of the BTK Strangler (as Beattie [2005] called him). Ressler (in Beattie, p. 190), for example, offered that BTK lived in the College Hill section of the city, was a student or professor at Wichita State University, in his mid- to late twenties, and was an expert in the methods of serial killers.

How important were the profiles in eventually solving the case? To be quite honest, they probably played no role in this case at all. As in most cases, the resolution was a result of good police work and a cooperative relationship between the police and the media. As you can see, profiles are helpful in directing many investigations, but very seldom close a case and lead to the arrest of the offender. Good police work does this, and the profile is designed to help.

The BTK murderer confessed to the police about his murders. He reveled in the manner in which he could "control" the police with his letters, and he viewed them as intellectually inferior to him. Narcissism, psychopathy, sexual sadism, triolism were all components of his personality. Even to date, he has never expressed any remorse over any of his killings.

His wife divorced him after he was arrested, and the BTK killer is now spending the remainder of his life in a Kansas prison. Perhaps if he could be studied and was truthful, valuable information could be learned that would assist in the knowledge of profiling.

Dennis Rader's Victims

Victims	Year
Four members of the Otero Family	1974
Kathryn Bright	1974
Shirley Vian	1977
Nancy Fox	1977
Marine Hedge	1985
Vicki Wegerle	1986
Dolores Davis	1991

❖ PROFILE OF A RAPE CASE

Police departments often seek the help of profilers, usually when they have exhausted all of their leads. Recently, a suspected serial rapist was apprehended in a southern state. In the trunk of his car, the police found videos of more than 20 women he had raped. The police wondered why someone would carry such incriminating evidence in his car. The alleged rapist was visibly seen in the 20 rapes along with the protesting victims. When it was explained that the man had a sexual paraphilia called triolism and that by seeing the videos, he was reliving the acts of rape, it led to a better understanding of the person and his personality attributes and suggested a plan of interrogation.

In another state, another rapist was involved in multiple rapes. He would be invited into the home, posing as a repair technician. After gaining control of the situation, he would ask each victim a simple question: Did she have a sewing kit in the home? Each victim admitted that she did. He would then rape each in their beds. Remarkably each bed was a four-poster bed. This suggests that there was some stalking occurring before selecting each victim. After the rape, the women were forced to stand by one of the posters, with it between her breasts. He would then insert needle and thread into the nipples and in effect attach her to the poster as he made his getaway. Where would one learn of such a horrific act? Did this have something to do with an earlier experience in his life? Did he learn it in a movie? This is a type of case for which profiling is especially potentially fruitful.

Another serial rapist terrorized women in a southern city. When the investigators became convinced that they were dealing with a serial rapist, they sought the help of an outside agency that studied the crimes and produced a "criminal personality profile." These profilers believed that there were actually two rapists involved in the total of 34 incidents under investigation: One was responsible for 29 rapes and the other for the remaining 5.

❖ CASE PROFILE: MRS. CHARLENE L. MILLER

Dear Detective Rivers:

Thank you for the opportunity to review the case of Charlene L. Miller. I have reviewed the two-page fact sheet, the pathologic diagnoses of the body document, the forensic anthropologist report, the map of the county and surrounding area, the photos, and the video. I have not talked with you or anyone else about a potential suspect and am offering the following as my general impressions of the type of person you may be looking for as a viable suspect in this case.

Age:

The age of the suspect would be in the cohort of 32–36. Perhaps the age could be a couple of years older. There are several reasons for this belief. First of all, I don't see this as the first time this person has done this type of murder. What I am saying is that he has fantasized about killing a woman in this manner for several years. His fantasies have to become real, and to do the acts that he did to this victim would take a long time to finally act out as well as perhaps a murder or two before this particular murder. There are other items that would indicate that he would be about this age: These include the age of those who "hang out" in the bars in this community as well as the energy taken in the commission of this crime.

Sex:

The sex of the offender is male.

Race:

I would believe that this suspect is White. There are several reasons for this. First of all, most murders are committed by persons who are of the same race as the victim. There was no reported evidence that would indicate that the race of the offender is of any other race than White.

Intelligence:

I would think that this person is of average to less-than-average intelligence. I would not believe that this person is a "rocket scientist," but one who would blend in well with the other people he associates with, and he probably has the ability to work in jobs with little supervision. I would also think that he is not viewed as mentally retarded but as one who is a loner and one who is viewed by others who know him as being of average ability but a little strange or weird.

Education:

This suspect has a high school education or less. Also, while in school he adjusted well and presented no behavioral problems of any significance. He attended a local school in the area of your part of the state. He did not attend college for any significant part of time—if indeed he did attend college, he stayed less than a semester. His mental ability would not stop him from enrolling in college, but his mental status and personal disorganization would prohibit him from staying in college. In the school situation, he would have been an average student, probably not a behavioral problem.

Family:

This person is either an only child or one from a small family with no other siblings. His father was a passive person while the suspect was growing up and may have been deceased or absent from the family. The mother was a domineering person, aggressive, and was the center of power within the family. She was the chief judge, jury, and executioner. What she said was law for the family. I would also believe that she has only recently died, perhaps within the last 6 months. In the family, the child lived under her control, and the mother was constantly verbally abusing the offender.

Residence:

At the time of the present murder, the suspect lived in this local area and still does. There is something of a comfort zone in the manner in which he brings the dying victim back to the area where he is most familiar and most comfortable. There appear to be four dump sites here. The first one is the place in your jurisdiction where the torso was found; the other three sites are less comfortable for him and the dumping occurred at a later date. He lives closer to the first dump site than to the others.

The place where the torso was dumped is interesting for consideration. The residence of this offender is within a close driving distance and perhaps even within walking distance. The house itself would be nondescript and would blend in with the other homes in the area. This person is a longtime resident of this community. He would be a person who is well known and probably lived with his mother for a long period, perhaps to the time of her death.

Vehicle:

This person drives a car that is in poor cosmetic condition. The car is 8–10 years old, a domestic car, Ford, Chevrolet, etc., and is also dirty, unkempt, and also in relatively poor mechanical condition. The trunk of the car would also be littered, and there would be blood in it that would match the blood of the victim.

Employment:

This person is involved in a steady work situation. He is working in some type of construction work and something that demands physical labor. He may also be a truck driver. He is not, however, in a white-collar position. He is involved in a job on a steady basis. He shows some knowledge of the various police jurisdictions, and the manner in which the body parts were dumped shows some knowledge that police don't always share information. He may at one time have been or currently be a volunteer, an auxiliary police officer, deputy sheriff, medical technician, foreman, etc.

Psychosexual development:

This killer is a seriously disturbed individual. The savagery of the dismemberment depicts someone who has anger directed toward women, appearing in the manner in which he disfigured the face of the victim—i.e., the "smile" on her face. The manner in which he cuts the parts of the body shows determination and anger, while making the victim less than a human being: "Not only are you nothing, now you are little bits of nothing."

The killer has placed the parts in descending order of preference. First of all, the hips, or lower torso, are found days before the other parts. This illustrates that he has a lower interest in the torso area, and other parts are more important since they were kept longer. What is especially interesting is that the person has kept—or at least it has not been found—the body from the neck to the waist. This is the most important part for him. I can see him skinning this body part and wearing it at night around the house, where he lives alone.

This person may be a preoperative transsexual and may have tried to get counseling for sexual problems. I must stress here that I do not believe he is a homosexual. I think he has a tremendous problem with his sexuality. On the one hand he admires women for who they are, he wants to be like them, and that is the reason he keeps the breasts and looks inside the body cavity at the reproductive organs. But on the other hand, he hates women for the manner in which they (the mother?) have treated him. He also demonstrates this in the manner in which he selects his victims. The victimology shows that this victim was sexually active and frequented lower-class bars, drank excessively, and "ran around on her family." The "victim was deserving" may have been a theme in the fantasy of the killer.

Interrogation:

I would be happy to talk with you concerning interrogation strategies once you have effected an arrest.

According to the profile, the offender was White, a high school graduate, of average intelligence, and a loner. This profile proved to be correct, but it was rather limited.

The first author of this volume was also asked to provide a profile in this case. According to the profile, all 34 rapes were committed by one offender, who was White (as described by the victims), married, a Roman Catholic, and employed. He probably lived near where most of the rapes had taken place and had likely been raised in a sexually repressive home atmosphere. Given that he was Catholic, it was probable that he was not the product of a broken home; that is, it was unlikely that his parents had divorced. He probably now lived in his own home with his wife and children, maybe two or three children, and drove his well-maintained car to the scenes of his rapes.

This profile proved to be remarkably accurate. When the rapist was apprehended, it was found that he was indeed responsible for all the rapes. He was Catholic and lived in his own home with his wife and two children. His parents lived not far from his home, and he worked as a skilled worker for a manufacturing company. He stalked his victims and drove his pickup truck, which was in excellent condition, to the sites of attacks.

It would be impressive evidence of the usefulness of profiling if this profile had led directly to the apprehension of this rapist, but this did not prove the case. Rather, one of the man's victims happened to recognize him when she saw him later at a shopping center; she followed him to the parking lot and copied down his truck's license number. He was soon arrested, and the case was quickly resolved.

This rapist received 666 years in prison. He is in prison, is a model prisoner, and is now eligible for parole. However, when released on parole, a neighboring state is waiting to prosecute him on an additional rape charge.

❖ CONCLUSION

The profile developed by Delaney in *The Third Deadly Sin* illustrates a point we will emphasize again later in this book: The daily activities of police officers provide them with learning experiences they can use in profiling cases. This point is also made by Captain Marino in Patricia Cornwell's novels. The knowledge base needed for psychological profiling is formed by an understanding of what both physical and non-physical evidence can reveal as well as an understanding of basic precepts and principles of the social and behavioral sciences.

The attention to detail in Sherlock Holmes's investigations offers plain and simple messages to investigators: The details, the trifles, are not to be ignored—often the answers are in the crime scene if one pays attention. As Doyle (1891e) said himself, "There is nothing so important as trifles" (p. 89).

During an interview with serial killer Ted Bundy, he said that police officers take their cases too personally. Because of the total personal immersion in their cases, they lose their objectivity. In *Red Dragon,* Will Graham loses his objectivity, and his total immersion in the crime and into the mind of the killer lead him to emotional and health problems, early retirement, and almost fatal consequences (Harris, 1981). Of course, profiling in reality is not as neat and precise as it appears in fiction, and sometimes the profiles go unused. As we have shown, the profile of Hitler developed by Langer was never actually utilized, and the profiles developed in the serial rape case discussed above did not lead directly to apprehension. Some profiles do lead to arrests, however, and we will discuss some of these at length later in this book.

❖ REFERENCES

Beattie, R. (2005). *Nightmare in Wichita: The hunt for the BTK strangler.* New York: New American Library.

Bruno, A. (1993). *The Ice Man: The true story of a cold-blooded killer.* New York: Delacorte.

Carlo, P. (2006). *The Ice Man: Confessions of a Mafia contract killer.* New York: St. Martin's.

Carr, C. (1994). *The alienist.* New York: Random House.

Carr, C. (1997). *The angel of darkness.* New York: Random House.

Cornwell, P. (1991). *Postmortem.* New York: Avon Books.

Cornwell, P. (1996). *From potter's field.* New York: Berkley.

Cornwell, P. (1999). *Black notice.* New York: G. P. Putnam's Sons.

Douglas, J., & Olshaker, M. (2000). *The cases that haunt us: From Jack the Ripper to JonBenet Ramsey, the FBI's legendary mindhunter sheds light on the mysteries that won't go away.* New York: Scribner.

Doyle, A. C. (1891a). The Bascombe Valley mystery. In *The original illustrated Sherlock Holmes*. Secaucus, NJ: Castle.

Doyle, A. C. (1891b). A case of identity. In *The original illustrated Sherlock Holmes*. Secaucus, NJ: Castle.

Doyle, A. C. (1891c). The five orange pips. In *The original illustrated Sherlock Holmes*. Secaucus, NJ: Castle.

Doyle, A. C. (1891d). The red headed league. In *The original illustrated Sherlock Holmes*. Secaucus, NJ: Castle.

Doyle, A. C. (1891e). The man with the twisted lip. In *The original illustrated Sherlock Holmes*. Secaucus, NJ: Castle.

Ferrero-Lombroso, G. (1911). *Criminal man: According to the classification of Cesare Lombroso.* New York: Putnam.

Harris, T. (1981). *Red dragon.* New York: Putnam.

Harris, T. (1988). *The silence of the lambs.* New York: St. Martin's.

Harris, T. (1999). *Hannibal.* New York: Delacorte.

Harrison, S., & Maybrick, J. (1994). *The diary of Jack the Ripper.* London: Smith Gryphon.

Langer, W. (1943). *A psychological analysis of Adolph Hitler: His life and legend.* Washington, DC: M. O. Branch, Office of Strategic Services.

Langer, W. (1972). *The mind of Adolf Hitler.* New York: New American Library.

Patterson, J. (2000). *Roses are red: A novel.* Boston: Little Brown.

Sanders, L. (1981). *The third deadly sin.* New York: Putnam's Sons.

Sandford, J. (1994). *Winter prey.* New York: Berkley.

Sandford, J. (1995). *Mind prey.* New York: G. P. Putnam's Sons.

Sandford, J. (1997). *Sudden prey.* New York: Berkley.

Sandford, J. (1998). *Secret prey.* New York: G. P. Putnam's Sons.

Sandford, J. (1999). *Certain prey.* New York: G. P. Putnam's Sons.

Sandford, J. (2000). *Easy prey.* New York: G. P. Putnam's Sons.

Sandford, J. (2001). *Chosen prey.* New York: G. P. Putnam's Sons.

3

The Rationale for Psychological Profiling

❖　❖　❖

W hen a particularly bizarre and sadistic crime has been discovered, an immediate question comes to mind: What kind of person would commit such an act? Most crimes of this nature defy understanding and leave one with a sense of bewilderment and astonishment.

The appropriate questions, however, are more like these: What makes someone do something like this? What makes up a personality who enjoys mutilation, necrophilia, rape, child molestation, setting fires, and other forms of perversion and pain? To address such questions, profiling reconstructs a personality sketch for evaluation.

❖ PERSONALITY AND CRIME

Some understanding must come to the forefront to meet the challenge of apprehending and prosecuting perpetrators who commit crimes such as sadistic torture, rape, and other forms of violent crime, and what should be called for is personality profiling. The profile endeavors to share some understanding on the type of person who would rape, pillage, mutilate, and kill.

A personality is the sum total of what a person is. It is that person's total set of values and attitudes, the way he or she views motherhood and fatherhood, law and order, Democrats and Republicans, and all the other social, cultural, religious, and personal experiences that have ever been a part of his or her life. Each person, criminal or not, has a unique personality. Regardless of past experiences, parental background, or biology, each person relates differently, behaves differently, and possesses a different set of values and attitudes. What accounts for this difference? It is a variety of blending five personality components: biology, culture, environment, common experiences, and unique experiences.

❖ BIOLOGY

There is no extant data that suggest that an individual personality is determined solely by the biological inheritance from his or her parents, grandparents, or other ancestors. It does appear, however, that intellectually superior parents have intellectually superior children. It is also true that tall people tend to have tall children, and short people tend to have short children. The key phrase here is "tend to." There are always exceptions.

As far as intelligence is concerned, it simply may be that intelligence is only a score on a test. Some children score higher on standardized tests because of social factors rather than simple biological inheritance. These factors include social class, educational experiences, life's rewards, personal relationships, and varied other experiences that shape and mold the personality of the individual.

❖ CULTURE

The culture in which a person is reared provides rules and regulations, words, ideas, customs, and beliefs for the formation of a personality. Culture provides the normative structure for the society in which a person lives.

But within each culture there are subcultures: male, female, rich, poor, criminal, and noncriminal. These subcultures have certain distinguishable characteristics that set them apart from the overall, prevailing culture. Each subculture insists on certain patterns of behavior. Each also rewards its members in its own unique fashion.

In other words, a person brought up in one part of a society will be exposed to elements of that particular society, which will differ from other parts of that society and culture because of the unique exposure to a varied set of subcultures. These exposures will have an influence on personality development.

❖ ENVIRONMENT

The total surroundings of a person affect the perception and behavior of that person. A person from the elite upper class, for example, will be exposed to a far different set of life experiences than will a person from the lower class. It is not only these day-to-day experiences that become an integral part of the personality, but the social class of an individual also places that person into an arena where he or she will come in contact with a far different set of experiences and opportunities than other people in other social classes could ever experience.

❖ COMMON EXPERIENCES

All of us encounter common daily experiences: going to school, having a job, and so on. Most members of Western society have been exposed to baseball, automobiles, marriages, and unfortunately, perhaps, divorce. These activities are part of our cultural identity. Not all of us, however, have been to the same school or have been taught by the same teacher. Not all of us have been reared in the same family, and not all our parents were happily married. Not all children are brought up by their biological parents. Some may have been reared by their grand-parents, by foster parents, or others. But enough of us reared in the United States have developed a modal personality type. This personal-ity type contains ideal values—trustworthiness, loyalty, honesty, and reverence, among others—that we have learned to hold dear and true.

❖ UNIQUE EXPERIENCES

What separate each of us are not the common experiences but the unique ones. This is the element that explains our individual personal-ities. Consider identical twins. The biological inheritance is the same, but identical twin studies report marked personality differences (Bouchard & McGue, 1990; Eaves, Eysenck, & Martin, 1989; Keller, Bouchard, Arvey, Segal, & Dawis, 1992; Loehlin & Nichols, 1976; Tellegen et al., 1988; Vernon, Jang, Harris, & McCarthy, 1997).

The answer to the question of why identical twins are not identical in their personalities must certainly rest with unique experiences. After all, twins have the same set of parents and usually share much of their genetic makeup. The daily happenings, feedings, diaper changes, and verbal exchanges are all performed in slightly different sequences. This accounts, at least in part, for the difference in personalities.

❖ NEW WAYS OF VIEWING THE PERSONALITY

The personality of a violent offender must be viewed as more than sim-ply someone who has gone through life much the same way as others in the same society. This cannot be the case. The personality of the very violent is different in substance from the modal personality type of American society at large. Those people who commit the crimes suit-able for profiling are substantially different from law-abiding citizens, as are their personalities. Theories attempt to define these differences, but no satisfactory differences has been discovered. Because the very violent do not share in the modal personality, and because impersonal violence is so difficult to understand, it is assumed that such perpetration of violence reflects a pathological personality condition, which is then reflected in the perpetrator's crime scene or scenes.

This is really not an extraordinary assumption. This same comment could be made about the law-abiding but neurotic person. The social and behavioral sciences have been doing this for years. Take, for example, the obsessive-compulsive personality. These people are anal retentive in all they do. This will be evident in their homes, cars, personal effects, and personal hygiene. This personality disorder will take over their daily life's activities. So it is with the very violent. When I visited Ted Bundy on death row in Florida, his cell was immaculate. His correspondence was all arranged in labeled shoe boxes against one wall of his cell. His clothing was arranged neatly, and his comb and hairbrush were side by side on a small counter next to his sink. Ted was neat and orderly. So were his crimes. He was a "five window killer," or one who exhibits all of the stages that many serial killers do (fantasy, stalk, abduction, kill, disposal). Thus, the traits of this personality will be reflected in the perpetration of his or her crime, much as it is with the obsessive-compulsive personality.

The crime scene of the very violent reflects the violent personality. If one accepts this premise, then viewing crime scenes will take on a totally fresh and unique perspective. This new perspective, however, will be evident only if the profiler knows what to look for and where to look for it.

❖ ASSUMPTIONS OF THE PROFILING PROCESS

Several assumptions can be made regarding psychological profiling. These assumptions are important to consider because they deal directly with the reasons why profiles are important and the manner in which certain information can be obtained and used to formulate a creditable criminal investigation assessment. These assumptions are as follows.

The Crime Scene Reflects the Personality

The basic assumption of psychological profiling is that the crime scene reflects the personality of the offender. After all, how effective would profiling be if the crime itself were not indicative of the pathology assessment? The assessment will aid in the direction and scope of the investigation of the crime.

Not only is the manner in which the homicide victim was fatally dispatched important, but the physical and nonphysical evidence will also lend, to some degree, an assessment of the type of personality involved in a particular murder. The amount of chaos, for example, might indicate that a disorganized personality was involved in this crime. If this is true, then we can make certain assumptions about particular social core variables of the unknown perpetrator. On the other hand, if the crime scene is "neat and clean," then other assumptions might lead us to an offender who possesses a different set of social core variables.

The focus of the attack may also indicate certain information that aids in the apprehension of an unknown offender. For example, in a Midwestern state, an elderly woman was killed in her own home. She was stabbed repeatedly and suffered multiple deep wounds to the upper legs and genital area. The profile offered an assessment of the crime itself that, in part, resulted in the arrest of a man who was considered a suspect in the beginning stages of the law enforcement investigation.

In essence, the total picture of the crime scene must be viewed and evaluated to obtain a mental image of the personality of the offender. One sadistic offender reported to us in a personal communication the following:

I had once read a pornographic book in my father's garage. This book was about rape. I believe I memorized the whole book. There was one part of the book which described a rape of a young girl. I made all the girls I raped repeat the words of the girl in the book. This was the only way I could enjoy the rapes. Eventually, it was not enough to rape. The girl in the book was killed, so I had to kill.

This killer learned from an experience with violent pornography. But because of the constellation of his other experiences, combined with his family background, social and biological inheritance, and common experiences constituting his personality, he found sexual pleasure and personal satisfaction from the rapes and killings of scores of women. This killer was unable to stop his raping and killing as long as he was physically free to do so. These urges develop similarly to an addiction. This urging, compulsion, or addiction became part of the killer's personality. The manifestation of the urging became part of the crime scene, which was part of each of his crimes. Again and again, he acted out the scenario found in his father's pornography.

There is no denying that once the cycle of violence is set into motion, violence itself becomes a habit, a need that must be satisfied repeatedly thereafter. And in this general sense, we're sure it can be said that the offender is addicted to impersonal violence.

The Method of Operation Remains Similar

The behavior of the perpetrator, as evidenced in the crime scene and not the offense per se, determines the degree of suitability of the case for profiling (Geberth, 1983). The crime scene contains clues that experienced profilers determine to be signatures of the criminals. Because no two offenders are exactly alike, it is equally true that no crime scenes are exactly alike. As certainly as a psychometric test reflects psychopathology, the crime scene reflects a personality with pathology.

Many serial offenders are very aware of the nonphysical evidence that is present at a crime scene. One murderer remarked,

> First of all, any investigative onlooker to my crime scene would have immediately deduced that the offender was extremely sadistic in nature. The visible markers of bondage, nature of the victims' wounds, and evidence of unhurried, systematic abuse should have indicated that these sadistic acts were not new to me. And that I had committed such brutal crimes in the past and would likely to do so again. (authors' files)

The offender further stated that

> From these points, it could have then be correctly assumed that although brutally violent, the offender was nevertheless intelligent enough to attach method to his madness, cautious and aware enough of his surroundings to make sure he proceeded unseen in the commission of his deeds. Further, because such a brutal offense was unprecedented in this location, it could have been correctly assumed that the offender was very new to the city; if he was a drifter, he was at least someone who very possibly could decide to leave town as suddenly as he arrived [which is exactly what he did].

The remarks from this killer show one dimension of personality—the conscious dimension—that profiling often neglects. This murderer and rapist illustrates by his remarks the elements within his crime scenes that truly reflect his personality. The method of operation, the MO, was repeated many times in the course of his rapes and murders.

The Signature Will Remain the Same

A signature is the unique manner in which a certain offender will commit a crime. It may be the manner in which he will kill, certain words he will use in the rape, or a certain way in which he will leave something at the crime scene.

In a Midwestern state, two elderly women were murdered. Neither was raped. They were left in a public park in full view. Their driver's license and their keys were placed on their bare stomachs. In another state, several hundred miles away, a female impersonator was killed in the same fashion, strangled and knifed, and his driver's license and his car keys were also left on his bare stomach. If we examine just the perpetrator's ideal victim type, it would appear that there are two killers. After all, why would a killer of elderly females also kill a female impersonator? However, the placement of the licenses and the keys should be considered a "signature" and an indicator of the uniqueness of the crime. This signature should alert the investigators that the crimes were committed by the same person and some sense of cooperation should exist between the various jurisdictions.

Hazelwood (1994), a retired FBI agent who spent the latter part of his career with the Behavioral Science Unit, lectures to law enforcement units across the United States about the importance of considering the signature and its influence on the profiling process.

The Offender Will Not Change His Personality

As many people believe, the core of our personalities does not change fundamentally over time. We may change certain aspects of our personality, but the central core is set, and we make only minor alterations due to time, circumstance, pressure, and so on. We may want to make fundamental changes in our personalities but find it is most difficult or impossible to do so. So it is with the criminal personality. It has taken him years to be the person he now finds himself. He will not, over a short period, radically change. It is not simply a matter of not wanting to change; he is not able to change. This assumption has fundamental importance to the profiling process. The inability to change will result in the perpetrator committing a similar crime in a similar fashion. Not only will the criminal commit the same crime, but he may force the victim to act out a scenario that he has also forced previous victims to perform.

The Worth of the Psychological Profile

Not all profiles are as accurate. Some are very general, missing key details, and others are too specific, detailing the manner of dress the victim will be wearing when caught or the type of car the perpetrator drives. Case in point: Perhaps the most accurate on record concerned the Mad Bomber, George Metesky. Dr. James Brussel, a psychiatrist, developed the profile for the Bomber case. Amazingly, he accurately predicted that when the Bomber was eventually caught, he would be wearing a double-breasted suit.

Despite the accuracy of this particular profile, there is a thought that profiling still has not proven its worth:

> Nine out of ten of the profiles are vapid. They play at blind man's bluff, groping in all directions in the hope of touching a sleeve. Occasionally they do, but not firmly enough to seize it, for the behaviorists producing them must necessarily deal in generalities and types. But policemen can't arrest a type. They require hard data: names, dates, none of which the psychiatrists can offer. (Godwin, 1978, p. 2)

Even the Federal Bureau of Investigation's research on the reliability and validity of profiling shows less than a unanimous endorsement of the profiling process. In its study of 192 cases where profiling was performed, 88 cases were solved. Of that 88, in only 17% did a profile help in the identification of a suspect (FBI, 1981). The Bureau does claim, however, that its profile in the Wayne Williams case helped break Williams's composure on the witness stand (Porter, 1983).

Jenkins (1994, pp. 70–79) levels a scathing attack against the worth of the profiles offered by FBI agents/authors Douglas, Ressler, and Hazelwood. The latter agent, now retired, offered the most "inaccurate profile in the Bureau's history" in the Charlie Hatcher case, in which Hazelwood attempted to link two cases based on the MOs from New Jersey and Maine (Ganey, 1989, p. 22). Another debacle was the Clayton Hartwig profile concerning the explosive aboard the U.S. battleship *Iowa* (Jeffers, 1992, pp. 177–229). In this profile, Hazelwood and his fellow agent Richard Ault stated that Hartwig committed suicide by sabotaging a 16-inch gun that killed 47 sailors. Paul Lindsey, a former special agent with the FBI, denounced the claims made by Ressler in his autobiography, *Whoever Fights Monsters* (Jenkins, 1994, p. 71). In addition, Smith and Guillen (1990) cite a case where Douglas was brought in to offer a profile and the case is still unsolved 18 years later.

Despite the claims of the FBI concerning the validity of their profiles and huge resources available to the Bureau, there is less than agreement among those in law enforcement that profiles specifically from the Bureau or generally from others are key elements in the investigatory process. Regardless, profiles will continue to be a part of many such investigatory efforts.

❖ CONCLUSION

The personality of the violent offender is a result of a special combination of factors, which include his biological inheritance, the culture, the environment, as well as common and unique experiences. Because of this unique combination, the violent personal offender will commit crimes as an outgrowth of his existing pathological conditions.

The crime scene reflects the pathology in his personality, and the personality is a part of the crime scene. The nonphysical evidence will have important ramifications for the psychological profiling process. Because the personalities of individuals, either noncriminal or criminal, remain relatively inflexible, the criminal personality will continue to commit the same or similar crimes utilizing the same or similar MOs.

Inflexibility of personality and perpetration of crimes aid the profiler in the task of developing a character sketch. Chaos and order, sexual torture or a quick kill, mutilation or not all indicate a personality that has evolved over the years. It is no easier for the violent personality to suddenly and completely change patterns of behavior than it is for the law-abiding citizen.

❖ REFERENCES

Bouchard, T. J., & McGue, M. (1990). Genetic and rearing environmental influences on adult personality: An analysis of adopted twins reared apart. *Journal of Personality, 58*, 263–292.

Eaves, L. J., Eysenck, H. J., & Martin, N. (1989). *Genes, culture, and personality: An empirical approach.* London: Academic Press.

Ganey, T. (1989). *St. Joseph's children: A true story of terror and justice.* New York: Lyle Stuart/Carol.

Geberth, V. (1983). *Practical homicide investigation.* New York: Elsevier.

Godwin, J. (1978). *Murder USA: The ways we kill each other.* New York: Ballantine.

Hazelwood, R. (1994, March). Lecture delivered at the Southern Police Institute, Ft. Lauderdale, FL.

Jeffers, H. (1992). *Who killed precious?* New York: St. Martins.

Jenkins, P. (1994). *Using murder: The social construction of serial homicide.* New York: Aldine de Gruyter.

Keller, L., Bouchard, T., Arvey, R., Segal, N., & Dawis, R. (1992). Work values: Genetic and environmental influences. *Journal of Applied Psychology, 77*, 79–88.

Loehlin, J., & Nichols, R. (1976). *Heredity, environment, and personality: A study of 850 sets of twins.* Austin: University of Texas Press.

Porter, B. (1983, April). Mind hunters. *Psychology Today*, 1–8.

Smith, C., & Guillen, T. (1990). *The search for the green river killer.* New York: Onyx.

Tellegen, A., Lykken, D., Bouchard, T., Wilcox, K., Segal, N., & Rich, S. (1988). Personality similarity in twins reared apart and together. *Journal of Personality and Social Psychology, 54,* 1031–1039.

Vernon, P., Jang, K., Harris, J., & McCarthy, J. (1997). Environmental predictors of personality differences: A twin and sibling study. *Journal of Personality and Social Psychology, 72,* 177–183.

4

Criminal Theories and Psychological Profiling

❖ ❖ ❖

Theories of Crime and Criminality

Individual Theories of Crime
Psychology and Crime
Psychiatry and Crime
Constitutional Theories

Social/Ecological Theories of Crime
Social/Ecological Approaches

Combining the Disciplines

The questions of why some people commit crime and how to stop them are questions that have perplexed mankind since the dawn of civilized society. Despite the fact that we can build a station in outer space, talk to others via a cell phone almost anyplace in this country, and investigate the causes of a plane crash with utmost precision, mankind still cannot answer these age-old questions with any precision.

In our classes, students routinely ask us why a certain offender would commit a heinous and bizarre offense against another. After all, we are the experts, so we should know. However, more often than not, there is no simple explanation of why some people behave the way they do. Despite our experience, education, and simply our best guess, our explanations concerning the reasoning behind the actions of many criminal offenders are just theoretically grounded guesses and nothing more.

We suppose that many students may be caught off guard by the admission that even some of the most educated people and professed experts simply have no simple answer to why many offenders behave the way they do. But to say something else or to pretend that we or any other expert in this field knows with certainty what makes a violent offender tick is a lie. And any firm educational experience, of course, mustn't base its foundation on lies, mistruths, or suggestive interpretations.

Thus, we intentionally choose to start this chapter with the basic idea that most of the time, theories concerning the basis of deviant or criminal behavior are based on nothing more than a series of educated guesses. No, there is no crystal ball, nor are there any people in the forensic sciences (that we know of) that see visions of the criminals committing their crimes when they come in contact with the victim's personal effects. So, what we are left with is a series of theories about why some people behave the way they do, and what motivates others to refrain from these types of personal indiscretions.

The collection of knowledge that helps us explain human behavior is often referred to as theories of criminal behavior. These theories are often a series of propositions linking one concept to another. For instance, strain theory purports that persons of the lower economic classes commit crime because they feel that the only way they can achieve their legitimate goals of wealth and capital accumulation is through illegitimate means (Cloward, 1959; Merton, 1968).

Other social theories have been purported that take not a sociological perspective but rather a biological one. Biological explanations of criminal behavior state that some people are born with a predisposition toward crime, aggression, and violent behavior (Goring, 1913; Lombroso, 1876, 1917). Goring and many other theorists of this field believed that just as children inherit their parents' genes (eye color, body build, susceptibility to diseases, etc.), they also inherit their parents' moral and mental sentiments. Thus, if a parent had a drinking problem, addictive personality, or a problem with aggression management, so will the child.

While these theories are based on sound arguments and often statistical proof, none that we will discuss later are capable of explaining in aggregate sense why people commit crime or egregious deeds. Thus, it should be apparent that there is no one answer why people behave the way they do. It may be that the offender lacks attachment to the rest of society, was born with bad genes, or has a problem with aggression management, or it might simply be that this offender is just insane. There truly is no one answer that any of us can point to that explains the typical makeup of all violent criminal offenders, despite society being in continual search for one (Ainsworth, 2001).

Thus, the well-grounded student must force him- or herself to be well schooled in the variety of theoretical explanations of criminal behavior and be able to draw from this knowledge when he or she sees the indicators in the offender's modus operandi, crime scene, or victim attributes as necessary.

Hence, the purpose of this chapter. It is designed to introduce students to many of the traditional criminological theories concerning violent or criminal behavior so that students can develop a background database to assist them in profiling actual cases or simply cases they hear about or see on television or elsewhere.

What this chapter is not is a complete collection of these theories and thought. Whole books have been written on these topics, and due to space constraints, we are forced to summarize a selection of what we feel are the most pertinent criminological theories. Should students wish to gain a fuller and more detailed explanation of these theories, we suggest that they peruse resource texts like Vold and Bernard's (1986) *Theoretical Criminology* or Lilly, Cullen, and Ball's (1996) *Criminological Theory: Context and Consequences.*

❖ THEORIES OF CRIME AND CRIMINALITY

In the past, sociologists, psychologists, and criminologists have all argued about the source and nature of crime. Some sociologists claim that the root cause of criminality lies in the relationship of man to the existing social structure. They state that people commit crime to acquire the resources needed for survival that they do not believe they can get through legitimate means. Psychologists, on the other hand, have tended to claim that the root causes of crime lie within the individual and their personality formation. Contemporary criminologists are not so sure that the root causes of crime can be attributed to either of these two sources but rather a combination of these two and many more.

This simple segregation of beliefs regarding the root causes of criminality is by no means conclusive. Presently, most sociologists and psychologists recognize that there is no one factor that we can attribute as the root causes of criminality. During the past 30 years most people interested in this study of crime and its causes have begun to adopt an interdisciplinary approach—that crime has many dimensions. One person may be motivated by individual causative factors, another by social/structural factors, and another by biological or hereditary factors such as an aggressive personality, but most now would agree that most criminals are motivated and seduced into a life of crime by a combination of these elements.

In this chapter, for the sake of brevity, we will introduce students to the two major sources of theories about crime. The theories that compose these traditions will be explained in a brief manner with the sole purpose of introducing students to the many dimensions of crime. Thus the rest of this chapter will focus on individual-level and social/structural theories.

❖ INDIVIDUAL THEORIES OF CRIME

Under the rubric of individual-level explanations of crime there are many different types of explanations of why one would commit crime and participate in a criminal career. In the past, many believed that demons or evil spirits possessed those that had committed heinous crimes or barbaric acts. While our research and knowledge of the human psyche has evolved quite a bit since those days, demonic possession is still considered an individual explanation of crime causation in many parts of the world. Today, many individual-level theorists are more advanced and point to factors such as personality formation as one of the most formidable reasons why one engages in a life of crime.

To differentiate individual-level explanations more thoroughly, we will divide this section into three different subsections. In the first, we will look at psychological explanations; the second, psychiatric explanations; and in the final subsection we will examine biological factors that are believed to contribute to one's engaging in a life of crime.

Psychology and Crime

Contemporary theories detailing psychological explanations about criminal conduct tend to emphasize both individual and environmental influences on criminality. These theories claim that something in the environment has triggered an internal response in the individual's own personality and its development that allows the individual to engage in immoral behavior and criminal activity with relative impunity.

In fact, many psychological explanations tend to denote various personality attributes exhibited by offenders that if identified early could predict future criminal behavior (Vito & Holmes, 1994). Thus, the emphasis for these theories is the identification of aberrant behavior or tendencies, and how these are acquired, evoked, maintained, or modified (Bartol & Bartol, 1999).

Crime and Personality Formation

As discussed above, many psychological theories of crime have focused on an individual's personality and its formation. It is believed that impulsivity, the lack of an ability to delay gratification, and an innate aggressiveness are all components of a criminal's personality. As Neitzel (1979) noted, it is believed that "crime is the result of some personality attribute uniquely possessed, or possessed to a certain degree, by the potential criminal" (p. 350).

One of the most prominent theorists of the psychological school of criminality was Hans Eysenck. Eysenck (1977) professed that sociological theories offered little to the discussion of crime and antisocial tendencies. Instead he remained convinced that psychological factors (more specifically, inherited features of the central nervous system) in interaction with environmental influences were the key to revealing the crime causation origin.

While many of the constructs and suppositions put forth by Eysenck have failed to withstand empirical scrutiny when tested alongside other causative factors, other research has found that personality may indeed play a role in many serial offenders' behavior patterns (Cochrane, 1974; Farrington, Biron, & LeBlanc, 1982; Feldman, 1977). For instance, in one study, Holmes, Tewksbery, and Holmes (1999) claimed that many serial murderers report a phenomenon in their past where they had developed a fractured or split identity. While this split may not meet the clinical definition of a split personality, the offenders interviewed claimed that they developed a side of them that allowed them to operate in society without being noticed, and another side (the dark side) where they were all powerful and wanted to serve notice to others about who they were, demonstrating their power through the commission of violent acts or murder. Holmes et al. labeled this phenomenon Fractured Identity Syndrome. While this theory has not been empirically validated, it is based on Freud's and later Goffman's (1986) principle that behavior in adults is based on traumatic experiences in childhood that left a lasting mark on the individual and his or her personality (Redl & Toch, 1979).

Personality Characteristics

Other theories of criminal or antisocial behavior have focused more specifically on personality characteristics instead of personality formation. While these theories are difficult to empirically test, most law enforcement agents, homicide detectives, and profilers will attest that, based on their experience, they can tell you some of the personal attributes exhibited by those who commit grisly and heinous crimes. These personality attributes are a critical part of any profile and are often contingent on evidence (either physical or nonphysical) left at a crime scene.

Typical crime scene profiles involving violent crimes will attest that the offender is aggressive, withdrawn, argumentative, isolated, antisocial, organized or disorganized, suspicious, and paranoid. These personality characteristics of serial offenders have been recognized for ages. Some are based on firm theoretical grounding and others on the investigators' experience and intuition.

One the first large-scale studies completed to link personality attributes with criminal tendencies was conducted by Schuessler and Cressey (1950). This study found that of all the studies published prior to 1950, 42% found differences between the personality attributes of criminals and non-criminals. While a 42% concordance rate is not overwhelming evidence or conclusive of a distinct personality difference, other studies have found that those who choose to live life in the criminal element may indeed share some personal attributes.

For instance, Glueck and Glueck (1950) in examining the behavior and personality patterns of 1,000 delinquent and non-delinquent boys found that the delinquents are more likely to be

extroverted, vivacious, impulsive and less self-controlled than the non-delinquents. They are less fearful of failure or defeat than the other delinquents. They are less concerned about meeting conventional expectations, and are more ambivalent toward or far less submissive to authority. They are as a group, more socially assertive. To a greater extent than the control group, they express feeling of not being recognized or appreciated. (p. 275)

Based on the results of this study, these researchers and many others developed quantitative predictive instruments in an attempt to predict which youths or even which adults might later choose a delinquent or criminal career. The Gluecks developed three such predictive inventories: one based on a potential offender's social background, the second based on character traits, and the third was based on personality attributes as determined through an in-depth psychological interview (Glueck & Glueck, pp. 257–271). They found that for those youths scoring the best, only 10% could be expected to engage in delinquency. Moreover, these researchers concluded that among those scoring the lowest, up to 90% would later participate in a criminal career (Craig & Glueck, 1963).

Other classical research such as the one conducted by Dollard, Doob, Miller, Mowrer, and Sears (1939) found similar results. Dollard and his colleagues at Yale University stated that "aggression is always a result of frustration" (p. 1). The policy implications of this research finding were clear: The real violent and aggressive criminals were those that were frustrated by their life chances and conditions. And if these frustrated people could be singled out, and provided counseling, then their aggressive behavior could be held in check. While this theory was oversimplistic, it did foster further research.

Researchers such as Berkowitz (1962, 1969) began to revise this hypothesis and found that while frustration may be linked with aggression, each individual deals with frustration differently. Some individuals may behave aggressively, while others may repress their emotional reactions to frustration and vent in other ways. Nonetheless, Berkowitz found that frustration is not an innate reaction to blocked goals but rather a learned reaction. Individuals must acknowledge their goals and learn that someone or something prevented them from acquiring these goals (Berkowitz, 1962, 1969).

In our own conversations with serial killers and other violent offenders, we found evidence that many of these individuals do lack the ability to receive criticism and withstand frustration. This frustration often serves as a catalyst for action, which serves to validate the offender's sense of importance and being in control. As one offender told us:

So when I murdered this first person, it was not to fulfill an inner craving, but only because this person frustrated my aims by being completely unresponsive to my brutality. As this victim was seemingly in a catatonic state, oblivious to my violence, I derived no gain or gratification from my acts, and this individual, therefore, was useless to me.

Obviously, more research needs to be done in this area, but the data thus far do not support any strong indication that any particular combination of personality characteristics produces a criminal mind. Even the contemporary widespread use of such tests as the Minnesota Multiphasic Personality Inventory (MMPI) or the *DSM-IV* has shown inconsistent results as far as particular personality traits and the criminal mind are concerned (Fisher, 1962; Funtowicz & Widiger, 1999; Tracey & Chorpita, 1997). While not downplaying the importance or utility of these tests, subjective inventories are simply not valid with all people at all times.

Mental Deficiency

Other psychological theories are related but not directly linked to the idea of personality formation. For instance, many early forensic psychologists suggested that crime and delinquency are directly related to mental deficiency or lack of intellectual ability. Deficits in intelligence may have direct influence on social adjustment and may indeed "cause" certain individuals to adopt a criminal or delinquent lifestyle. Research like that conducted by Hirschi and Hindelang (1977) stated that despite how politically correct it may be to ignore intelligence as a predictor of future criminality, the correlations across studies appear to hold. They found that previous studies indicate that young persons with relatively low IQs may be more prone to delinquency than those with at least average IQs. However, they are quick to note that there may not be a direct relationship between the two. High IQ may lead to better test scores and school grades, and this, in turn, may lead to more opportunities and ability to reach goals. Thus, just because some individuals have low intelligence scores does not mean that they are or will be delinquent; it simply means that chances are greater for them to experience later life stress as a result of their inability to function as efficiently as others (Block, 1995; Fergusson & Horwood, 1995; Lynam & Moffitt, 1995).

There may be another side to the issue of whether IQ is a causal factor in criminal behavior. Individuals with higher intelligence may be more apt to elude capture. It may be that the person with limited mental capacity simply lacks the ability to recognize the opportunity to avoid detection and subsequent apprehension, and thus offenders of lower intelligence may be more visible than more intelligent persons in the criminal justice enterprise. However, there are few empirical data available to validate this possibility.

Criminal Thinking Patterns

Separate but related to the concept of mental deficiency is the notion that while criminals may be just as capable of processing information as others, they may just process information and stimuli from the environment in different ways. For example, Greenberg (1988) stated that human beings constantly scan their environment and organize information about the world around them. From this type of cognitive constructionist viewpoint, it may be that delinquents and other criminals are no different than law-abiding citizens in their personal makeup, but they just store the meanings of external stimuli in their minds in different and often distorted ways (Greenberg, 1988). Other researchers tend to agree. For instance, Yochelson and Samenow (1976) interviewed scores of criminals in hospital settings and concluded that the personality of the criminal is not fundamentally different from that of the non-criminal. In fact, the only difference between the two lies in the criminal's manner of reasoning. Yochelson and Samenow place emphasis on the general irresponsibility of the criminal, coupled with his or her erroneous thinking pattern. Samenow (1984) goes further, however. He states that "it is not the environment that turns a man into a criminal. Rather, it is a series of choices that he makes starting at a very early age" (p. 34).

From this perspective, the solution to the problem of crime rests with changing criminals' thought patterns and making it beneficial for them to restructure their perceptions of their world. Only by changing the way criminals think can we change their behavior.

Character Defects

Psychologists have expended great energy on research into the antisocial personality. Cleckley's *The Mask of Sanity* (1982) was the first major work to describe the behavioral and personality characteristics of individuals with the character defect of psychopathology. According to Cleckley, the psychopath is charming, has no sense of remorse or guilt, is narcissistic, is a habitual liar, has an inadequate sex life, and continually gets into trouble with the law.

There is no single accepted theory regarding what causes psychopathology. It may be that psychopathic individuals have a form of brain damage and tend to come from homes where they have suffered mild rejection. There is less than unanimous agreement that psychopathy actually exists. In his study of hospitalized patients, Cason (1943) found common agreement for only 2 of the 54 behavioral traits supposedly typical of psychopathy. Cason's data suggest that there are no real personality differences between those who exhibit psychopathic behavior and those who do not.

Another possibility posited by some is that psychopathy may indeed be a reality, but that it disappears from the personality by the time a person reaches his or her 30s. It is theorized that this change is based on the argument that the psychopath matures at a much slower rate than most people, reaching maturity around the age of 30. An alternative theory is that the psychopath adjusts to society, and by his or her 30s is accomplished at masking his/her behavior and thus able to avoid identification.

Regardless of the various theories concerning the origins of the criminal mind, psychology offers a perspective unlike any other discipline. Perhaps most important, methodological psychology offers statistical probabilities regarding demographics and propensity to commit criminal acts and display sometimes violent behavior.

Psychiatry and Crime

A second common area of explanation for the involvement of individuals in criminal acts falls under the rubric of psychiatric explanations. Psychiatric models of criminality follow the traditional psychoanalytic perspective advanced by its founder, Sigmund Freud. This perspective derives its impetus for explaining criminality through an exploration of the unconscious drives and motivations of individuals to participate in deviant and sometimes criminal deeds.

Figure 4.1   Sigmund Freud

According to Freudian thought, the quest to understand the motivations or tendencies toward criminal behavior begins with the assumption that all people are born with innate drives to fulfill their wishes and whims. These drives include the motivation to eat, sleep, and engage in sexual behavior. According to Freud, these drives are a natural part of the evolution of mankind. They have allowed him to adapt to inclement weather and conquer his environment. However, these drives and innate motivations have also caused war, famine, and civil distress.

Freud's Building Blocks of Personality

The theory of psychoanalytic building blocks is based on the concept that the human psyche comprises three primary component parts.

These parts, the id, ego, and superego are the building blocks of an individual's personality.

The first of these and the core element of human behavior is called the *id*. The id contains the unconscious instinctual part of the personality and the savage impulses of the individual that center on instant gratification. Most of these impulses lie in the area of sex and aggression (Brill, 1966; Holmes, 1983; Redl & Toch, 1979).

The second part of the inner human psyche is called the *ego*. The ego is best conceptualized as an insulating layer that attempts to protect the individual from the savage impulses of the id. While the ego still wants what it wants, when it wants it, the ego-dominated person understands that there is a time and a place for everything. It is the conscious part of the personality that is able to delay gratification for the savage impulses of the id. However, in this layer, no attempt is made on the part of the ego to measure the social cost and benefit of engaging in illicit activities. This activity is left to the third layer: the *superego*.

The superego is the mediator between the unconscious self and its external environment. This is the level of the individual's psyche that tells the person which types of behavior are appropriate and which are not. While the superego is influenced by the outside world, most lessons about the consequences of behavior stem from experience and not perceptions of how the self would look relative to its environment.

This building block theory has set the stage for researchers over the past 50 years to explore and test Freud's theories. While we still do not have definitive proof that any of these three layers exist, our understanding of the human psyche is premised on their existence. This is not to say that serious research has not been attempted. Aichorn (1935), for example, has related an underdeveloped superego to the criminal personality. Abrahamsen (1944) views the criminal as an id-dominated person. That is, the criminal responds to the basic aggressive and sexual urges of the id and fails to evaluate or appreciate the pain and suffering of the victim. As Abrahamsen notes, "The criminal rarely knows completely the reasons for his conduct" (p. 137).

The criminal may have either an overdeveloped or an underdeveloped superego. Whichever the case, this leads to a psychological state of guilt and anxiety, or *anomie*. Because of this feeling of anomie, the individual is in a constant state of desire for punishment—punishment that will remove the guilt and anxiety and restore the person to a state of psychological equilibrium.

Figure 4.2   Freud's Elements of the Human Psyche

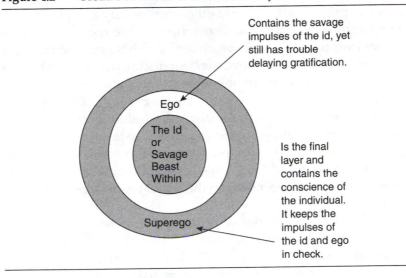

Contains the savage impulses of the id, yet still has trouble delaying gratification.

Ego

The Id or Savage Beast Within

Is the final layer and contains the conscience of the individual. It keeps the impulses of the id and ego in check.

Superego

Freud's View of the Source of Crime

According to Freudian tradition, the source of trauma to the super-ego originates in early childhood. The unregulated id is the direct link to crime, but, because of early conflict, the guilt is evident in youth. Freud (1930) was aware of this and stated:

> In many criminals, especially youthful ones, it is possible to detect a very powerful sense of guilt which existed before the crime, and is therefore not its result but its motive. It is as if it was a relief to be able to fasten the unconscious sense of guilt onto something real and immediate. (p. 52)

Psychoanalytic Treatment

With psychoanalytic treatment, the psychiatrist or other qualified mental health professional tries to reach deep inside the individual and uncover the base reason why people behave the way they do. Hypnotherapy is one type of treatment in which the focus is not on the conscious mind but rather the unconscious one. If Freud was right, then the target of traditional psychotherapy is the ego or even the id. And if criminals, with help from their therapists, can delve into these levels, well below what the conscious mind is able to do by itself, they will be able to uncover the root causes of antisocial behavior and make amends from the inside out.

Other types of treatment, like that received by the majority of inmates in prison facilities across the country, rely on appealing to the superego and attempting to redefine for the individual which behaviors are acceptable and which are not. These traditional forms of treatment do little to remove the hedonistic drive, brought about by some type of pain or emotional scar, but rather try to apply a temporary fix, like a Band-Aid to a gushing wound. For these reasons, it is easy to see that if we are indeed able to delve into the unconscious mind and discover the root causes of behavior, this type of treatment offers a lot more promise than the Band-Aid treatments that the criminal justice system has become so famous for. That is all, however, dependent on the actual presence of the id, ego, and superego.

The factor that many people believe psychiatrists ignore in their approach and interpretation of criminal/violent behavior is the environment. This simply is not true. While the psychiatric model relinquishes the importance of the environment, it does not ignore it. Most theorists belonging to this perspective believe that the source of most personality disorders is held within the individual, and it is the individual that is in need of treatment, although the environment may trigger responses in an already wounded individual.

In summary, theories under this framework hold that violent offenders at some point in their lives have experienced a fissure in their personality and psychosocial development in which the offenders do not truly understand why they desire or engage in these socially and oftentimes legally prohibited acts (Abrahamsen, 1952; Roche, 1958). This perspective's main contribution to criminal theory is the creation of an awareness of the unconscious and the role of guilt and anxiety as they relate to crime.

Constitutional Theories

In today's world, almost all would agree that a person's psyche and the environment they are brought up in play an important role in his or her propensity to engage in a life of crime. We all have heard and have come to accept that the major correlates of criminal behavior are poverty, inadequate educational opportunities, alcohol/drug dependency, and being a product of a broken home. There have, however, been several criminological theorists—constitutional criminologists—who have posited that one's decision to engage in a life of crime or even homicide is not so much a product of a lack of social bonding or a break or fissure in the personality of the individual as a function of the genes that one was passed by a previous generation.

While very few theorists at present now believe that heredity is the sole cause of criminality, constitutional criminological theories still stand. And while these theories may not be as strong predictive elements as some of the contemporary social/structural models, researchers and students of the social sciences simply cannot discount their importance either. One does not have to look too far to see proof of the effect of heredity.

One of the most famous studies in the constitutional school of criminality was the study of the descendants of the Jukes. This study traced the descendants of Ada Jukes. Ms. Jukes was from an unusually large family with a high incidence of alcoholism, sexual promiscuity, mental retardation, and insanity. The researcher found that most of her family members were criminals, prostitutes, or welfare recipients (Dugdale, 1877). Other studies tracing criminal lineages, such as the one conducted by Goddard (1912), reached similar conclusions.

Perhaps the best test of constitutional criminality lies in the research that looked at the criminal propensity of biological twins raised since birth in separate homes. These studies have consistently found that identical twins are more likely than fraternal twins raised in the same surroundings to subscribe to similar lifestyles than their fraternal counterparts (Christiansen, 1977; Lange, 1929; Rowe, 1985; Wilson & Hernstein, 1985).

Despite consistent findings over the years confirming that crime and aggressive propensities may indeed have a biological root, social scientists have continued to argue over how strong a predictor biology is and what parts of our genetic makeup contribute to our innate violent and aggressive tendencies. As it is too much to address all the indicators that researchers have been able to discern that may predict a propensity to engage in violence, we will focus in this section on three. These are heredity, physical characteristics, and chemical/hormonal determinants of criminality.

Heredity and Atavists

Cesare Lombroso (1836–1890) was perhaps the most famous and well-known constitutional criminologist. Lombroso was an Italian physician and amateur criminal anthropologist who proposed that crime and heredity were intricately related. In his book *l'Uomo*

Delinquente (Criminal Man), published in 1876, he stated that some men were born with strong innate propensities to engage in a life of crime (Lombroso, 1876). Borrowing from the works of Darwin, Lombroso felt that the criminal was a separate species of mankind who had not yet evolved as much as the rest of the population (Savitz, 1972). The traditions and ideas of Lombroso were solidified into what we currently call the positive school of criminology.

In the positivist tradition, crime was a "natural phenomenon" for those individuals who were biological throwbacks to an earlier time (Goring, 1913; Lombroso, 1876). Lombroso professed that criminals could be identified by a series of distinguishing physical characteristics, such as their large appendages, insensibility toward pain, an asymmetrical head, and many others (see Table 4.1).

It is important to note that Lombroso retracted many earlier claims that these biological atavists were responsible for the majority of crime. In his third revision of *l'Uomo Delinquente* (1917) he acknowledged that it was possible that this theory could help explain the criminality of only 35% to 40% of habitually violent criminals. Further, he even acknowledged that mental illness, psychological deficiencies, or even social-structural causes may better explain why the majority of individuals engage in violent crime.

Table 4.1   Characteristics of Lombroso's Born Criminal Type

Physical Attributes of the Born Criminal
Asymmetrical face Unusually large or small ears A low receding forehead Prominent eyebrows, jawbones, or cheekbones
Ancillary Attributes of the Born Criminal
Have more acute sense of touch on the left side of the body instead of the right Show a greater insensibility toward pain Sharp vision, but more often than not colorblind Less than average sense of hearing, smell, and taste Are extremely agile, even at advanced ages Ability to recover quickly from wounds Have little to no ability to distinguish between right and wrong Complete lack of shame, remorse, honor, or pity A passion for gambling and alcohol

Physical Characteristics and Crime

Other theorists claimed that different biological factors determined the likelihood that an individual would engage in a life of crime. For instance, Sheldon and Stevens (1940) introduced a theory linking physical attributes of a person's body and his or her personality, a process they called *somatotyping*. After collecting and coding data on the physical measurements of 200 university men, Sheldon, Hartl, and McDermott (1949) claimed to be able to delineate between three main body types: the *endomorph, ectomorph*, and the *mesomorph*. They then took these body types and correlated them to three clusters of temperament that were displayed by their sample. These temperament classifications were *viscerotonia* (a pleasure from eating and socializing), *somatotonia* (a tendency toward assertiveness and dominance, physical adventure, and exercise) and *cerebrotonia* (a tendency toward restraint in movement and emotional expression, and a love of privacy) (Sheldon & Stevens, 1942).

According to these classifications, the endomorph is a person who is fat and soft. In his relationship with others, he is gregarious, jolly, and easy to get along with. According to Sheldon et al. (1949), the endomorph is the least likely to get into trouble with the law because his body type determines his personality and disposition. The second body type that he described was the ectomorph. The ectomorph is a thin and fragile individual. They are easily excitable, afraid of people, and introverted. Sheldon et al. postulated that the ectomorph is less likely to engage in criminality because of a lack of self-confidence and an inability to have and hold sustainable interpersonal relations with others.

The final body type that Sheldon identified was mesomorph. According to his theory, the mesomorph was the real problem. Mesomorphs he described as being athletic and muscular and craving adventure. Similar to Lombroso's biological atavist, Sheldon et al. (1949) described the mesomorph as being ruthless, psychopathic, and indifferent to pain.

While Sheldon's theory was innovative at the time, he never developed a full or complete classification system that could precisely identify offenders. In Sheldon and colleagues' study, respondents were scored on three items (attributes of each body type) using a seven-point scale. Thus, any individual would receive only three scores ranging from 1 to 7, denoting whether they scored high or low on the attributes of that particular body type. While it is not exactly clear, it is believed that if a person scored higher on one scale relative to the other two, they were categorized into that specific group.

Sheldon and colleagues' primitive study looking at personality and body type sparked a series of other studies, each finding some link. For instance, Child (1950) found similar correlations between self-reported temperament and body type for a similar sample of 414 university students for mesomorphs and ectomorphs only. And Cortes and Gatti (1965) studying adolescents found significant correlations across all three measures. A comparison of the correlations between the works of Sheldon and Stevens, Child, and Cortes and Gatti can be found in Table 4.2.

The results and findings of these somatotyping theories sparked interest in the study of body type as it relates to the development of personality, especially violent and aggressive personality types. So powerful was this influence that even the Gluecks alluded to their findings on delinquency and body types when they reported that delinquent boys were larger and stronger than non-delinquent boys (Glueck & Glueck, 1956). Even a follow-up study by Cortes and Gatti (1972) found that male delinquents in their sample were significantly more mesomorphic than their control, non-delinquent sample (Cortes & Gatti, 1972).

While Sheldon and Stevens's (1940) somatotyping theory has recently run out of favor with traditional criminological theory construction, it is clear that biology and heredity do appear to play some role in the display of violence and aggression.

Chemical Imbalances and Hormonal Influences

Another perspective within individual-level theories of crime is the biological school of criminology. This school of thought proposes that many children and adults engage in violent acts because of some type of chemical or hormonal imbalance within their body. Biological theories are now abundant in the current literature. Some researchers

Table 4.2   Correlations Between Physique and Temperament

Study	N	Endomorphy & Viscerotonia	Mesomorphy & Somatotonia	Ectomorphy & Cerebrotonia
Sheldon & Stevens (1942)	200	.79*	.82*	.83*
Child (1950)	414	.13	.38*	.27**
Cortes & Gatti (1965)	73	.32**	.42*	.31**

Note: *Significant at the .001 level; **Significant at the .01 level have found that children who do not ingest the proper balance of vitamins and minerals have problems with their intellectual development, which then in turn may affect their choice to engage in later aggressive, violent, and abnormal sexual activity (Krassner, 1986; Neisser, 1996). The studies linking crime or aggressive behavior to biological factors or chemical imbalances run the scale. For instance, one researcher was able to demonstrate a link between crime and insufficient ingestion of vitamins C, B3, and B6 (Hippchen, 1978, 1981). And another found that for women, most crime was committed in the days leading up to or during the perpetrator's menstrual cycle (Dalton, 1971).

Due to the variety of research that has been done in this area and the consistent findings that hormonal or chemical imbalances have significant effects our bodies, this school of thought remains one that must be contended with and considered when attempting to explain the root causes of criminality. However, the ingestion of certain types of high-protein or fatty foods should never be used as a defense. It may explain why some people feel more agitated and thus are less likely to inhibit their aggressive tendencies, but it does not explain how the motivation to commit crime or other random acts of violence is placed in a potential offender's repertoire of behavior.

❖ SOCIAL/ECOLOGICAL THEORIES OF CRIME

The second group of theories that we will discuss in this chapter have to do with social and structural theories. These theories are more concerned with social and environmental pushes and pulls into a life of crime than with individual-level explanations. The primary focus of these explanations is on how society is structured and the stratification in social life that predisposes some classes of people to commit crimes more so than others.

According to the structural/functionalist perspective, society attempts to function as a well-oiled, integrated, and orderly machine. Ideally, citizens would unanimously agree on society's values and goals, and social structures would function to implement these values and goals. Deviance and crime represent breakdowns of this mechanized system where people stray outside the rules of expected conduct and exhibit self-expressive behavior to alleviate their inadequate social positions.

The structural/functionalist approach can be traced to the writings of Emile Durkheim (1965), who suggested that different interest groups have varied and conflicting views about what types of behavior in civil society are acceptable and which are not. Durkheim's main contribution rests in his emphasis on the organization of social life rather than on psychological causes. He originated his theory of crime in the context of a movement toward modernization, the progression of a society from an organic to a mechanistic state.

He stated that the high rate of crime in mechanistic (modern industrialized) societies rests with the general feeling of anomie, a feeling of helplessness or normlessness that people develop because they lack attachment to society and others. He states that in primitive or organic societies, everyone performs all the work they need for subsistence and no one is dependent on others for their wellbeing or survival. However, when modern industrialized societies began to form, people began to divide labor and live separate and independent lives from the collective group. He states that people in these societies began to lose touch with who they were and what they stood for and instead began to identify themselves with their profession and biological family. According the Durkheim, this progression away from the collective group to more divided, diverse, and segregated groups left many in society suffering from anomie. In this condition, there is no social bond attaching people to society, and the collective sense of what is right or wrong, just or unjust, got lost in the quest for personal/familial, not communal betterment. Simply put, Durkheim felt that modern society, through the division of labor, caused a significant amount of strain to be placed on its constituents as they searched for who they were and how they fit into a larger society.

Other sociologists have addressed the strain between society and the individual. Robert Merton (1968), for example, offered a theory that maintains that both social ends and the means to achieve those ends are learned. Some people in a society will have high aspirations; some will not. In American society, economic rewards are a socially approved goal. The socially approved ways of acquiring these goals are through hard work, education, and the delay of gratification. However, many in society are not able to reach these goals by employing these methods. Maybe they are not able to go to school, cannot afford it or simply do not have the requisite skills necessary to be admitted. These people can, however, achieve the goal of wealth and capital appreciation if they short-circuit the system. If they cheat, lie, or swindle others, or use some other illegitimate means, they may find that they can still achieve their goals. Thus for many in the criminal element, the means are not as important as the ends, since the means are not rewarded in our society.

Social/Ecological Approaches

Following the works of Durkheim and Merton, in the 1930s, an important sociological perspective developed among a group of scholars at the University of Chicago. Important theoreticians such as Burgess, Reckless, Dinitz, Glaser, and Sutherland all became well-known names associated with this social/ecological approach.

These theorists argued that crime and criminal proclivity was not something that could be found innate in the individual but was something that environmental stressors created. For instance, Park (1952) felt that individuals in cities could be compared to animals in their natural habitat. Thus, humans in a collective space practiced the natural processes of invasion, dominance, and succession (Morris, 1966; Park, 1952; Warming, 1969). Thus crime is a natural part of organized life, and the more like individuals that inhabit an area, the more likely they are to invade the property and turf of others not belonging to their social group.

Crime as Learned Behavior

Scholars of the social/ecological perspective broadened the discussion of the root causes of criminality. Durkheim taught us that crime was a normal and functional part of society and these authors found that crime was a natural evolutionary process. But that did not explain how people learned that criminal activity or the enactment of violence against others would bring them status or wealth. Those ideas were left to the theorists belonging to the social learning perspective.

One of the first theorists to adopt this perspective was Gabriel Tarde. Tarde and his colleagues believed that criminality was not biologically determined, as the positivists believed, but rather crime was learned in the interaction with others in a deviant social group (Tarde & Clark, 1969; Tarde & Parsons, 1903). According to Tarde and his colleagues' theory, people learn criminal proclivities in interaction with others and imitate each other in direct proportion to the amount of time they spend together. While it was well known that people often mimic the behavior of others in peer groups, he went one step further. He stated that people of inferior social stature often imitated people of superior stature. The addition of this second clause meant that even normal, well-adjusted youth could be seduced into a life of crime simply by being in the company of a stronger, more aggressive individual or group. Thus, it was not likely that the good would rub off on the evil, but rather evil would always trump decency (Curtis, 1953).

Cultural Transmission Theories

Other theorists took this idea a step further. For instance, Edwin Sutherland's (1937) theory of differential association began to examine this phenomenon as a theory of cultural transmission. According to Sutherland, criminal behavior is learned in primary group relationships, not through exposure to mass media, such as television, movies, radio, and comic books. This is not to say that some techniques for committing crimes may not be learned from these sources, but the inculcation of the necessary motives, drives, direction, and rationalization for the commission of crime takes place on a conscious level. The rearing of an individual with a criminal mindset rests on the person's affiliation with those who favor violation of the law versus those who favor obeying the law.

Social Bond Theories

Perhaps the most recent influential theory of deviance has been offered by Travis Hirschi (1969), who asserts that there is a bond between people and conventional society. There are several basic elements in the theoretical construct of norms of a society that are internalized: *Attachment* refers to a person's sensitivity to the way people think about him or her. *Commitment* is the extent to which a person's social rewards are connected to social conformity. Finally, *involvement* refers to the amount of time a societal member devotes to conventional activity. The higher the level of involvement, the lower the probability of criminal activity.

In essence, social theorists have taken the position that the criminal has learned or has been compelled to commit crime by social situations often triggered by environmental influences. The core of the criminal commitment lies within the personality of the offender and the fiber of the society. The society contains the goals, both legitimate and illegitimate means, objectives, and opportunities, as well as proscriptions concerning criminal behavior. Sociologists place little emphasis on the role of the unconscious in deviance, or on mental deficiency as a causal determinant in crime.

❖ COMBINING THE DISCIPLINES

Clearly, each of the types of theories of criminal and violent behavior are applicable in one way or another for each type of crime or violent behavior that you may investigate or hear about through media outlets.

As stated at the beginning of this chapter, when trying to understand human behavior, especially behavior that is seen as vile and heinous, investigators must take a multidisciplinary approach. Exactly what makes an offender behave the way he or she does cannot simply be explained by individual factors but must also take into account the environment in which he or she was raised and how this environment transmitted justifications for his or her behavior.

The value of the various theories that come from these disciplines is found in the profiler's ability to blend them to reach an understanding of the personality of the perpetrator. There is nothing magical or mystical about this process; its success depends on the "truths" of the disciplines and how they add to the knowledge base of the law enforcement professional. Academic theories will never take the place of on-the-street police work, and the psychological profile is not intended to bolster or refute academic theory; it is simply another tool available for use in the total investigative process.

❖ REFERENCES

Abrahamsen, D. (1944). *Crime and the human mind.* New York: Columbia University Press.

Abrahamsen, D. (1952). *Who are the guilty?* Westport, CT: Greenwood Press.

Aichorn, A. (1935). *Wayward youth.* New York: Viking.

Ainsworth, P. (2001). *Offender profiling and crime analysis.* Portland, OR: Willan.

Bartol, C. R., & Bartol, A. M. (1999). *Criminal behavior: A psychosocial approach* (5th ed.). Englewood Cliffs, NJ: Prentice-Hall.

Berkowitz, L. (1962). *Aggression: A social-psychological analysis.* New York: McGraw-Hill.

Berkowitz, L. (1969). The Frustration-Aggression Hypothesis revisited. In L. Berkowitz (Ed.), *Roots of aggression.* New York: Atherton.

Block, J. (1995). On the relation between IQ, impulsivity, and delinquency: Remarks on the Lynam, Moffitt, and Stouthamer-Loeber interpretation. *Journal of Abnormal Psychology, 104*(2), 395–399.

Brill, A. A. (Ed. and Trans.).(1966). *The basic writings of Sigmund Freud.* New York: Modern Library.

Cason, H. (1943). The psychopath and the psychopathetic. *Journal of Criminal Psychopathology, 4,* 522–527.

Child, I. (1950). The relation of somatotype to self ratings on Sheldon's Temperamental Traits. *Journal of Personality, 18,* 440–453.

Christiansen, K. (1977). A review of studies of criminality among twins. In K. Christiansen (Ed.), *Biosocial bases of criminal behavior.* New York: Gardiner.

Cleckley, H. (1982). *The mask of sanity.* New York: Plume.

Cloward, R. (1959, April). Illegitimate means, anomie, and deviant behavior. *American Sociological Review, 24,* 164–179.

Cochrane, R. (1974). Crime and personality: Theory and evidence. *Bulletin of the British Psychological Society, 27,* 19–22.

Cortes, J., & Gatti, F. (1965). Physique and self description of temperament. *Journal of Consulting Psychology, 29,* 432–439.

Cortes, J., & Gatti, F. (1972). *Delinquency and crime: A biopsychosocial approach.* New York: Seminar Press.

Craig, M., & Glueck, S. (1963). Ten years experience with the Glueck Social Prediction Table. *Crime and Delinquency, 9*, 249–261.

Curtis, J. (1953). Gabriel Tarder. In C. Mihanovich (Ed.), *Social theorists* (pp. 142–157). Milwaukee, WI: Bruce.

Dalton, K. (1971). *The premenstrual syndrome.* Springfield, IL: Charles C Thomas.

Dollard, J., Doob, L., Miller, N., Mowrer, O., & Sears, R. (1939). *Frustration and aggression.* New Haven, CT: Yale University Press.

Dugdale, R. (1877). *The Jukes: A study in crime, pauperism, disease and heredity.* New York: Putnam.

Durkheim, E. (1965). *The division of labor in society* (G. Simpson, Trans.). New York: Free Press.

Eysenck, H. (1977). *Crime and personality* (2nd ed.). London: Routledge and Kegan Paul.

Farrington, D., Biron, L., & LeBlanc, M. (1982). Personality and delinquency in London and Montreal. In D. Farrington (Ed.), *Abnormal offenders, delinquency, and the criminal justice system.* Chichester, UK: Wiley.

Feldman, M. (1977). *Criminal behavior: A psychological perspective.* London: Wiley.

Fergusson, D., & Horwood, L. (1995). Early disruptive behavior, IQ, and later school achievement and delinquent behavior. *Journal of Abnormal Child Psychology, 23*(2), 183–200.

Fisher, S. (1962). The MMPI: Assessing a famous personality test. *American Behavioral Scientist, 6*, 20–21.

Freud, S. (1930). *Three contributions to the theory of sex* (Monograph Series 7). Washington, DC: Nervous and Mental Health Disease.

Funtowicz, M., & Widiger, T. (1999). Sex bias in the diagnosis of personality disorders: An evaluation of the *DSM-IV* criteria. *Journal of Abnormal Psychology, 108*(2), 195–212.

Glueck, S., & Glueck, E. (1950). *Unraveling juvenile delinquency.* Cambridge, MA: Harvard University Press.

Glueck, S., & Glueck, E. (1956). *Physique and delinquency.* New York: Harper and Row.

Goddard, H. H. (1912). *The Kallikak family: A study in the heredity of feeblemindedness.* New York: MacMillan.

Goffman, E. (1986). *Stigma: Notes on the management of spoiled identity.* New York: Simon & Schuster.

Goring, C. (1913). *The English convict.* London: His Majesty's Stationary Office.

Greenberg, L. (1988). Constructive cognition: Cognitive therapy coming of age. *Counseling Psychologist, 16*, 235–238.

Hippchen, L. (Ed.). (1978). *Ecologic–biochemical approaches to treatment of delinquents and criminals.* New York: Von Nostrand Reinhold.

Hippchen, L. (1981). Some possible biochemical aspects of criminal behavior. *Journal of Behavioral Ecology, 2*, 1–6.

Hirschi, T. (1969). *The causes of delinquency.* Berkeley: University of California Press.

Hirschi, T., & Hindelang, M. (1977). Intelligence and delinquency. *American Sociological Review, 42*, 571–587.

Holmes, R. (1983). *The sex offender and the criminal justice system.* Springfield, IL: Charles C. Thomas.

Holmes, S., Tewksbury, R., & Holmes, R. (1999). Fractured identity syndrome: A new theory of serial murder. *Journal of Contemporary Criminal Justice, 115*(13).

Krassner, M. (1986). Diet and brain function. *Nutrition Reviews, 44*, 12–15.

Lange, J. (1929). *Crime as destiny.* Leipzig, Germany: Scott-Townsend.

Lilly, J., Cullen, F., & Ball, R. (1996). *Criminological theory: Context and consequences.* Thousand Oaks, CA: Sage.

Lombroso, C. (1876). *Criminal man.* Milan: Torin.

Lombroso, C. (1917). *Crime, its causes and remedies.* Boston: Little.

Lynam, D., & Moffitt, T. (1995). Delinquency and impulsivity and IQ: A reply to Block. *Journal of Abnormal Psychology, 104*(2), 399–402.

Merton, R. (1968). *Social theory and social structure.* Glencoe, IL: Free Press.

Morris, T. (1966). *The criminal area.* New York: Humanities Press.

Neisser, U. (1996). Intelligence: Knowns and unknowns. *American Psychologist, 51,* 77–101.

Neitzel, M. (1979). *Crime and its modification: A social learning perspective.* New York: Pergamon.

Park, R. (1952). *Human communities.* Glencoe, IL: Free Press.

Redl, F., & Toch, H. (1979). The psychoanalytic explanation of crime. In H. Toch (Ed.), *Psychology of crime and criminal justice.* New York: Holt, Rinehart, and Winston.

Roche, P. (1958). *The criminal mind: The study of communication between criminal law and psychiatry.* New York: Farrar.

Rowe, D. (1985). Sibling interaction and self-reported delinquency behavior: A study of 265 twin pairs. *Criminology, 23,* 223–240.

Samenow, S. (1984). *Inside the criminal mind.* New York: Time Books.

Savitz, L. D. (1972). Introduction. In G. Lombroso-Ferrero (Ed.), *Criminal man.* Montclair, NJ: Patterson-Smith.

Schuessler, K., & Cressey, D. (1950, March). Personality characteristics of criminals. *American Journal of Sociology, 55,* 476–484.

Sheldon, W., Hartl, E., & McDermott, E. (1949). *Varieties of delinquent youth: An introduction to constitutional psychiatry.* New York: Harper.

Sheldon, W., & Stevens, S. (1940). *The varieties of human physique.* New York: Harper.

Sheldon, W., & Stevens, S. (1942). *The varieties of temperament.* New York: Harper.

Sutherland, E. (1937). *The professional thief.* Chicago: University of Chicago Press.

Tarde, G., & Clark, T. (1969). *On communication and social influence; Selected papers.* Chicago: University of Chicago Press.

Tarde, G. D., & Parsons, E. W. C. (1903). *The laws of imitation.* New York: H. Holt and Company.

Tracey, S., & Chorpita, B. (1997). Empirical evaluation of *DSM-IV* Generalized Anxiety Disorder criteria in children and adolescents. *Journal of Clinical Child Psychology, 26*(4), 404–415.

Vito, G. F., & Holmes, R. M. (1994). *Criminology: Theory, research and policy.* Belmont, CA: Wadsworth.

Vold, G., & Bernard, T. (1986). *Theoretical criminology* (3rd ed.). New York: Oxford University Press.

Warming, E. (1969). Plant communities. In E. Burgess (Ed.), *Introduction to the science of sociology* (pp. 175–182). Chicago: University of Chicago Press.

Wilson, J., & Hernstein, R. (1985). *Crime and human nature: the definitive study of the causes of crime.* New York: Simon & Schuster.

Yochelson, S., & Samenow, S. (1976). *The criminal personality.* New York: J. Aronson.

5

The Analysis of the Crime Scene

❖ ❖ ❖

Beyond the Physical Evidence

Psychological Profiling Typology
   The Disorganized Asocial Offender
   The Organized Nonsocial Offender

Crime Scene Differences

Conclusion

Obviously, some crimes are more appropriate for profiling than others. We have listed these crimes in Chapter 1: sadistic torture in sexual assault, evisceration, postmortem slashing and cutting, motiveless fire setting, lust and mutilation murder, and rape (stranger rape, not date or acquaintance rape). Such crimes as check forgery, bank robbery, and kidnapping, in contrast, are usually not appropriate candidates for profiling, nor are "smoking gun" or "dripping knife" murders. In this chapter we focus on those crimes to which the process of profiling is directly applicable.

❖ BEYOND THE PHYSICAL EVIDENCE

Perhaps one of the most difficult things for investigators to accept is the need to look beyond the physical evidence. Homicide detectives are generally trained to reconstruct a crime based on the physical evidence found at the scene, such as blood spatter, fingerprints, and semen. This kind of evidence is often mistakenly thought to hold the key to the successful resolution of any criminal case.

While lecturing in classrooms and across the country on psychological profiling we repeatedly tell our students that when they begin to profile a case, they should disregard the physical evidence and concentrate on nonphysical factors. Oftentimes, students and law enforcement officials are reluctant to do so. We say this, however, because it helps the investigator tie the nonphysical evidence with the physical evidence, once introduced, to produce a total picture of a crime scene. We have found that many people become too caught up in the physical evidence and it limits their ability to think outside the box to reconstruct the totality of a crime scene. However, once they are able to ignore the physical evidence, they can often deduce information about a suspect, including race, sex, employment status, residence, and so on. Thus from our point of view, it is the interrelationship of physical evidence and nonphysical evidence that is the key to the profiling process.

❖ PSYCHOLOGICAL PROFILING TYPOLOGY

The Federal Bureau of Investigation has developed a typology of lust offenders that many profilers find particularly useful; it divides offenders into two categories—disorganized asocial offenders and organized nonsocial offenders. In their book *Sexual Homicide*, Ressler, Burgess, and Douglas (1988) delete the labels "asocial" and "nonsocial" in describing this typology. We believe this is unfortunate, because the descriptive nature of these words is useful. There is a fundamental difference between nonsocial and asocial behaviors, and these adjectives add valuable information that can help clarify the differences between organized and disorganized offenders. For the purposes of this text, we use the full original label to identify each type of offender. (The FBI also has dropped the words *nonsocial* and *asocial* from the labels in its typology, but, as explained, we retain both terms here because we believe they have important meanings.)

This typology can be useful when the crimes at issue involve sex as a primary motive. The offenders who commit such crimes as rape, sexual assault, mutilation, necrophilia, and picquerism are particularly amenable to categorization as organized nonsocial or disorganized asocial offenders.

The Disorganized Asocial Offender

Personal Characteristics

As the list of characteristics in Table 5.1 shows, the personality of this kind of offender is reflected in the label. The disorganized asocial offender, who is almost always male, is disorganized in his daily activities as well as in his general surroundings, including home, employment (if he is employed), car or truck, clothing, and demeanor. In other words, he is a totally disorganized person in all areas—appearance, lifestyle, and psychological state. We should note that this is a general description, and it has not been empirically validated. Nonetheless, in the cases where a "pure" such personality has been found, these general characteristics have proven to be amazingly accurate.

According to the FBI's research data, the typical offender with a disorganized asocial personality tends to be a nonathletic, introverted White male. As children, many of these offenders have been victims of physical or emotional abuse. Their fathers were often absent; if the fathers were present and employed, their work was unstable. During their childhoods, these offenders had few real playmates; they tended to have solitary hobbies, to have imaginary and secret playmates, and to take part in few social activities. The disorganized asocial offender is a loner. The reason for this aloneness, however, is fundamentally different from that behind the aloneness of the organized nonsocial offender. The disorganized asocial offender is a loner because he is perceived by others to be "weird" or strange—his neighbors are often aware of his strangeness.

This perpetrator has usually experienced a great deal of difficulty in educational pursuits. While in high school, he participated little in extracurricular activities, and he probably dropped out of school as soon as legally possible. He is possibly below average in IQ (the FBI

Table 5.1   Profile Characteristics of Disorganized Asocial Offenders

Personal Characteristics	Post-Offense Behavior	Interview Techniques
Below-average intelligence	Returns to crime scene	Show empathy
Socially inadequate	May attend victim's funeral/burial	Introduce information indirectly
Unskilled worker	May place "in memoriam" in newspaper	
Low birth-order status		Use counselor approach
Father's work unstable	May turn to religion	
Received harsh/ inconsistent discipline in childhood	May keep diary or news clippings	Interview at night
Anxious mood during crime	May change residence	
Minimal use of alcohol	May change job	
Lives alone	May have a personality change	
Lives/works near crime scene		
Minimal interest in news media		
Significant behavioral change		
Nocturnal		
Poor personal hygiene		
Secret hiding places		
Usually does not date		
High school dropout		

estimates the IQ of the typical disorganized asocial offender to be between 80 and 95), but this may be more a product of his social and cultural experiences than his native intelligence.

His status in his community is the product of several components of his personality. Limited intelligence, involvement in unskilled work (often as a menial laborer), and few dates or other social contacts with women all reflect a person who is alone not by choice but because of societal segregation.

Because of the combination of components described above, the disorganized asocial offender lacks the ability to plan out his crimes efficiently, and the crimes tend to be spontaneous acts. This kind of offender does not feel comfortable venturing far from his home or work, so he often commits crimes in his own neighborhood. He may walk or ride a bicycle to his crime sites ("Crime Scene," 1985). Generally, this kind of offender does not feel the need to follow his crimes in the news media.

The disorganized asocial offender normally lacks the initiative to practice good personal hygiene. This same characteristic carries over to his domicile, as well as to any car or truck he may own. This trait, then, may theoretically carry over into the crime scene. Finally, as with all lust offenders, he will repeat his crimes.

Post-Offense Behavior

According to the researchers at the Behavioral Science Unit (BSU) of the FBI, the disorganized asocial offender will tend to exhibit certain behavior patterns after he has committed a crime. First, he will need to return to the scene of the crime relatively soon afterward, to envision and relive what has taken place. He may attend the funeral services of his victim, even the burial ceremony. It is not unheard of for such an offender to place an "in memoriam" message in the newspaper for his victim.

This offender may keep a diary in which he records his activities and victims. With the widespread availability of instant photography and video equipment, this type of offender will often keep a visual collection or a collage of his criminal events. Included in collage may be pictures or videos he took of the victim before, during, or after the crime. A part of this type of offender's diary, in addition to accounts of his acts, may be devoted to stories of his fantasies. One serial rapist related the following fantasy:

My preference is for tight teenage girls—the tighter the better. [Talking with another rapist] We've got to do this the right way.

You really blew it, but you were inexperienced. The first thing is to get a house with a windowless, underground basement. Equip it with steel cages [for holding victims], and make sure to soundproof it. Only then will we go out and hunt.

But not just for anyone. Take your time, and find exactly what you want—you don't want to be attracting attention by snatching up a new one every little while. Find one that's perfect. Then we'll keep her locked up before you kill her and grab another. But if we torture, we'd best grab two so that we will always have one recovering while we're busy on the other. (Author's files)

After an offense, the disorganized asocial offender may change his address, but it would be unusual for him to move to a far different environment, because he feels comfortable only with the familiar. If he moves to an area that is drastically different, he may suffer great feelings of anomie. He may therefore move to a similar domicile in a similar area. He may even change jobs. Some may try to enlist in the military, but this is usually unsuccessful, because they either cannot pass the physical or psychological tests or, once enlisted, receive a general discharge.

Interviewing Techniques

Once in custody, the disorganized asocial offender may respond differently to questioning than would the organized nonsocial offender. This perpetrator may be more likely to respond to an interrogator who uses a relationship-motivated strategy. It may be a good idea for the interrogator to appear to empathize with him. For example, if an offender says that he has seen a demon and that the demon demanded that he kill, it might be wise for his questioner to tell him that although the questioner has not personally seen this demon, if the killer says it exists, it does indeed exist.

Because this kind of offender is not used to lengthy personal contacts with others, it may be beneficial for interrogators to keep up a constant stream of conversation, perhaps introducing something into the conversation that has to do with the crime scene. The establishment of a positive personal relationship may also prove beneficial in securing some statement concerning the involvement of the suspect in the case.

Another characteristic of the disorganized asocial offender that may be useful for interrogators to know is that he tends to be a night person. Considering this, the interviewer might take the opportunity to interview this person when he is at "his best"—at night.

The Organized Nonsocial Offender

Personal Characteristics

The organized nonsocial offender is the disorganized asocial offender's opposite. He has an organized personality that is reflected in his lifestyle, home, automobile, and personal appearance. This kind of offender may suffer from some type of obsessive-compulsive disorder in his life, in that there is a place for everything, and everything must be in its place.

Ted Bundy is an example of such an offender. Because of his personality, Bundy would have found it very difficult to deviate from his accustomed way of doing things. As a result, he was connected with at least four murders because he charged his gasoline and signed receipts for his purchases. He was placed in Golden, Colorado, on the day Suzy Cooley was abducted and killed; in Dillon, Colorado, when Julie Cunningham was murdered; and in Grand Junction, Colorado, when Denise Oliverson was reported missing. Michael Fisher was able to secure a murder indictment against Bundy in the Caryn Campbell case when Fisher was able to place Bundy in the immediate vicinity of the Snowmass Ski Lodge because of his gasoline purchases.

As Table 5.2 shows, organized nonsocial offenders are basically organized in everything they do. They are nonsocial because they choose

Table 5.2   Profile Characteristics of the Organized Nonsocial Offender

Personal Characteristics	Post-Offense Behavior	Interview Techniques
High intelligence	Returns to crime scene	Use direct strategy
Socially adequate	Volunteers information	Be certain of details
Sexually competent	Police groupie	Be aware that offender
Lives with partner	Anticipates questioning	will admit only to what he must
High birth order	May move body	
Harsh discipline in childhood	May dispose of body to advertise crime	
Controlled mood		
Masculine image		
Charming		
Situational cause		
Geographically mobile		
Occupationally mobile		
Follows media		
Model prisoner		

to be so. These offenders' solitariness is different from that of disorganized asocial offenders, who, as noted above, are loners because they
appear to be strange. Organized nonsocial offenders are loners because
they often feel that no one else is good enough to be around them.

In addition, there are precipitating factors involved in the crimes of
the organized nonsocial personality ("Crime Scene," 1985, p. 19). These
precipitating factors may be either real or imagined. As one serial killer
told us:

> One night I finally got a date with a young woman I had been try-
> ing to date for 6 months. We went out for a drink before dinner. We
> were sitting at the bar when a guy walked by. She watched him as
> he walked down the bar. I felt that she should not look at him
> while she was with me. So, what could I do? I killed her.

The young woman who was this killer's victim had challenged his
sense of self-importance. The killer believed he "had no choice"—he
had to kill to regain his rightful position. Although the damage this
offender perceived the woman had done him was only imagined, it
was enough.

Another attribute of the organized offender includes average intelligence; some such offenders may have done well in school, and many
are at least high school graduates. (Ted Bundy was a college graduate
and a law school student.) These offenders are socially competent, have
sex partners, and some are married. Many come from middle-class
families and are high in the birth order. Their fathers held stable jobs
and were often inconsistent about discipline. For many such offenders
there is a history of some drug use, especially alcohol and marijuana.
Bundy, again as an example, was a heavy user of alcohol and marijuana
during his crimes.

The organized offender feels comfortable venturing away from his
home. He is able to work and carry on personal, although superficial,
relationships. He also is psychologically able to widen his network of
relationships and can travel farther and farther away from his home
and work to cruise for victims, and, more important, to hinder his
apprehension.

Because of his personality, this type of offender has no trouble
making friends. He is also able to change employment as often as he
chooses because he makes such a good impression and appears to have
qualifications that he may in reality not possess. Many have good positions. John Gacy owned a construction company. Chris Wilder was a
race car driver. Ken Bianchi was a "psychologist" and security officer.

The organized nonsocial offender has a masculine personality. He often dresses in a flashy manner and drives a car that reflects his personality. As mentioned above, unlike the disorganized asocial personality offender, he feels comfortable in widening his range when cruising for victims, or when trying to avoid detection. Using Bundy again as a prime example, he was suspected of abducting Roberta Kathy Parks from the campus of Oregon State University. He drove her (apparently still alive) almost 300 miles back to Seattle. This was not an isolated incident. He also was alleged to have driven from Seattle to Ellensburg, Washington, for the abduction and murder of Susan Rancourt. The disorganized offender, in contrast, ranges only within his immediate neighborhood, because this is the only place he feels comfortable.

With a positive self-image bordering on egomania, the organized nonsocial offender may be said to have a character disorder. Commonly, he is termed a full-blown sociopath. He believes that he knows best, not only for himself but for everyone else as well. Because he is always right, he is reluctant to accept criticism, even when it is meant constructively; this offender perceives any kind of criticism to be destructive.

Post-Offense Behavior

For the organized nonsocial offender, the crime becomes, at least partially, a game. Such an offender will often return to the scene of the crime for the purpose of reliving the sensations he felt there. Some, like Edmund Kemper, will be tempted to return to the scene but will not because they have "seen one too many stories of one too many people" who have been caught by the police when they did so—a piece of information Kemper picked up from watching television. The organized nonsocial offender often learns many details of police work from television and other sources. He may even associate with police or other law enforcement agencies, because the police talk about the cases that are special to them. As Kemper said of his relationships with police, "I became a friendly nuisance" (Horvath, 1984).

In interviewing one serial killer, we mentioned to him that although the man was suspected of killing scores of young women, only a few of the bodies had ever been found. The killer's reaction was, "You only find the bodies they [the serial killers] want you to find." When asked why a killer would want some bodies to be found and not others, he said, "To let you know he's still there."

Because of his charm and charismatic personality, this person may be the last to be suspected of a crime. Even if suspected, because he often possesses intelligence and social graces, he may be able to anticipate investigators' questions and prepare responses to suit his own situation.

Interviewing Techniques

The BSU recommends that this kind of offender be confronted directly during the interviewing session. Offenders of this type respect competence, even when it may lead to their arrest and conviction. However, when using such confrontation in the interrogation, the interviewer must be absolutely confident about his or her information. If the interviewer presents "the facts," he or she must be certain that they are true and accurate. This type of offender will know immediately when he is being conned, and he will understand immediately that if false "evidence" is presented to him the police actually have no case. This can close the door on the successful resolution of a case, because the offender will never volunteer any information that can be taken as any kind of admission of guilt. This type of offender will admit to only what he must. The interrogator should not hope that once he is confronted with all the known facts the floodgates of information will open.

Some believe that a single-interviewer strategy is best. In the Ted Bundy case, Donald Patchen and Steven Bodiford (personal communication, 2000) interrogated Bundy frequently during a short period. The interviews took place mostly at night. Finally, after several sessions, Bundy admitted, "There's something deep inside me, something I can't control." However, after he had the chance to sleep and psychologically regroup, Bundy denied having admitted even that.

❖ CRIME SCENE DIFFERENCES

It has been theorized that the crime scenes of organized nonsocial offenders and disorganized asocial offenders will differ along the same lines as the differences in their personalities (see Table 5.3). That is, those who are organized in their lives in general will also be organized in the perpetration of their crimes, and those who are disorganized in their everyday lives will be disorganized in the perpetration of their crimes, and so differing degrees of organization and disorganization should be evident in crime scenes.

The organized nonsocial offender takes great care in the perpetration of his violence. This offender makes certain that the evidence will be destroyed. Also, in the case of homicide, he will often kill at one site and dispose of the body at another site. The disorganized offender, on

Table 5.3   Comparison of Crime Scenes of Organized Nonsocial and
Disorganized Asocial Lust Killers

Organized Nonsocial Kilter	Disorganized Asocial Killer
Planned offense	Spontaneous event
Targeted stranger	Victim unknown
Personalizes victim	Depersonalizes victim
Controlled conversation	Minimal conversation
Controlled crime scene	Chaotic crime scene
Submissive victim	Sudden violence
Restraints used	No restraints
Aggressive acts	Sex after death
Body moved	Body not moved
Weapon taken	Weapon left
Little evidence	Physical evidence

the other hand, attacks his victims suddenly, in unplanned or barely planned violence. The surprise, or blitz, attack results in a crime scene that holds a great deal of physical evidence.

The following case provides an example.

Case study: A 75-year-old widow had lived in the same housing project since 1937 and had been living alone since the mid-1960s. On July 4, when her son came to pick her up to spend the holiday with his family, he found his mother's body in her bed. She had been stabbed repeatedly and decapitated. The weapon was a butcher knife that had belonged to the victim. Blood spatter was found on the walls by her bed as well as on the ceiling, showing that the attack had been carried out in a frenzy. The woman had been sexually assaulted, and semen was found in her vaginal vault as well as on the bedspread and in the bedclothes.

There was a great deal of physical evidence at the scene. No other murders similar to this one were known, and a profile was requested.

The profile suggested that the offender was a Black male, early 20s, single, living within the immediate neighborhood, and living with his mother or alone. He probably had a history of mental illness and probably had been hospitalized or institutionalized for his mental condition. In addition, the profile suggested that once the offender was apprehended, the interrogators might try to establish a personal relationship with him.

Within 6 weeks, three other elderly women were attacked. All had lived within a 1-mile radius of the original attack. Of these three women, the first was 70 years old. She was stabbed 21 times in the neck with such force and rage that a half-inch of the scissors was left lodged in her neck. The next victim, who was also attacked in her home, was stabbed in the neck 11 times. The last victim succeeded in warding off the attacker and called the police. A suspect was apprehended.

In the course of the interrogation, the suspect admitted that he had been in the homes of the victims. In the case of the decapitated victim, he denied stabbing her but did say that he had "killed a demon" that had been chasing him. Elaborating on his story, he stated that the only time he was safe from the demon that had been after him was when he was on a city bus or in jail. On the evening of the first attack he got off a bus, and the demon was there waiting for him. He ran and entered the house at the first door he came to. The demon ran past him and then into the victim's bedroom. The killer grabbed a butcher knife from the kitchen, ran into the bedroom, and repeatedly stabbed the demon.

The profile in this case was accurate. The amount of evidence, the chaos evident in the crime scene, the weapon's belonging to the victim as well as its being left at the crime scene, the violence done to the victim, the lack of restraints, the body left at the death scene—all suggested a profile that did indeed narrow the scope of the investigation. (Author's files)

Organized nonsocial offenders and disorganized asocial offenders also tend to have different relationships to their victims. Both types select "strangers" as victims, but the character of the strangers is different. The disorganized asocial offender may be aware before the crime of the existence of his victim, but he has no personal relationship with that person. In the case related above, for example, the killer lived in the neighborhood and knew the addresses and locations of the apartments in which the murders occurred. For the organized nonsocial offender, however, the victim is a targeted stranger. One offender told us in an interview about his typical choice for a victim:

> If I had made a composite of my "typical" victim, it would read like this: The individual would be White, female, between the ages of 13 and 19, given the adolescent dress and manner. I would say that perhaps 75% of my victims fell under this general description. Obviously there is a pattern of selectivity here, else this large percentage figure would not so closely fit the description I've laid forth. Just as obviously, it wasn't a matter of my victims' "just being there."
>
> But just how conscious was this selectivity and why did roughly three-quarters of my victims fit this mold? In answer to the first question, I would have to say that it was not entirely conscious in that I didn't hold a general picture of an 18-year-old adolescent, White female in my mind. Certainly more and more often than not, I was roaming the streets in search of females in general, but with no specific age group in mind. Yet 75% of the time the person who "clicked" and "registered" in my mind was the girl I described above. More accurately, I was reacting to the "click" in my gut, more so than to predetermined, sought-after characteristics. Yet the predisposition toward victims of that general description, subconscious or not, was there. (Author's files)

This violent personal offender seemed to have some understanding of the reason for his selection of young White females. He went on to discuss how very popular female students rejected him in high school. Of another nationality, he was averse to dating young women of his own ethnic group, and he provided some insight into this reluctance, citing some shame about his own background. The slightest resistance to his social overtures met with rage.

Minimal conversation takes place usually between the disorganized offender and his victim. It is a blitz attack, and the establishment of any relationship is not a requirement. In contrast, conversation between the organized offender and his victim is a language of intimidation once the victim is within the offender's "comfort zone." The vehicle for the initial contact now becomes the vehicle for control. The organized nonsocial offender appears able to assay the vulnerability of his stalked victim. One serial killer remarked, "I can tell by the way they walk, the way they tilt their heads. I can tell by the look in their eyes" (author's files).

Victims of organized nonsocial offenders often suffer vicious attacks prior to death. Sometimes these offenders use restraints to render their victims helpless and to heighten victims' fear, which the offenders may need to see to gain full satisfaction. Disorganized offenders, in contrast, usually have no need for restraints, because their purpose is not to intimidate or to instill fear. One organized offender described to us his reaction to one victim's failure to show the fear he wanted to see:

> When I sighted the women [his two victims] they meant absolutely nothing to me as human beings. Indicative of the worthlessness they held in my eyes was my extreme rage toward the first woman, who I felt was defying me through her "unwillingness" to "suffer well." Undoubtedly she was instead paralyzed by cold and fear, but, in my own distorted mind, her silence and lack of struggling was a defiant sign against being reduced to brokenness and worthlessness, and therefore, the contempt I felt for her defiance was such that I killed her right away, forgetting her almost instantly as I went to the second woman. (Author's files)

In an organized nonsocial crime scene, normally the weapon not only belongs to the offender but is taken from the crime scene. This is not true of the disorganized asocial offender. This violent personal offender does not think through what he is about to do; the act is spontaneous. Bringing a weapon to a crime scene shows at least some form of rudimentary planning, and this offender does not think ahead.

The moving of a body from the crime scene may be an indication that the unknown suspect is an organized nonsocial type. The disorganized type has no desire or need to move the body. Once the killing has been accomplished, his mission is over.

❖ CONCLUSION

In this chapter we have discussed a typology of offenders that has important implications for law enforcement profiling of lust killers. We have addressed the typical personal characteristics and post-offense behaviors of disorganized asocial and organized nonsocial offenders, as well as the interviewing techniques recommended for use with each type of suspect. We have also discussed the differences that may be found in the crime scenes associated with the two types of offenders.

Investigators will find the guidelines laid out in the typology discussed here to be useful in their profiling of violent crimes, as they take into account the chaos or lack of chaos in a crime scene, the presence or absence of a weapon, the presence or absence of mutilation of the victim, and other details. Of course, not all crimes are lust killings. In the next chapter we will address arson and the types of individuals who commit these crimes.

❖ REFERENCES

Crime scene and profile characteristics of organized and disorganized murders. (1985). *FBI Law Enforcement Bulletin, 54*, 18–25.

Horvath, I. (Director). (1984). *Murder: No apparent motive* [Motion picture]. United States: Vestron Video.

Ressler, R., Burgess, A., & Douglas, J. (1988). *Sexual homicide: Patterns and motives.* Lexington, MA: Lexington Books.

6

Arson and Psychological Profiling

❖   ❖   ❖

T he deliberate setting of fires has a long history, as varied as the fires themselves. There is no reason to believe that the motivation for all firesetters is the same or even similar (Forehand, Wierson, Frame, Kempton, & Aristead, 1991; Holt, 1994; Orr, 1989; Sakeheim & Osborn, 1986; Webb, Sakeheim, Towns-Miranda, & Wagner, 1990). To the contrary, arsonists are as varied as their motivations and anticipated gains and different from offender to offender (Kolko & Kazdin, 1992; Sakeheim, Vigdor, Gordon, & Helprin, 1985). This may seem strange at first blush, but the motivating factors as well as the planned gains may be indigenous only to a few. The purposeful firesetter, for example, may be an arsonist for property gain or erotic gratification (Law, 1991). However, it may be that the exact role of sex as a motivating factor may have been grossly exaggerated (Quinsey, Chaplin, & Uphold, 1990; Rice & Harris, 1991).

❖ WHAT IS ARSON?

Arson is defined by the U.S. Department of Justice (2004) as "any willful or malicious burning or attempting to burn, with or without intent to defraud, a dwelling house, public building, motor vehicle or aircraft, personal property of another." This is one simple definition, but there is more to arson than a rudimentary denotation. In addition, there are three components to the crime of arson:

- There has been a burning of property. This must be shown to be actual destruction, at least in part, not just scorching (although some states include any physical or visible impairment of any surface).

- The burning is incendiary in origin. Proof of the existence of any effective incendiary device, no matter how simple it may be, is adequate. Proof must be accomplished by cases that have been considered and ruled out.

- The burning is shown to be started with malice—that is, with the specific intent of destroying property (DeHaan, 1997).

There is both a legal component as well as a behavioral dimension to arson. These forms may come in the construct of types of arson.

Forms and Types of Arson

In an early study, Macy (1979) classified the crime of arson and placed it into five forms:

1. Organized crime (loan sharking, extortion, strippers, and other crime concealment)

2. Insurance/housing fraud (over-insurance, block busting, parcel clearance, gentrification, stop loss, and tax shelters)

3. Commercial (inventory depletion, modernization, and stop loss)

4. Residential (relocation, redecoration, public housing, and automobile)

5. Psychological (children and juveniles, pyromania, political, and wildlands). (p. i)

But what might be a better strategy to use to understand the phenomenon of arson is to examine the various types of arson, and later in this chapter, the personality and the behavior of the firesetter.

❖ STATISTICS ON ARSON

Data concerning arson is collected nationally by two federal agencies: the National Fire Protection Association (NFPA) and the Federal Bureau of Investigation. The former agency collects data from structural fires as well as "suspicious" fires. The FBI's statistics are gathered from reports that identify fires that have been termed and identified as arsons by the reporting local agencies. However, as Douglas, Burgess, Burgess, and Ressler (1992) reported, "the statistics compiled by both the NFPA and the FBI closely agree" (p. 164).

The U.S. Department of Justice reports there were 61,304 suspected cases of arson in 2006. Of this total, only 18.4% were cleared by arrest. Further, when you examine these data more closely, approximately 39.5% of those solved by arrest were committed by youth under the age of 18 (U.S. Department of Justice, 2007).

While alarming, it is important to note that other official data sources appear to state that the problem is not that large. For instance, data collected by the U.S. Fire Association (2007) in 2006 lead us to believe that the number of incidents of arson is significantly on the decline. As shown in Table 6.1, the number of arsons in 1997 was 78,500, and in 2006 it was 31,500. That represents a downward change of 60.5%.

One problem in the accumulation of data is that the process obviously depends on the method by which the data are collected. One would expect that all of the numbers match. However, this does not always appear to be true.

The Bureau of Alcohol, Tobacco, Firearms, and Explosives also collects data on arson. They claim that most arsonists attack immoveable structures like residences and businesses (42%) and another 28.2% of the fires were directed at mobile property like automobiles. Dealing specifically with structural damage, they claim that on average a typical arson will cause approximately $66,000 in damage (U.S. Department of Justice, 2007).

Regardless of the relative agreement of gathered data, it is apparent that arson is indeed a very serious personal and financial problem. There are millions of dollars expended on combatting and repairing

Table 6.1   Arson Fires and Deaths in the United States

Year	Fires	Deaths
1997	78,500	445
1998	76,000	470
1999	72,000	370
2000	75,000	505
2001	45,500	2,781
2002	44,500	350
2003	37,500	305
2004	36,500	320
2005	31,500	315
2006	31,500	305

damage from this crime. This does not, of course, include the immeasurable cost of human lives lost because of the firesetter. In the 10-year period from 1997 to 2006, approximately 6,166 people were killed as a direct result of these fires. If we remove the bombing of the World Trade Center from these statistics, still more than 3,700 people lost their lives to this type of crime (U.S. Fire Association, 2007).

There is no way to measure the financial impact of lost lives. And of course, what is intended here is to look not only at the fires themselves, which is actually secondary in this discourse, but to look at the person who sets these fires. We will try to develop a mental image, a psychological profile, of the type of person who intentionally sets fires for varied reasons. We shall see that the motivations vary from one firesetter to another, as do the social core variables, the motivations, and the anticipated gains.

❖   A VIEW OF THE FIRESETTER

Arson is, among all age groups, almost equally split between adults and juveniles. Approximately 39% of all reported arsons are committed by juveniles (U.S. Department of Justice, 2007). We can even break down the demographics of those arrested and charged with arson. As shown in Table 6.2, we see that 28.5% of all reported arsons

Table 6.2   Arson Arrests in the United States, 2006

		Number	Percent
Race	White	4,455	73.0
	Black	1,516	24.8
	American Indian or Alaskan Native	67	1.1
	Asian or Pacific Islander	66	1.1
		6,104	100.0
Age	Under 15	3,416	28.5
	Under 18	5,888	49.1
	18 and older	6,114	50.9
		12,002	100.0
Gender	Male	9,967	83.0
	Female	2,035	17.0
		12,002	100.0

Table 6.3   Portrait of an Arsonist

Prior Arrest History
87% had a felony arrest
63% had multiple felony arrests
24% had a prior arrest for arson
Location of Residence
21% lived within 5 blocks
30% lived within 1/2 to 1 mile
20% lived within 1–2 miles
16% lived more than 2 miles away
7% lived in a home or institution
Motivation for Crime
41% revenge
30% excitement
7% vandalism
5% profit
5% concealment of crime

are committed by children younger than 15 years old. And 49.1% of all arsons are committed by those under the age of 18.

Using these same data it is clear that arson is a crime predominately practiced by males. In this case, almost 83% of all arrests involve a male suspect. Regarding race, it seems that Blacks are slightly over-represented, accounting for about 25% of all who are arrested for arson, while they only made up 12.8% of the population in 2006. Whites account for slightly less than three of four arson arrests, while composing 80.1% of the U.S. population in 2006. Native Americans, Native Alaskans, Asians, Hispanics, and Pacific Islanders account for the remainder.

These statistics are important to consider when one commences the profiling process. By combining what is typically known regarding the statistics of arson, examining the various typologies, the principles of profiling, etc., a psychological assessment of the arsonist may develop.

There are other basic characteristics common to many serial arsonists. Sapp, Huff, Gary, Icove, and Horbert (1994) reported basic data that included social core variables such as marital status and education. This information is contained in Table 6.4.

Table 6.4   Attributes of Serial Arsonist

Occupation	Percent
Menial laborer	28.2
Retail sales	2.6
Service worker	5.1
Maintenance worker	7.7
Police/security	7.7
Fire service	2.6
Office/clerical	10.3
Food service	5.1
Homemaker	2.6
Medical service	5.1
Marital Status	*Percent*
Single	65.9
Significant other	5.8
Married	6.1
Separated	3.7
Divorced	14.6
Widowed	1.2
Gender	*Percent*
Male	94.0
Female	6.0
Childhood Family Status	*Percent*
Both parents	57.5
Father only	3.8
Mother only	12.5
Father, stepmother	1.3
Mother, stepfather	10.3
Foster home	8.8
Other relatives	6.3
Ethnicity	*Percent*
White	81.9
Black	9.6
Hispanic	7.2
Native American	1.2

(Continued)

Table 6.4 (Continued)

Marital History	Percent
Never married	53.7
Married once	36.6
Multiple marriages	9.7

Highest Grade Completed	Percent
3	1.3
4	2.7
5	2.7
6	6.7
7	1.3
8	5.3
9	13.3
11*	16.0
12	26.7
13	1.3
14	4.0
15	1.3
16	2.7

Type of Institution	Mean Times in Institution
Orphanage	1.3
Foster home	1.6
Juvenile detention	4.1
State juvenile home	1.7
County jail	4.9
State prison	2.0
Federal prison	1.3
Mental health	3.2
Other institution	1.3

Sex Preference	Percent
Heterosexual	75.4
Homosexual	8.7
Bisexual	15.9

Psychological History	Percent
Depression	3.8
Dyslexia	3.8
Stress related	3.8
Multiple diagnosis	34.6
Alcoholism	11.5
Hyperactive child	7.7
Brain damage	3.8
Suicidal	19.2
Borderline personality	3.8
Unspecified problem	3.8
Psychotic outburst	3.8
Felony Arrest Records	Percent
Multiple arrests	63.4
Arson	23.9
Aggravated assault	1.4
Burglary	2.8
Grand theft auto	1.4
DWI	1.4
Robbery	1.4
Attempted arson	1.4
Child molestation	2.8
Method of Apprehension	Percent
Turned self in or confessed	21.1
Informant	7.0
Witness	12.7
Key evidence recovered	4.2
Law enforcement investigation	38.0
Caught in act	9.9
Arson while in jail	4.2
Caught fleeing the scene	1.4
Multiple events	1.4
Plea Offered	Percent
Guilty	52.6
Not guilty	28.9
Changed to guilty	10.5
Combination	7.9

(Continued)

Table 6.4 (Continued)

Area of Arsons	Percent
Work/school	2.5
To/from work/school	7.5
After work hours	42.5
Days off/weekends	10.0
Multiple locations	12.5
Home or other	25.0

Distance From Home to Arson Site	Percent
0–1 block	2.7
1–2 blocks	5.4
2–5 blocks	12.2
1/2–1 mile	29.7
1–2 miles	.3
2–5 miles	4.1
5–10 miles	5.4
10–40 miles	2.7
> 40 miles	2.7
Varied distances	6.8
Home/institution	6.8

Mode of Transportation to Scene	Percent
Walked	60.8
Bicycle	5.1
Motorcycle	2.5
Automobile	16.5
Truck	1.3
Already at scene	7.6
Mixed modes	6.3

Living Arrangements at Time of Arson	Percent
Parents	23.3
Alone	16.3
Female roommate	4.7
Male roommate	7.0
Both sex roommates	2.3
Spouse	2.3
Spouse and children	4.7
Grandparents	7.0

Institution	14.0
Mixed	18.5

Type of Residence	Percent
Rooming house	18.1
Hotel/motel	2.4
Apartment	23.8
Single-family house	42.9
Institution	11.9

Method of Victim/Site Selection	Percent
Knew the People	2.9
Worked there	5.9
Random selection	17.6
Walking distance	5.9

Means of Gaining Access	Percent
Open entry	37.8
Broke in	18.9
Had a key	2.7
Lived there	10.8
Set outside premises	13.5
Multiple means	16.2

Ignition Devices	Percent
Wooden matches	7.9
Book matches	57.9
Cigarette lighter	17.1
Combination	6.6
Molotov cocktail	2.6
Cigarette device	2.6
Road flare	1.3
Candle	1.3
Gunpowder	1.3

Items Left at Scene	Percent
Gas can	13.9
Matches	47.2
Devices	11.1
Cigarette lighter	5.6
Multiple items	25.0

Note: *Data for Grade 10 omitted in the original source.

❖ TYPOLOGIES OF FIRESETTERS

There are typologies that indicate the various differences among fire-setters. Rider (1980), in reviewing the work of Lewis and Yarnell (1951), suggests several types of firesetters.

First, there is the Jealousy Motivated Adult Male who does this as a reaction against an incident that impaired the vanity and personality of the firesetter himself. The next is the Would-be Hero type. This fire-setter rushes into his fire scene, saves a life, etc., and is the apparent hero because of his swift and decisive action. Another type reported is the volunteer fireman who joins the department to fight the fires, many of which he will set himself. The fire buff is similar to the police groupie, and he will want to associate with professional firefighters, frequents the fire station, and many times is an active person in the community and has a special interest in the work of the fire depart-ment. The Excitement Firesetter ignites the fires because of his need for personal excitement, which does not include a sexual component or a sexual fantasy. The Pyromaniac is the final type.

Table 6.5   Additional Elements in the Profile of the Typical Pyromaniac

Age	Heaviest concentration between ages 16–28; highest frequency at age 17
Gender	Male
Race	Predominately White
Intelligence	Ranged from mentally defective to genius (approximately 22% of those with no explanation for their firesetting were low-grade defectives)
Physical defects	Found to be frequently present
Enuresis	Present in some
Mental disorders	Psychopathy, as well as psychotic disorders, was identified within the category; the compulsive urge also appears to reflect a neurotic obsessive-compulsive pattern of behavior.
Academic adjustment	Poor educational adjustment, although some pyromaniacs were intellectually bright. Their academic performance was marginal or scholastically retarded—underachievers.
Rearing environment	Pathological, broken, and harsh rearing environment with inconsistent discipline and parental neglect. Pyromaniacs noted an unhappy home life.

Social class structure	Some pyromaniacs emerged from middle or even upper socioeconomic levels, while others were products of lower class environments.
Social adjustment	Social maladjustment present, severe problems in developing and maintaining interpersonal relationships.
Marital adjustment	Although some pyromaniacs were married, their marital adjustments were poor.
Sexual adjustment	Sexually maladjusted and inadequate; limited contact with women.
Occupational/ employment history	Most frequently unskilled laborers, if employed. They accept subservient positions and become resentful when they realize that their work is degrading.
Personality	The pyromaniac has been described as a misfit and feeble person, a physical coward with feelings of inadequacy, inferiority, insufficiency, and self-consciousness. They are introverted, reclusive, aloof, frustrated, and lonely people. They have unconscious fears of being unwanted and unloved and suffer from a wounded self-esteem and a lack of pride and prestige. They often project an image of calmness and indifference (anxiety and tension are present nonetheless). They have vague feelings, however, that their defenses will fail them and that these repressed impulses will emerge. They tend to be defensive and obstinate in attitude and ambivalent toward authority. Although they have an inner dependency on authority, they also have contempt for it. In fact, they have repressed their rage and hatred toward society and authority figures. They lack ambition and aggressiveness. Some stated that they did not want to really hurt anyone. They are apologetic but ashamed for being apologetic. They seek expression through excitement. Some pyromaniacs have been found to be quite intelligent, neat, and methodical in their behavior. They have a need to be recognized and have a sense of worth. They have a craving for power and prestige. They fail to express remorse or to accept responsibility for their firesetting behavior.
Criminal history	Many had histories of delinquency and criminal behavior to include: runaway, burglary, theft, and other property offenses.
Use of alcohol	Alcohol was frequently used as a method of escape and to remove social inhibitions, but they did not set fires because they drank.
Suicide	Some attempted suicide after arrest and incarceration.

(Continued)

Table 6.5 (Continued)

Motives	The exact motivation in each case was unknown; however, the following motives were identified: (a) Desire to be a hero and center of attention (craving for excitement and prestige), play detective at the fire, render first-aid, help rescue victims, assist firemen. (b) Desire to show themselves sufficiently clever to cause the "experts" (the firemen and detectives) problems and to render them helpless. They have grandiose ambitions to be the executive who directs the firefighting activity and puts the firemen into action. (c) Enjoy destruction of property (vagrants exhibiting pyromania receive sadistic pleasure in watching the destruction of buildings). (d) Irresistible impulse (could not offer an explanation except driven by unexplainable force or impulse to set fires). (e) Revenge, although not consciously present, was also considered to be a possible factor. (f) Sexual satisfaction (this was noted in only 40 cases).
Irresistible impulse	No single precipitating factor produced this impulse. It was believed to be the result of an accumulation of problems that caused stress, frustration, and tension. Examples included thwarted sexual desires, loss of employment, refusal of employment, death of parent or loved one, threats to personal security and masculinity, explosive protest over imagined immorality or promiscuousness of mother or spouse, fear of impotency.

❖ FIRESETTING EXPERIENCE

Types of Fires

The fires set by pyromaniacs are generally made in haste and in a disorganized fashion, often set in rubbish, basements, and in and around inhabited dwellings, office buildings, schools, hotels, and other structures in thickly populated sections of cities. Frequently, they were made in rapid succession. Matches, newspapers, and other available materials were used in starting the fires.

Number of Fires

Frequently they start numerous fires, sometimes hundreds, until they were caught.

False Alarms

They were also known to set false alarms.

Time of Day

Their fires were often nocturnal.

Regard for Life

There was no regard for life. Fires were frequently set in and around occupied buildings.

Emotional State and Behavior Just Prior to Firesetting

Pyromaniacs frequently expressed the following symptoms preceding their firesetting: Mounting tension and anxiety; restlessness—an urge for motion; conversion symptoms, such as headaches, pressure in the head, dizziness, ringing in the ears and palpitations; a sense that the personality was merging into a state of unreality; and an uncontrollable urge or irresistible impulse to set fires.

Emotional State and Behavior During Firesetting

While setting the fire, pyromaniacs felt that the act was so little of their own; they described the emergence of a sort of dissociative state (a transient sensation of being controlled by an external force, a feeling of being automated). They recognized that the firesetting was senseless, but they did not have the control to prevent it. To a casual observer, they would appear normal.

Emotional State and Behavior After Setting the Fire

Pyromaniacs expressed a sense of relief and even exaltation. After setting the fires their tensions subsided. Few expressed sexual satisfaction in setting fires. They often stayed at or near the fire as a spectator, or to assist the responding firemen by rendering first-aid or rescuing victims from the fire. Some enjoyed playing detective at the fire scene. Some pyromaniacs after setting the fires and ensuring that the firemen would respond went home to a restful sleep.

Arrest

Some pyromaniacs ensured that they would be identified and arrested; some even turned themselves into the police. Many continued to set fires till apprehended. The arrest seemed to release the magical hold the irresistible impulse had on them. It was a relief for them to be stopped from setting fires.

Confession

Pyromaniacs often readily confessed or admitted guilt, although they expressed no remorse or regret for their behavior; neither did they generally accept responsibility for their firesetting activity. They were most often quiet and cooperative under arrest.

Selection of Target

Firesetting targets were often randomly selected for no apparent reason. Douglas and colleagues (2006) reported several motives for arsonists' actions:

1. Vandalism

2. Excitement

3. Revenge

4. Crime concealment

5. Profit

Vandalism

The arsonist of this ilk tends to be younger, and oftentimes he will act in groups. The typical target is an educational facility, but he will also select residential areas as well as bush and vegetative areas. The young person will often come from a lower class background, live close to where the crime occurs (usually within 1 mile), and lives at home with his parents. This person is not one, at least at this time of his life, who abuses drugs or alcohol. In addition, sex is not a motivating factor in his crime or the target that he selects to spark. The time that he will usually victimize is the afternoon and also during the weekdays. There are some obvious reasons for this. For example, this person may still be in high school and attends classes during the day. Because of this, setting fires will occur after the school day. From the information we have seen regarding the typical firesetter according to age, 49% of all arsons are committed by young people, and most of them are between the ages of 10 and 14.

After the fire is set, the vandal will flee the scene and tends not to return. However, if the arsonist does indeed return, he will watch the scene from a safe distance.

Excitement

Douglas and colleagues (2006) reported subtypes of the Excitement arsonist: the thrill seeker, the attention seeker, the recognition seeker, and finally the sexual perversion type.

This Excitement arsonist craves attention and finds that setting fires is one way to gain such needed attention. He will set fires and watch the activity from a guarded distance. If the firesetter does remain at the scene, he will try to blend in with the other bystanders.

The targets for the firesetting include vegetation, dumpsters, construction sites, as well as residential areas. This firesetter will use rather simple incendiary materials; however, it seems that the older the victim, the more complex the firesetting device. For example, if one is close to 30, there may be a time-delayed mechanism involved. There appears to be some type of learning involved with the setting of multiple fires. The younger Excitement arsonist is more likely to use matches, cigarettes, etc.—that is, simple methods. Unlike the Vandal firesetter, this arsonist tends to come from a middle-class family where he lives with both parents.

This offender will often have an arrest record, and the older the offender the longer the arrest history. The arsonist will typically commit his crime alone but may on occasion commit arson in the company of another. Again, sex does not play an important motivation role unless the firesetter is one who has attached a sexual component. In this case, the alert investigator will look for sexual paraphilia—e.g., semen at the scene, pornography.

Revenge

This firesetter operates from a perspective of trying to right a real or imagined injury. This arsonist may be quite different from other arsonists especially those who could be termed as serial arsonists. This firesetting may be a one-time occurrence since it may be centered on the destruction of a particular dwelling, business, or facility of someone who has done this offender an injustice. The focused direction of the attack may be toward an individual, a business (e.g., a former employer's business structure), or a government structure or an toward a group of persons such as a rival gang, etc.

This arsonist usually comes from a lower class background and is more educated than the first two arsonists already discussed, usually completing more than 10 years of formal education.

Women are often of the Revenge arsonist type. If this is the case, she will burn personal items of her former paramour or husband. These items would include such things as clothing, bedding, or other forms of intimate items. The typical target for the Revenge arsonist, if a male, is residential and personal property units.

This firesetter will often commit his crimes on the weekends. The location of the attacks usually is within a 1-mile radius of the home of the offender. He will flee the crime scene, trying to personally distance himself from the fire, and moreover will seldom return to the scene of the crime. Also, unlike the other two previously discussed arsonists, this firesetter will often use alcohol as a means to lower inhibitions.

Sex is not a motivating factor; spurned love may be, though, especially to the women, as noted above.

The precipitating factor in this form of arson is something that the arsonist believes was a personal affront. This affront may be real or imagined. However, it is sufficient that it will result in the firesetter setting a fire, sometimes several, which victimizes the personal property of the victim. It must be also remembered that this affront may have occurred several months or even years before the arson.

Crime Concealment

With this form of firesetting the arson is really secondary to the commission of another crime. The purpose of the fire is to conceal or hide the more primary crime. For example, a man killed his wife, decapitated her, buried her head in the backyard, and then burned her corpse inside the house. The purpose of this fire was to hide the original crime of homicide.

Many of these crimes of arson are set with an abundance of liquid accelerant, but because of the naiveté of the firesetter, the original crime is usually not totally destroyed. Ressler, Burgess, and Douglas (1988) stated that this form of crime scene tends to be more of the disorganized variety. Consequently, there is apt to be more physical evidence at this type of crime scene because the disorganized offender is more likely to leave physical evidence than the organized variety.

Concerning some of the social variables and personality traits of this arsonist, the offender is likely to be male, an adult from a lower class background, commits his crime in the evening or in the early morning hours, lives alone, lives slightly farther away from the crime scene than the other types we have mentioned thus far, will often commit the crime in the company of another person, and will flee the crime scene once the fire has started.

As with most firesetters we have mentioned in this section, sex is not a primary motivating factor. The goal here is simple and utilitarian: to get rid of evidence from a crime that has already occurred—e.g., a homicide, a burglary, a motor theft. If the primary crime is murder, then this arsonist is usually not a serial arsonist since, predominately, with this type of person the crime of homicide is a one-time occurrence. If this is the case, the firesetter usually acts alone. However, if the fire is set to hide other crimes—e.g., burglary, robberies—this may be the work of a serial arsonist, and he will usually be accompanied by another person when he sets the fire.

Alcohol plays an important role in the commission of this crime. Here, the alcohol lessens the inhibitions of the firesetter and enables the perpetration of the crime. Drugs may also play a role here.

Nothing is mentioned by Douglas et al. (2006) concerning the education, employment, and arrest record of this form of firesetter. It may be inferred that he too is limited in his educational pursuits. If employed, it is in menial jobs that require little education, and he may have a long history of involvement with the criminal justice system because crimes such as burglaries and robberies are common serial crimes. In addition, almost four of five are single.

Profit

The least passionate arsonist is the adult male who sets fires for material gain. Sometimes, this firesetter is hired by a failing business owner who wishes to collect insurance monies, deplete an inventory, etc., because the business is not succeeding as expected. The times of the fires are typically after business hours, in the evening hours or the early morning hours. There is no motivation to cover a crime, a sexual motive, or one vented on revenge. The motivation here is to set a fire because of material gain. This person who is hired by others to commit this crime may indeed be a serial arsonist. The anticipated gain may be in the form of money or goods.

The marital status of this firesetter tends to be single and he lives alone. He lives usually more than a mile away from the scene of the fire and travels by a vehicle to the scene of the crime. Often, by the time the fire or explosion occurs, he may already be far away from the scene. He may have an accomplice, one who will assist him in setting up the fire itself, and this second person may be in the position of an apprentice.

His experience with the criminal justice system may be quite extensive. He may have an arrest record in robbery, burglary, public disorderly conduct, and public drunkenness. In addition, since we have noted that this man may be a serial arsonist, he also may have an arrest record as an arsonist.

Douglas et al. (2006) reported that this firesetter is usually 25 to 40 years old and has less than a high school education, usually about the 10th grade. This is a crime of premeditation, which suggests that the arsonist is at least of average intelligence and his lack of academic performance rests with outside forces rather than intellectual abilities. In addition, the crime scene itself would be organized.

Of course, each crime should be approached as if the perpetrator is a unique individual. However, it is usually accepted that the crime scene reflects the personality of the offender. Still, recognizing the individuality of the offender, we can make certain assumptions about the personality of the offender, which might hopefully lead to his or her apprehension, which is, of course, the goal of psychological profiling.

❖ ORGANIZED VERSUS DISORGANIZED PERSONALITY

As might be surmised from reading previous chapters, it is apparent that some of the concepts we have already discussed have important implications regarding organization (or the lack of organization) at the crime scene. Some arsonists may be better organized than others, and this will be reflected in the crime scene. Therefore, the same concepts that apply to other organized offenders may be true of the arsonist who also possesses the organized personality.

We might look for social and personal items that send this person into the "fall," especially if the crime is committed for motives that are intrinsic to the personality of the offender. A negative social happening or breakup of an intimate relationship, for instance, may cause the offender to resort to arson as a means of medicating for his own pain.

Douglas et al. (2006) reported that the organized arsonist will display certain elements at the crime scene (see Table 6.7). These points are also well illustrated in the writings of Rider (1980) and Sapp et al. (1994).

❖ CONCLUSION

The crime of arson costs millions of dollars a year as well as the loss of human lives. An initial step toward a successful resolution of this very serious crime is to come to some understanding of the person who

Table 6.6   Search Warrant Suggestions for Five Types of Arsonists

Vandalism

Spray paint can
Items from the scene, especially if a school was the target
Explosive devices: fireworks, firecrackers, packaging, or cartons
Flammable liquids
Clothing: evidence of flammable liquid, evidence of glass
    particles, for witness identification
Shoes: footprints, flammable liquid traces

Excitement

Vehicle

Material similar to incendiary devices used: fireworks,
    containers that components were shipped in, wires, etc.
Floor mats, trunk padding, carpeting: residue from accelerants
    (not conclusive evidence, but indicative)
Beer cans, matchbooks, cigarettes: to match any brands found
    at the scene

House

Material similar to incendiary devices used: fireworks,
    containers that components were shipped in, wires, etc.
Clothing, shoes: accelerant and soil samples if vegetation fire
Cigarette lighter, especially if subject does not smoke
Diaries, journals, notes, logs, recordings and maps documenting fires
Newspapers, articles reporting fires
Souvenirs from the crime scene

Revenge

If accelerants used: shoes, socks, clothing, glass particles in
    clothing (if break-in; or homicide victim's blood, glass
    fragments of windows broken during burglary attempt)
Discarded, concealed clothing
Bottles, flammable liquids, matchbooks
Cloth (fiber comparison), tape (if device used)

Crime Concealment

Refer to category dealing with primary motive
Gasoline containers
Clothing, shoes if liquid accelerant used (or if homicide victim's blood)
Glass fragments if windows broken during burglary attempt
Burned paper documents

Profit

Check financial records
If evidence of fuel/air explosion at the scene, check emergency
    room for patients with burn injuries
Determine condition of utilities (gas, electric) as soon as
    possible (eliminate gas, the common accidental cause of fires)

Table 6.7   Crime Scene Elements Common for the Arsonist

Organized Arsonists
Elaborate incendiary devices (electronic timing mechanisms, initiators, etc.)
Less physical evidence; if forced entry, more skillful (no footprints, fingerprints, etc.)
Methodological approach (trailers, multiple sets, excessive accelerant use, etc.)
Disorganized Arsonists
Materials on hand
Matches, cigarettes, more common accelerants (lighter fluid, gasoline)
Physical evidence (handwriting, footprints, fingerprints, etc.)

would commit the crime of arson. Recognizing that there are different types of arsons, we can also understand that those who set the fires also have different kinds of personalities. Investigating the crime and then assessing the type of person who would commit such a crime is the first step toward a successful resolution of the crime of arson.

❖ REFERENCES

DeHaan, J. (1997). *Kirk's fire investigation* (4th ed.). Upper Saddle River, NJ: Prentice-Hall.

Douglas, J., Burgess, A. W., Burgess, A. G., & Ressler, R. (1992). *Crime classification manual*. Lexington, MA: Lexington.

Douglas, J., Burgess, A. W., Burgess, A. G., & Ressler, R. (2006). *Crime classification manual* (2nd ed.). San Francisco: John Wiley & Sons.

Forehand, R., Wierson, M., Frame, C., Kempton, T., & Aristead, L. (1991). Juvenile fire-setting: A unique syndrome of an advanced study of antisocial behavior. *Behavioral Research Therapy, 29*, 125–128.

Holt, F. (1994, March). The arsonist profile. *Fire Engineering*, 127–128.

Kolko, D., & Kazdin, A. (1992). The emergence and recurrence of child firesetting: A one year perspective study. *Journal of Abnormal Child Psychology, 20*, 17–36.

Law, D. (1991, January). The pyromaniac vs. the hired torch. *Fire Engineering*, 50–53.

Lewis, N., & Yarnell, H. (1951). *Pathological firesetting (pyromaniac)* (Vol. 2). New York: Coopridge Foundation.

Macy, J. (1979). *To the reader: In arson: The federal role in arson prevention and control* [Report to Congress]. Washington, DC: Federal Emergency Management Association, U.S. Fire Administration, Office of Planning and Evaluation.

Orr, J. (1989, July). Profiles in arson: The vanity firesetter. *American Fire Journal*, 24–47.

Quinsey, V., Chaplin, T., & Uphold, D. (1990). Arsonists and sexual arousal to firesetting: Correlation unsupported. *Journal of Behavior Therapy and Experimental Psychiatry, 20*, 203–209.

Ressler, R., Burgess, A., & Douglas, J. (1988). *Sexual homicide: Patterns and motives.* Lexington, MA: Lexington Books.

Rice, M., & Harris, G. (1991). Firesetters admitted to maximum security psychiatric institution. *Journal of Interpersonal Violence, 6,* 461–475.

Rider, A. (1980). The firesetter: A psychological profile (Part 1). *FBI Law Enforcement Bulletin, 49,* 7–17.

Sakeheim, G., & Osborn, E. (1986). A psychological profile of juvenile firesetters in residential treatment: A replication study. *Child Welfare, 64,* 495–503.

Sakeheim, G., Vigdor, M., Gordon, M., & Helprin, L. (1985). A psychological profile of juvenile firesetters in residential treatment. *Child Welfare, 64,* 453–476.

Sapp, A., Huff, T., Gary, G., Icove, D., & Horbert, P. (1994). A report of essential findings from a study of serial arsonists. Unpublished manuscript.

Sharn, L., & Glamser, D. (1994, March 24). One man, more than 100 fires: Seattle area's wave of terror. *USA Today,* p. 9A.

U.S. Department of Justice (Federal Bureau of Investigation). (2004). Crime in the United States, 2004. In *Sourcebook of Criminal Justice Statistics.* Washington, DC: U.S. Government Printing Office. Retrieved from: www.fbi.gov/ucr/cius_04/offenses_reported/property_crime/arson.html.

U.S. Department of Justice (Federal Bureau of Investigation). (2007). Crime in the United States, 2006. In *Sourcebook of Criminal Justice Statistics.* Washington, DC: U.S. Government Printing Office. Retrieved April 4, 2008, from: www.fbi.gov/ucr/cius2006/offenses/expanded_information/data/arsonatble_02.html.

U.S. Fire Association. (2007). Arson fire statistics. Retrieved April 1, 2008, from: www.usfa.dhs.gov/statistics/arson/index.shtm.

Webb, N., Sakeheim, G., Towns-Miranda, L., & Wagner, C. (1990). Collaborative treatment of juvenile firesetters: Assessment and outreach. *American Journal of Orthopsychiatry, 60,* 305–309.

7

Profiling Serial Murderers

❖   ❖   ❖

The motives, gains, and etiology of serial murder differ from those of other forms of homicide (Fox & Levin, 1994; Godwin, 1978; Holmes & Holmes, 1998). Fundamentally different from conventional homicide, serial murder claims more than 5,000 victims a year by an estimated 35 identified serial murderers currently at large in the United States (Holmes & Deburger, 1985b; Norris & Birnes, 1988; A. Rule, personal communication, 1985). Some researchers assert that as many as one-third of all yearly homicides are attributable to serial killers (Linedecker & Burt, 1990, p. ix). It has been suggested that serial murder is on the rise and that there is an epidemic of such homicides, as reflected in a statement made by Robert Ressler, a retired FBI agent who was instrumental in the formation of the Bureau's Behavioral Science Unit:

> Serial killing—I think it's at an epidemic proportion. The type of crime we're seeing today did *not* really occur with any known frequency prior to the fifties. An individual taking ten, twelve, fifteen, twenty-five, thirty-five lives is a relatively new phenomenon in the crime picture of the U.S. (Jenkins, 1994, p. 67)

Some scholars have expressed the fear that such statements may cause some members of the public to become unduly alarmed, and some believe that authors in this field are deliberately creating their own monsters (Jenkins, 1994; Sears, 1991). In actual terms, there is no real measurement to ascertain if serial murder is increasing. Eric Hickey states that it is a tricky game to play to make a statement of infallibility in one direction or another (E. Hickey, personal communication, 2001).

It would be an error to assume that we are all potential victims of serial killers, or that there is a serial killer around every corner. However, from our own experiences with police departments across the United States, we believe that current estimates concerning numbers of victims may be too high, but estimates of numbers of killers may actually be too low. In lecturing across the country, we seldom come away from a lecture site without a police officer telling us about a serial murderer he had previously not known about. It is our estimate that there are at least 100 serial murderers currently active in the United States. Estimates of the numbers of victims have been questioned by many experts, including Egger, Jenkins, and Hickey (Egger, 1990; Hickey, 1991; Jenkins, 1994, pp. 20–29, 60–64). It should be kept in mind that some serial killers may kill no more than one victim a year, or none at all during particular periods of time (perhaps because they are prevented from doing so by illness or incarceration). But there is no doubt that a substantial number of the victims who fall prey to serial predators, including killers, each year are not recognized as serialists' victims because of lack of communication among law enforcement agencies (aka "linkage blindness"; Egger, 1990, 1998), law enforcement turf issues, and some law enforcement personnel's simple refusal to identify or accept some cases as instances of serial murder.

The number of victims any given murderer has had is a defining characteristic for applying the label *serial killer*. The most common number given is a minimum of three victims (Holmes & Holmes, 1998); however, some researchers, such as Jenkins (1994), prefer to reserve the label for killers of four or more persons, and others believe the number should be as low as two, as Egger states in his book, *The Killers Among Us* (1998, p. 5). If two murders were to be adopted by authorities and those within the criminal justice system as the defining number, clearly the number of offenders defined as serial killers would increase drastically.

❖ TYPOLOGY OF SERIAL MURDERERS

Despite the similar motivations of all humans, individuals behave differently from each other (Drukteinis, 1992; Holmes & Holmes, 2001). These differences derive from a variety of factors. Social and behavioral scientists have formulated models to explain the behavior of various categories of people. The typology of serial murderers presented below has been developed based on interviews with and case studies of serial murderers, many of whom are currently incarcerated in U.S. prisons (Holmes & Deburger, 1985a).

❖ SPATIAL MOBILITY OF SERIAL KILLERS

The initial distinction that may be made among serial murderers is in their degree of spatial mobility (see Table 7.1). Some serial murderers live in one area and kill in that same area or a nearby area. These offenders are termed *geographically stable* killers. There are many examples of this type of killer: John Wayne Gacy (Chicago), Wayne Williams (Atlanta), Ed Gem (Plainfield, Wisconsin). *Geographically transient* serial murderers, in contrast, travel a great deal in their killings. These offenders will cruise not necessarily to look for victims but, more important, to avoid detection. As several serial killers have told us in personal interviews, if you are looking for victims, you can find them down the block. Geographically transient offenders log thousands of miles a year in their cars in pursuit of murder. They travel to avoid detection and to confuse law enforcement. Henry Lucas, Ted Bundy, Larry Eyler (Kolarik, 1992), and Chris Wilder (Gibney, 1990) are all examples of transient serial killers. See also the work of Hickey (2001b), who adds a "place specific" trait to the typology predicated upon mobility. This "place specific" category is on a micro level—e.g., bathroom, bedroom. In our manner of thinking concerning the profiling process, this may have more to do with a "signature" than a "place." Regardless, Hickey has many valid points to make, and the disagreement is only minor.

The Visionary Serial Killer

Most serial murderers are not psychotic (Andrews & Bonta, 1998, pp. 319–321); they are in touch with reality and respond to that reality. Such nonpsychotic killers tend to be psychopathic; that is, they possess a character disorder (Holmes & Deburger, 1985b; Holmes & Holmes, 1998). By contrast, the visionary serial killer is propelled to kill by voices he hears or visions he sees. These breaks from reality demand that he kill certain kinds of people. This type of killer is "outer directed" by these voices, sometimes from an apparition of the devil or a demon. Harvey Carignan was convinced that God spoke to him, demanding he kill young women. He judged women to be "evil," and he believed he was God's instrument in killing them (author's files).

The visions and the voices experienced by the visionary serial killer may be perceived to be from God or the devil. The visions and voices legitimate for the offender his violence against others, who are usually strangers to him. This kind of offender is truly out of touch with reality. In psychiatric terms, he is psychotic. A competent defense

Table 7.1   Spatial Mobility and Serial Murderers

Geographically Stable	Geographically Transient
Lives in same area for some time	Travels continually
Kills in same or nearby area	Travels to confuse law enforcement
Disposes of bodies in same or nearby area	Disposes of bodies in far-flung areas

attorney for this kind of killer will typically encounter little difficulty in having his client declared "insane" or "incompetent" in court.

The visionary serial killer does not engage in any crime scene "staging" or the deliberate altering of the crime scene to disguise the manifest purpose in the commission of the crime (Douglas, Burgess, Burgess, & Ressler, 1992).

There are other psychotic killers who are not serial murderers. Some are mass killers; others are killers who only strike once. We must also bear in mind that usually a psychotic person is not under the control of a vision or a voice every hour of the day. There are some times when the person is lucid and aware, but other times reality becomes distorted and demanding.

The Mission Serial Killer

The mission serial killer feels a need on a conscious level to eradicate a certain group of people. This type of offender is not psychotic; he does not hear voices or see visions. He is very much in touch with reality, lives in the real world, and interacts with that world on a daily basis. However, he acts on a self-imposed duty to rid the world of a class of people: prostitutes, Catholics, Jews, young Black males, or any other specific identifiable group. Such a killer may be either an organized nonsocial personality or a disorganized asocial type, but the former is more typical. Usually, when such an offender is arrested for his crimes, his neighbors are amazed at what he has done, often saying such things as, "He was such a fine young man."

In one recent case, four young women were murdered in similar ways. One was a known prostitute, and the others had alleged reputations for casual sexual encounters. The way they dressed appeared to convey their sexual availability and their willingness to participate in impersonal sex for money. The killer also mentioned that he stalked the women in the early morning hours after he got off from work. In his mind, their availability in the early morning hours signaled to him that they were prostitutes and thus deserving to die at his hands. The murderer of these women had a personal mission to rid his community of prostitutes. When the killer was arrested, and during his interrogation, he showed not only an awareness of his killings but a sense of pride based on the service he felt he had done for his community in eliminating such women, who were, in his mind, responsible for the rise in the rate of venereal disease. He also mentioned that he had sex with the women prior to killing them. The women were, according to his statement, given a choice of having sex with him or being shot. These victims chose to have sex rather than die. This judgment was fatal to them; this was a sign that they were prostitutes. Only a prostitute would consent to sex; "good" women would rather die than to have sex with a stranger, even at gunpoint.

The Hedonistic Serial Killer

The "lust or thrill killer," a subtype of the hedonistic serial killer category, has made a vital connection between personal violence and sexual gratification. This connection of sex with violence is firmly established, and the offender realizes sexual gratification through the homicide, making it an eroticized experience.

Because of the pleasure he gets from killing, this type of hedonistic killer's crimes are process focused, generally taking some time to complete, in contrast with the quick kill more characteristic of a visionary or a mission murderer, whose crimes may be described as act focused. The processed-focused killing of the hedonistic murderer may include anthropophagy, dismemberment, necrophilia, torture, mutilation, domination, or other fear-instilling activities. Jerry Brudos, for example, surgically removed one foot from his first victim and dismembered the breasts of two other victims. He made epoxy molds from the breasts and mounted the molds on his fireplace mantle (Stack, 1983). Ken Bianchi and Angelo Buono took young women to Buono's home for the purpose of torture and murder. Often they covered their victims' heads with plastic bags until they passed out, reviving them later to continue their savage ritual (O'Brien, 1985). The hedonistic serial killer receives sexual pleasure from such interaction with a helpless victim. Other killers who may be classified as hedonistic include Robert Berdella (Jackman & Cole, 1992) and Jeffrey Dahmer (Bauman, 1991), as well as John Wayne Gacy (Cahill, 1986; Sullivan & Maiken, 1983).

Another type of serial killer who may also be classified as a hedonistic killer does not have sexual gratification as a prime motive. This is the *comfort-oriented* serial murderer, who kills for personal gain. Professional assassins, for instance, kill because there is profit to be realized from their behavior. Other comfort killers may kill for profit people to whom they are related or with whom they have some kind of relationship; H. W. Mudgett, for instance, killed a variety of people— wives, fiancees, employees—to collect monies and properties. Usually, women who are serial killers are of this type; Aileen Wuornos (Kennedy & Nolin, 1992) and Dorothea Puente (Blackburn, 1990) are examples.

CASE STUDY OF A HEDONISTIC SERIAL KILLER: DOUGLAS CLARK

In Los Angeles, a series of women were found dead by the local police. Some had been decapitated, some brutally humiliated, but all had been sexually assaulted and violated.

The killings went on for several months. The victims were all young. Marnette Comer was 16 and new to California. Exxie Wilson, also a teenager, was also new to the L.A. area, looking for fame and fortune. Some witnesses reported the young girl getting in a 1978 Buick LaSabre station wagon and others just as confident at seeing another young woman getting into a similar year, yellow Datsun B-210. Some of the young women were found on the hillsides outside the Hollywood area, while others, minus their heads, were found in other parts of L.A. County.

The detectives working the case knew there was a serial killer in their midst. There were commonalities that would fit and become integral parts for the construction of a profile. First of all, there was an "ideal victim type": young, attractive, picked up on the street of an urban area, taken away from the pick-up site in a car. Many were prostitutes; all were found on the street by the unknown offender and killer. The killings were similar in MO, and the bodies were found in similar geographical areas and locations.

We interviewed Douglas Clark (Hollywood Strip Killer, as he became known) on death row at San Quentin Prison. Sitting on death row with a man who admits to killing 60 young women—who cut a few of their heads off and placed them in his refrigerator freezer, retrieving them to have sex with them. He bragged about his murders.

Douglas was sitting with his wife, Kelly, at a small table. We asked him about the murders. He confessed that he had killed many more than the six he had been convicted of. He also confessed to the manner and the motive. He also admitted that a few of the women had been decapitated and both he and his accomplice, Carol Bundy, now deceased, had simulated sex with the heads before tiring of them and throwing them into trash cans in the nearby subdivisions.

Clark is a hedonistic killer. He was involved in "five window" murders—fantasy, stalk, abduct, kill, and dispose—and involved with the corpses after death, thus also a necrophiliac. He is a "lust type." He is also a geographically stable killer, living, killing, and disposing the bodies and body parts in the same area.

As we will discuss in a later chapter, a geographically stable serial killer will eventually be caught. Look at Dennis Rader, the BTK killer; John Gacy, the Killer Clown; and many others who were stable in their movements. It is not, however, only the transience of the killer that becomes totally integral to the profile but the combination of many things that add up to an emerging picture of the killer.

What is the total picture of Douglas Clark? He is still on death row at San Quentin. He has no firm date for his execution. Still married, he still fights for his freedom. He said to us that he doesn't deserve to be on death row because the police and the courts perjured themselves at his trial: It is not about the number of people he has killed, be it 6 or 60; it is really about how the criminal justice system is corrupt. This shows another part of the profile of the Hollywood Strip Killer. He is a psychopath; he has no feelings for others. Even for a team killer (killing with Carol Bundy), he believed that he should have been granted grace for what he had done and argued strongly about the way Bundy received a reduced sentence since she cooperated with the police in his trial. As he told us, "Yes, I killed more than 60, a lot more than the 6. But the police lied and the prosecution conducted an unfair trial."

Apprehension of lust or thrill hedonistic serial murderers can be especially difficult if they are geographically transient. Their methods of killing make investigation of these crimes troublesome. Also, this type of killer is often intelligent, and if he is geographically mobile, his apprehension may be delayed for years.

The Power/Control Serial Killer

The power/control killer receives sexual gratification from the complete domination of his victim (Holmes & Holmes, 1998). As one serial murderer told us in an interview, "What more power can one have than over life and death?" Contrary to one description of the killing of a young woman that reported the serial killer's sexual pleasure connected with the act, the integral origin of pleasure from this kind of killing is not sexual; it is the killer's ability to control and exert power over his helpless victim (Michaud & Aynesworth, 1983). He derives his gratification from the belief that he has the power to make another human being do exactly what he wants. By dominating his victims completely, he experiences a "sexual" pleasure akin to the pleasure of the hedonistic serial murderer of the lust or thrill subtype.

This murderer is psychologically rooted in reality. Like the hedonistic killer, he does not suffer from a mental disease; however, a case may be made for a diagnosis of sociopathy or character disorder. This type of killer is aware of social rules and cultural guidelines, but he chooses to ignore them. Like a true sociopath, he lives by his own personal rules and guidelines.

The killing of the power/control murderer is process focused; he will prolong the killing scene because of the psychological gain he gets from this process. Like an overwhelming number of serial killers, this type will kill with hands-on weapons; he especially has a tendency to strangle his victims.

❖ SERIAL MURDERERS: GENERAL CHARACTERISTICS

There should be a careful distinction drawn between the characteristics of serial murderers and the causes of serial murder. It is important to distinguish among the various types of serial killers as well as to inventory the characteristics of such murderers. In this context, *characteristics* are what appear to be commonalities among certain types of killers; *causes* are elements that may explain why certain behaviors occur (Holmes & Deburger, 1985b).

It is impossible to speak in absolute terms when dealing with aberrant personalities (Blair, 1993; Egger, 1998; Hickey, 2001; Holmes & Holmes, 1998), but the following generalizations may be asserted. The majority of serial killers appear to share certain characteristics:

- male
- White
- 25–34 years old
- intelligent (or at least street smart), charming, and charismatic
- police groupies or interested in police work

A perfect example of the embodiment of these characteristics was Ken Bianchi, a White male and a private security officer and applicant for a police department; he was intelligent, charming, and young. Ottis Toole, however, was on the other end of the continuum. By no stretch of the imagination could he be called charming or intelligent, and he was older than the average serial killer when he committed his crimes. One serial killer on death row in the same prison told us that Toole had the "IQ of Cool Whip."

As a serial killer's crimes progress, there appears to be a general tendency toward personality degeneration. There is less and less planning, the time between the killing episodes decreases, and the episodes increase in violence. Again, witness the case of Jerry Brudos. Brudos's second murder occurred 11 months after his first, and the third occurred 4 months after the second; his last killing occurred less than a month later. Brudos amputated the left foot of his first victim, the left breast of his second victim, and both breasts of the third victim; he sent electrical shocks throughout his last known victim's body.

A Serial Murderer's Perspective

From the minds and emotions of serial killers comes the "truth" about serial murder. Unfortunately, most killers are either unwilling to talk freely about their crimes or are working on court appeals and do not feel free to talk about their cases and their emotions. However, one convicted serial killer who felt the need to talk freely about what he had done consented to speak with us; the following material is drawn from the taped interview that resulted. The interview took place in a small interviewing room normally reserved for attorneys to talk with their imprisoned clients. The interviewee said that he had killed scores of people but would not elaborate on the details of those crimes because of the lack of legal confidentiality attached to such an interview. He did say, however, that he felt he was an authority on serial murderers, if for no other reason than that he was one himself. The complete interview lasted 8 hours.

> My comments pertain to various inner workings of serial murderers, offered from the perspective of someone who has been just such a killer: myself. There are various types of serial killers, so it is obvious that my input here will not be directly applicable to each and every murderer who bears that appellation. But there are many of this fold who, while appearing intelligent and rational and essentially normal to the unsuspecting eye, are nonetheless driven by a secret, inner compulsion to seize upon other human beings, usually complete strangers, for the purpose of subjecting them to deliberate terror, systematic brutalization, and then death. This is the type of killer I was. This is the type of killer I've endeavored to understand through many years of introspection. And it is upon the inner workings of this form of murderer—the sadistic serial killer—that I hope to present some insights for those who might benefit from my own unique, albeit unenviable, perspective.

> Among the issues I have heard discussed regarding serial killers is that of their victim selection process. The traditional school of thought has it that serial murderers, on the whole, select their victims on the basis of certain physical and/or personal characteristics that they, the victims, possess. This assertion presupposes that within the mind of each individual serial killer there evolves a synthesis of preferred characteristics and ultimately a clear, specific picture of his ideal victim emerges—male or female, Black or White, young or old, short or tall, large-busted or small, shy or forward, and so on. Then, as the reasoning goes, when a typical serial killer begins an active search for human prey, he will go to great lengths to capture and victimize only those individuals who closely fit the mold of his preferred "ideal."

We are personally convinced that every serial killer does indeed nurture a rather clear mental picture of his own ideal victim. However restrained the outer demeanor of many a serial murderer may appear, each is without question a hyperactive and exacting thinker, this thought-life obsessively preoccupied with the smallest details of how and what he will do to his future victims. For throughout each one, he pays particular attention to the varied modes of restraint, abuse, and destruction that will later be his options when a victim is on hand, his mind all the while deciding which of these options provide him the most in the way of self-gratification. And, just as he focuses so attentively on the methods of violence that gratify the most, so does he pay close attention to those physical details and personal characteristics that he has determined, through his imagination, to be the ones most gratifying to find and abuse as the objects of his later violence. The ideal methods and the ideal victim, then, are fairly well established in the mind of a serial killer long before he actually seeks out his prey.

Notwithstanding this point, however, we strongly believe that in the case of most serial killers, the physical and personal characteristics of those on their respective list of victims only infrequently coincide with the desired traits of their imagined "ideal." In this killer's case, he stated that a host of assorted factors contributed to what he finally deemed to be his ideal victim, this mental vision consisting of such specific traits: gender, race, size, shape, age, length and color of hair, dress, and certain characteristics concerning his ideal victim's bearing. Yet, despite this collection of "preferred" traits, none of his actual victims ever completely fit the mold of his "ideal," and only a very tiny fraction possessed more than half of the desired characteristics. The remainder of his victims fit no discernible mold or pattern whatsoever, beyond their common trait of gender. And such is the case, we believe, with most serial killers—their ideal victim, and those whom they actually victimize, seldom are one and the same.

There are two basic, interrelated reasons for this disparity. The first centers on the extreme caution exercised by a serial killer in his predatory search for a victim; the second on the nature of the compulsion that drives him to violence.

Addressing the first reason, it can be said that a serial killer is among the most alert and cautious of all human beings, this arising from his foremost concern to carry out his activities at the very lowest minimum of risk to himself. However, as much as he has inwardly justified his intentions, he nevertheless *does* have an unacknowledged sense or awareness of the heinous nature of the acts he will commit. He is aware of the stakes involved—that there is absolutely no room for error—and therefore will mark out no one for capture/killing unless he perceives the odds to be overwhelmingly in his favor. His motto might well be, "Whom I cannot seize safely and with ease, I will not seize at all."

This unremitting sense of caution has direct ramifications on victim selection in that, during the course of his search for human prey, a serial killer is seldom apt to find his preferred ideal victim in a position of safe and easy capture. However obsessed he may be with capturing his "ideal," he is frequently thwarted by the simple fact that, in actual practice, the opportunity for this hardly ever presents itself under the requisite circumstances demanded by his extreme caution. In truth, it is a difficult and time-consuming task to locate any potential victim who can be readily seized without risk of detection. And it is a task made all the more difficult and time-consuming when the parameters of selectivity are narrowed by any focus on an "ideal." A serial killer could, of course, bide his time. He could reject all other easy prey until, at last, his ideal victim appears in circumstances perfectly suited to his caution. In actual practice, however, he rarely will choose to wait very long.

Why is this so? Because as the second reason given above states, the nature of a serial murderer's compulsion for violence is such that it precludes any prolonged or self-imposed delay in acting out his brutal urges. Initially, he may set out fully determined to succeed at capturing his ideal victim regardless of how long he might have to remain on the prowl. But, as time passes without his promptly accomplishing this specific end—a common occurrence within his many hunts—his ballooning compulsion for violence itself will swiftly overtake any initially held obsession for a particular mold of victim.

This speedy shift of a serial killer's priorities might be likened to the conduct of a lion who finds himself hungry for a meal. Stirred to the hunt by his initial pangs of hunger, the lion sets out in search of gazelle—that is, a gazelle in particular—because he happens to favor the taste of gazelle meat over all other savanna fare. Early in his hunt, a hyena and then a zebra cross well within his killing range, but the lion lets them both pass unmolested and continues on with his search for the preferred gazelle. As time passes, however, he finds that the gazelles just won't cooperate; they smartly keep their distance each time the lion nears, remaining safely outside his killing range. His hunger and frustration mounting with every passing moment, the lion quickly decides that *any* meal will do, be it a skimpy long-eared hare or a sickly emaciated monkey. In the end, it's the *meal*, not the *type* of meal, that really counts.

So it is with a serial murderer. A serial killer just will not defer acting out his violent urges simply because his ideal victim adamantly refuses to materialize at his beck and call. Instead, his intense and mounting hunger for real-life violence against a real-life captive inevitably compels him to settle for any soonest-available victim of opportunity. And it is this, the increasingly mounting stresses of a serial killer's compulsivity, and not such concerns as preferred physical or personal characteristics, that ultimately determine the matter of victim selectivity.

Perception of Potential Victims

As a serial killer steps away from his home to begin a hunt for human prey, it is almost always true that he knows absolutely nothing about the person who is fated to become his next victim. And, in truth, he really doesn't care. He doesn't care whether the stranger he'll soon encounter is a person of hopes and fears, likes and dislikes, past disappointments and goals for the future. He doesn't care whether the person loves or is loved. Indeed, he doesn't even care whether the person has a name. All such personal characteristics fall within the sphere of real-life human beings. And, as far as he is concerned, his next victim is not at all a human being in the accepted sense of the term. So, well before he ever crosses paths with his next victim, he has already stripped that person of all human meaning and worth; he has unilaterally decreed, in absentia, that the person is deserving of no human consideration whatsoever.

This, then, is a serial killer's personal perception of all his future victims; each one is nothing more than a mere object, depersonalized in advance, with each existing only for the killer and only to be seized and used as he sees fit. Moreover, he perceives his unseen prey not just as objects to be used but as objects worthy of extreme contempt, vicious abuse, and certain destruction. In the mind of a serial killer, nothing is more worthless, and no one is more contemptuous, than the nameless, faceless stranger for whom he sets out to hunt.

Why does a serial killer hold such an extreme and irrational disregard for others? How can he so utterly despise and count worthless another human being whom he has even yet to meet? The answer to these questions is that, after years of nurturing and reinforcing his compulsion for violence within his imagination, each serial killer comes to a place where he finds it absolutely necessary to act out his brutal mind images. And this, in turn, thrusts him into the position of needing to perceive living human beings—the only pool from which he can obtain real-life victims—as *objects* deserving the violence he desires to mete out. So, he mentally transforms them into hateful creatures, because, in the twisted morality of his own making, it is only against such that he can justifiably and joyfully inflict his manifestly hateful deeds of violence.

Naturally, this outlook does not arise spontaneously or overnight. A serial murderer does not just wake up one fine morning with the desire to hate and kill other human beings. Instead, the entire sum of his initial violent activity takes place only in his imagination, and usually minus the presence of any outwardly directed feelings of hatred. At first, he is perhaps only intrigued by the inner visions he allows into his imagination. Then, gradually these begin to provide him with a sense of pleasure and self-gratification, this arising from the heady sense of control and power and accomplishment he feels as he places himself in the role of the aggressor within his make-believe arena of violence. He perhaps cannot identify or articulate these sensations for what they are, but, to him, all that matters is that they feel *good*, and so he continues mentally playing out the violence that causes them to surface. For the moment, however, his victims remain wholly imaginary, and he is content enough with this arrangement. Thus, at this early stage, he almost certainly gives no serious thought to the possibility of carrying out violence to actual, living victims.

As he continues dwelling on such images, however, he becomes like the budding heroin addict who finds he requires a more powerful jolt, a more powerful means of self-gratification. And it is at some point during this stage that a future serial murderer begins taking the steps that will help transform his developing appetite for mental violence into a full-blown compulsion for the same. Gradually, he grows more and more dissatisfied with the limited collection of images that his imagination has worn out to excess, so he begins to search out newer and more sophisticated imagery to play out in his mind. This imagery—which he obtains from the Internet, books, magazines, movies, and any other sources depicting new examples and new methods of violence—is introduced and tried out on his still-imaginary victims, this further reinforcing mental violence as his primary means of self-fulfillment.

The next step in the progression comes when the violence against imaginary victims, however refined, begins to lose its gratifying effects on the future serial killer. Thus, he switches gears anew and starts practicing his mental violence on real, living people—people he sees or knows from his school, his neighborhood, or his workplace—these acts taking the place of what previously had always been fictional, imaginary victims.

At the start of this new trend, he is probably convinced that, despite the fact that he might actually enjoy inflicting real violence upon, say, the librarian from his school, or on the girl who lives next door, he still would never consider doing such a thing to them, or to any other living human being, outside the space of his own imagination. As much as he might believe this lie, however, this imaginary brutalization of actual human beings has fateful ramifications on the course of future events. For, to inflict injury upon the librarian or the girl next door, even if meant to be done strictly within his mind, he first and necessarily learns techniques that will later be used to sanction actual and willful victimization. This is exactly what he does, and he continues reinforcing the development of these techniques as he plays out, in his mind, his new game of replacing imaginary victims with real people.

But even this new practice soon loses its novelty and gratifying effects. And, in part because he is now equipped with some experience at depersonalizing others, his deterring inhibitions gradually begin to dissolve in the face of his need for a more effective stimulus. For the first time, he begins seriously considering the thought of real violence against live human beings.

Finally, then, the decisive moment of choice arrives, and the inevitable occurs. He has practiced violence in his mind for so long and has derived such intense feelings of personal fulfillment from this imagery that his appetite for this, when it arises, is virtually insatiable. Imagery, however, no longer cuts the mustard. The future serial killer knows now that his brutal fantasies must be acted out, that only this real violence will give him the measure of relief that his compulsion craves. And, just as he never denied himself relief in the past, so will he not deny himself relief now. Indeed, by this time, he finds it psychologically impossible to deny himself the relief that now can come only through literal violence.

And so he crosses over the line and begins to look upon other human beings as potential victims and as the mere props they must later become on the stage of his acted-out violence. And as he continues thinking about them, he grows to despise them, even if for no other reason than they are walking free somewhere, as yet uncaptured, thereby denying him the relief he craves and is convinced he deserves. They are "denying" him, and he "deserves" them. By these and other such twisted rationalizations, he provides for himself all the reasons he needs to justify hunting people down as if they were vermin.

All such self-serving justifications, of course, are nothing but willful self-delusion and deliberate lies. To a serial killer, however, such lies are entirely necessary. For deep inside himself, each serial murderer does have an unacknowledged awareness of the fact that his future victims are innocent human beings deserving nothing of his wrath. Yet to admit to this fact directly, he would also have to openly admit that he, and the violence he intends to inflict, is altogether unjust and wrong. And, for a man grown accustomed to the goodness and the pleasure it provides, any such admission of actual wrong is intolerable. Not only intolerable, but impossible.

Perceptions During Violence

Once a serial killer is in possession of a live victim, the acts he carries out on this person are very often done as if on autopilot—being a close reenactment of what he previously did only in his imagination. The reason for this is that he already knows from the countless mental scenarios of his past the degree of self-gratification he can obtain through certain specific acts and specific methods of violence. So, from among all these violent fantasies, he picks and chooses the individual cruelties, which he feels will assure the most in the way of self-fulfillment. These selections, then, constitute the process from start to finish that he carries out upon the victim he has on hand.

Yet, if the serial killer places this kind of special emphasis on the careful and systematic acting out of his favorite fantasies, it is only because of the tremendous meaning and pleasure he derives from watching the degrading, dehumanizing effects they have on his victims as he methodically carries them out. To him, nothing is more important than to see his victim reduced to the very lowest depths of misery and despair.

This need for self-magnification is always, we believe, a mandatory prerequisite to any episode of violence. Just prior to his every decision to victimize, a serial killer always first experiences a sudden and precipitous psychological fall, an extreme low, which he can neither tolerate nor deal with in any rational fashion. Throughout his day-to-day existence, all of his meaning is derived from the fact that he thinks himself profoundly special, unique, and perfect over all other human beings on the face of the earth. So, with the sudden onset of this mental low, he finds it virtually impossible to respond to it, especially to the crushing sense of anomie it gives rise to, with anything else but unbridled inner rage. And it is this very same boiling rage that, in turn, fires up and triggers his preestablished compulsion for violence. The acting out of his cherished fantasies, he knows, will elevate him from his intolerable and infuriating psychological low; they will make things "all right" and cause him to feel good about himself; they will "prove," without any shadow of doubt, that he is really *somebody*.

This, then, aids in understanding the motivations and perceptions of a serial killer as he performs his actual deeds of violence. For when he finally has a live and helpless victim on hand, the violence he inflicts is not carried out just for the sake of violence alone but more so for the purpose of reestablishing and reaffirming his own great worth via the brutal degradation of his victim. The long experience of his imaginary violence has already reinforced and "proved" the notion that, to become a *real somebody*, he needs only to display his power to debase, his power to break, and his power to destroy whomever he succeeds at capturing. So, in the twisted logic of a serial killer, he "proves" his own personal power and superiority by "proving" his victim's "worthlessness" through the demeaning violence he metes out.

The specific methods of violence he chooses to act out, then, are perceived by most serialists as "good" and "righteous," perfectly appropriate for the present, as they have already been tried and tested in the imagination for their ability to restore his feelings of supremacy. And, once he actually begins, he is so intensely focused on the careful performance of this script-like process, and upon the restorative sensations they give rise to, that he leaves virtually no room whatsoever for perceiving his victim as anything other than a mere object, a lowly stage prop, a piece of meat necessary only for the literal acting out of his own self-serving drama.

The consequences of this outlook are that the struggles, the pain, and the outcries of a serial killer's victim inspire nothing in the way of pity; his victim is a worthless object, wholly depersonalized, and is therefore ineligible for such a human expression as pity. Rather than empathy, a serial killer feels a tremendous surge of excitement and euphoria at the sight of his victim's anguish, for this, to him, is what the whole violent episode is all about. His victim's misery is the elixir that thrills him beyond all measure, for it is his tangible assurance that all is proceeding according to his well-ordered plan; it is his visible "evidence" that he is the magnificent, all-powerful creature he always knew himself to be.

His real gratification comes from the subjugation, terrorization, and brutalization of his victim, and almost not at all from the actual murder of the victim. Thus, from a serial killer's viewpoint, his victim might be likened to a disposable paper cup, from which he takes a long and satisfying drink of water. Once the water is gone, his thirst quenched, the cup has served its purpose; it is useless and therefore can be crushed without thought and thrown away, as if it never existed.

Analysis of the Psyche of a Serial Killer

Although it would be a mistake to say that all serial killers think alike, it would also be foolhardy to assume that there are not some similarities among them. These similarities have important implications for psychological profiling. The initiation of the "process" of violence must depend on some external force or forces. The external stimuli may be either real or imagined, and the reality of the stimuli is important only to the violent offender.

As depicted in Figure 7.1, the usual initial psychological stage of the serial killer is *distorted thinking* (Stage 1). In this position, the killer is in a positive psychological equilibrium state. He is not in a position to ponder the repercussions of deviance because he has either blotted out the consequences or is at this time more interested in the intrinsic or extrinsic rewards of his behavior.

The serial killer will show many faces to society. Given that many (excluding visionary killers) are sociopaths, they use their charm to disarm others and to keep themselves in distorted thinking. No one, however, even the most charming, can remain in distorted thinking forever. Sooner or later, reality is going to challenge his position, and he will tumble into the *fall* (Stage 2). It may be one thing or an accumulation of events, real or imaginary, that set in motion the serial killer's movement into this second stage. For example, if A, B, C, D, and E are incidents, and event E sets the killer into the motion of the fall, then A, B, C, and D helped to set the stage for the fall. Event E might be trivial, but for the

Figure 7.1   Stages of Serial Murder

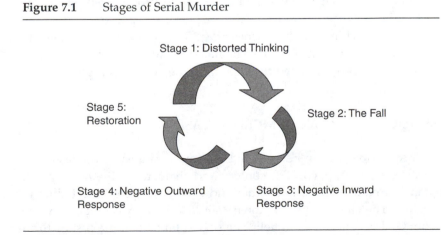

Stage 1: Distorted Thinking

Stage 5: Restoration

Stage 2: The Fall

Stage 4: Negative Outward Response

Stage 3: Negative Inward Response

violent offender it becomes all important. The stimulus may be personal or impersonal, but *the reaction is always personal.* The killer will store these incidents deep within his psyche because his ego is so large. The violent reaction that must follow is disproportional to the event.

This is not to say that each time the serial killer reaches this stage he will respond with personal violence. Sometimes his response may be symbolic—for example, violent pornography accompanied by masturbation—but such a symbolic response can be only temporary and short term. At some time the violent person finds physical release a necessity, and the stalking process begins. There can be no return to distorted thinking once the fall occurs.

Stage 3 is the *negative inward response.* The serial killer must deal with feelings of inadequacy, and he does so initially by mentally confronting these negative reality messages. His mental statement would be something like, "I'm too important, and I don't have to take this!" He must validate his self-status, and he will do this by the means he knows best, through the perpetration of violence. There is now the mental preparation to move to Stage 4, *negative outward response.* This becomes a compulsive and necessary element in the serial killer's self-affirmation of personal superiority. At this time, the killer has no thought relating to possible consequences of his actions. Once he commences to validate and affirm his personal superiority, he is not in command. He chooses only vulnerable victims because he cannot risk a further negative reality message.

With his status once again reestablished, *restoration,* Stage 5, has been reached. Once he has entered this psychological state, the serial killer will think of the potential dangerous consequences of his behavior and realize that he must take care in the proper disposal of the victim. Such concerns, about victim disposal, recognition, and so on, are not vital to him until he reaches Stage 5. He must now take steps to minimize his personal risk. Once he has done what he needs to do, he returns to Stage 1, distorted thinking, and the cycle is complete.

❖ PROFILING A SERIAL MURDER CASE

No act of violence can be executed without a fantasy (Douglas et al., 1992; Sears, 1991, p. 68). The content and character of the fantasy will change from one *person* to another and from one *type* of serial killer to another. The fantasy of the visionary serial killer may center on a voice from God or a vision from hell. The sexual fantasy of the lust or thrill hedonistic serial killer may focus on a victim who is faceless.

The role and existence of the fantasy can lend some direction to the profiling process. An alert law enforcement professional investigating a case of serial murder, for example, can make use of the knowledge that a serial killer is unlikely to commit violence while in the distorted thinking phase of the cycle described above. If the murders "stop" in a case of suspected serial murder, the inference may be drawn that something positive is happening in the life of the unknown killer. Maybe he has married, and a check on recently issued marriage licenses can turn up a possible lead. Whatever the exact events, something good may have occurred within the killer's life that has enabled him to remain—if only temporarily—in the distorted thinking phase. Only when something from reality challenges him and his self-perception will he tumble into the fall and start to kill again.

Elemental Traits in Crime Scene Evaluation

The crime scene characteristics common to organized nonsocial offenders and disorganized asocial offenders (Douglas et al., 1992), described in Chapter 5, can be combined with the typology of serial murderers. Take, for example, the visionary serial killer. This murderer modally reflects the disorganized asocial personality. The characteristics of this killer are reflected in the crime scene itself: There is ample physical evidence, overkill, the weapon belonged to the victim and is left at the scene, and so on. The personality characteristics are also similar. He is a loner, probably lives and/or works near the crime scene, and the victim is a victim of opportunity.

The mission serial killer is more likely to be of the organized nonsocial type. This serial killer selects one type of victim, stalks his victim, probably has an obsessive-compulsive personality, and uses his own weapon, which will usually not be found at the controlled crime scene.

Table 7.2 lists the elements of crime scenes and their relations to the various types of serial killers. Combining the typology of serial murderers laid out above with the FBI's typology of violent offenders, especially when sexual gratification is one of the prime motives in a murder, allows the profiler to make the best use of both theoretical models.

For example, the manifest motive of the power/control serial killer is the ultimate possession of his victim. Sexual gratification can take many different forms, and this serial killer's satisfaction emanates from his complete domination of his victims. Ted Bundy is an excellent example of such a killer. For the power/control serial murderer, as for other types, there are five "windows" in the killing process (see Figure 7.2). For the killing to commence, a fantasy must set the process in motion, and it is not the kill that terminates the process but the disposal of the body.

The crime scene traits listed in Table 7.2 can be examined and matched with the different types of serial killers. For example, usually a visionary, mission, or comfort serial killer will not move the body from the kill site. From a profiling point of view, the movement of the body denotes planning both before and after the kill. The physical evidence present in the kill site can be examined by the investigator. This is not to say that there is no evidence to be found in the dump site, but the movement of the body from the kill site to the dump site is in itself a valuable piece of information about the personality of the offender.

Only the visionary serial killer is not concerned with a specific victim type, because he is outwardly motivated by his voices or visions. The hedonistic, power/control, or mission serial murderer carefully selects a victim who will fulfill a psychological need or whose death will result in material gain. Only the comfort serial killer, a subtype of the hedonistic type, will kill victims with whom he or she has a relationship of some kind; the others will murder strangers, usually with hands-on weapons in a violent fashion. Pills and poison are weapons that are usually associated with the comfort killer.

The kill scene is often obviously different from the disposal site. Visionary, mission, and comfort killers will usually not move the body from where the kill itself has occurred. Therefore, if the kill site is also

Figure 7.2   The Windows of Serial Murder

Table 7.2   Crime Scene Analysis of Suspected Serial Murder Cases

Crime Scene Characteristics	Type of Serial Killer					
	Visionary	Mission	Comfort	Lust	Thrill	Power/ Control
Controlled crime scene	No	Yes	Yes	Yes	Yes	Yes
Overkill	Yes	No	No	Yes	No	No
Chaotic crime scene	Yes	No	No	No	No	No
Evidence of torture	No	No	No	Yes	Yes	Yes
Body moved	No	No	No	Yes	Yes	Yes
Specific victim	No	Yes	Yes	Yes	Yes	Yes
Weapon at the scene	Yes	No	Yes	No	No	No
Relational victim	No	No	Yes	No	No	No
Victim known	Yes	No	Yes	No	No	No
Aberrant sex	No	No	No	Yes	Yes	Yes
Weapon of torture	No	No	No	Yes	Yes	Yes
Strangles the victim	No	No	No	Yes	Yes	Yes
Penile penetration	?	Yes	Usually not	Yes	Yes	Yes
Object penetration	Yes	No	No	Yes	Yes	No
Necrophilia	Yes	No	No	Yes	No	Yes
Gender usually	Male	Male	Female	Male	Male	Male

the disposal site, then the perpetrator is probably one who lives close to the victim and shares many of the characteristics of the disorganized asocial personality type. Table 7.2 lists selected characteristics that can be ascertained by an attentive examination of the murder scene or the disposal site.

The weapon chosen, the owner of the weapon, evidence of necrophilia, evidence of penile and/or object penetration, and other elements revealed by the crime scene can help the investigator narrow the scope of the investigation. If, for example, a series of prostitutes has been murdered and necrophilia is involved, it may very well be that the killer believes he is receiving messages from God to rid the world of such "undesirables." This becomes more of a possibility if the crime scenes reflect a great deal of chaos with accompanying physical evidence. If necrophilia is not involved, the killer's motives may be more likely to have an inner source, a characteristic of the mission serial murderer.

The profiler can gain some basic information concerning the type of offender by matching the crime and disposal scene evidence with the type of serial murder category. Although computers may be of great help with such matching and their use is quite widespread, the value of the profiler's personal involvement should never be underestimated.

Additional Profiling Elements

The information in this section concerning crime scenes and disposal scenes has been obtained through interviews with serial murderers. It is interesting to note that the murderers have told us some things that are incongruent with the theories of profilers and those who are psychodynamically oriented, but the murderers themselves are well versed in their own killing and what they did to their victims. This information was obtained from killers whose victims numbered from fewer than 10 to "scores and scores."

Blindfolds

One element in many killings is the presence of a blindfold. Blindfolds can take many forms: masks, rags, or other pieces of cloth may be used, or victims can simply be kept in total darkness. One obvious reason for a blindfold is to hide from the victim the identity of the killer. One killer said that he blindfolded his victims, none of whom he knew on a personal level or believed would recognize him, to confuse and terrorize them. There may be another dimension to the blindfolding process—it may be that it further depersonalizes and objectifies the victim. Hence, the fantasy of the serial killer is aided by the blindfold, which helps to block out the personal nature of the crime. One serial killer who was also a serial rapist described this phenomenon:

After stripping off her clothes and tying her down to a cot, I prepared for the first part of my fantasy. [He wanted the woman to perform oral sex on him.] When I got on top of her, I felt very uncomfortable, nervous and unsettled by the woman's wide-eyed facial expression. I couldn't understand why I felt that way, but I did know I couldn't begin to go on until I covered her eyes. (Author's files)

Only after he had blindfolded her did he feel comfortable enough to proceed with his attack.

So, contrary to some common assumptions, a blindfold found at the crime scene does not necessarily mean that there was a previous personal relationship between the killer and his victim. As one murderer said in an interview, "I blindfolded my victims because faces scream at you."

Attacks at the Face

Slapping at the face of a victim depersonalizes the attack itself. Remember the remarks Will Graham made to the Red Dragon killer: "Is there something you're ashamed of?" (Harris, 1981, p. 26). Regardless of how ruthless a violent offender may be, he is still a human being, subject to the entire range of human emotions, shame included. When he is trolling for a victim, he more or less recognizes that his pseudo-contempt for this eventual captive is but a shoddy excuse to justify the hunt. And when he finally does seize a stranger to victimize, his unacknowledged awareness of his victim's actual innocence gives rise to a creeping sense of shame—or some similar emotion—that he has to deal with to proceed with what he knows is wrong.

Of course, being an expert at glossing over this emotion, he will not let this deter him from his ultimate, selfish aim. One of his key means of eliminating the "shame factor" (such as when in possession of a complete stranger), however, is to blot out the eyes, mask the identity—to keep the person a nonperson. When there is no "real person" to face, only a prop with a rag over its eyes, there is no shame.

On a more pragmatic level, violence directed at the face of the victim is a device manifestly intended to control. An attack at the eyes is especially important because of the obvious fact that injury can result in blindness and therefore reduce the possibility of a personal identification. This is usually not a factor in a serial murder case because the killer has already made the decision that the victim will not survive a process-oriented attack.

Oral sex can be viewed as a further attack upon the victim's face and a departure from the point of view that any such attack is an impersonal one. Of course, there is a utilitarian factor involved in oral sex; the offender wants his victim to arouse him sexually. In this stance, oral sex is not to be perceived as an attack; rather, as one serialist stated, oral sex "was an acceptable usage of a nameless receptacle" (author's files).

There is an inclination to believe that oral sex by itself can reveal little in terms of whether a crime has been perpetrated by a stranger or an acquaintance of the victim. Oral sex accompanied by blindfolding, however, would seem to point to a stranger-perpetrated offense. Oral sex with no evidence of blindfolding, especially when there has also been physical battering of the victim's face, tends to point to an acquaintance-perpetrated crime.

An attack in darkness combined with a blindfold is intended to terrorize as well as to depersonalize the victim. The blindfold, while reducing some of the personal element in the violence, renders the victim a nonentity and an object, but the attack at the face brings to the fantasy level of the perpetrator a personal but stranger dimension.

Disposal of the Body

Lust, thrill, and power/control serial killers are the most likely kinds of serialists to dispose of the bodies of their victims. These types of killers share many of the personality attributes of the organized nonsocial personality type. The reasons they dispose of the bodies are varied, and whether the killer intends for a body to be found can be a factor. One serial killer, when questioned about why many victims had never been found, said, "You only find the bodies of the ones [the killer] wants you to find" (author's files). He may have also been saying that the disposal of the body was a form of "advertisement" in his killing career.

Of those interviewed, not one serial killer related any concern about the bodies being found so that the victims' families could be relieved of doubt about their loved ones. The serial murderer is not concerned about his victims' families.

The disposal of the body is a signal that the killing process involving that particular victim is over. This completes the windows of serial murder, or the phases that serial killers go through in their killings. It is not a signal that the killing will start again. The murderer is now in a psychological state of euphoria, back in the distorted thinking stage of the cycle. He will remain in distorted thinking as long as reality does not challenge his position of self-importance.

For most serial murderers, learning how to dispose of bodies takes the same form as any other social learning process. In the same way one learns to do many everyday things, legal or not, the serial murderer learns the most personally beneficial manner of disposing of his victims. He will take care in the disposal because this is when he is most vulnerable. One serial murderer dumped many of his victims' bodies on a U-shaped curve in the road so that he could see in both directions at the moment of his highest vulnerability.

A recent case provides an example of how a profiler's knowledge can be useful even for locating a missing body. The police in the case requested a profile, after having first called in a psychic and an astrologer, both of whom believed that the killer had taken the body through town and dumped it in a large lake on the other side of the county. We, in contrast, offered the opinion that the body would be found somewhere between the murder site, where the victim's purse was found, and a road where the suspected murderer was seen later the same day the victim was killed. A triangle was drawn on a map delineating the search area, and the victim's body was eventually found within that triangle by hunters looking for game. Our reasoning was that a killer would not risk driving through a small town where everyone knew him to dump a body in an open area near a lake— nothing mysterious, nothing magical, just a hunch based in logic, accompanied by the luck of the two hunters' find.

Weapons

The weapon, as well as the torture used by the killer, moves the ritualist and the victim further apart from each other as human beings. Serial killers select their weapons of murder very carefully and usually kill with hands-on weapons for three reasons: (1) to touch the victim, (2) because the touch terrorizes the victim, and (3) because the touch degrades the victim. Hands-on weapons include straps (e.g., Jerry Brudos), women's hose (e.g., Ted Bundy), hands (e.g., Edmund Kemper), knives (e.g., Douglas Clark and Carol Bundy), hammers (e.g., Harvey Carignan), handguns (e.g., Beoria Simmons), and all other weapons that require or can be used in close contact. Fire is normally not a method preferred by serial murderers, because serial killers are socialized into the use of other weapons to kill and terrorize. This is not to say that some serial murderers will not burn their victims with cigarettes, hot spatulas, or other objects, but the final means of murder requires physical contact.

When the abduction initially transpires, the killer and the victim are close together on a social yardstick. The killer needs to establish a distance between them immediately to prove his superiority. The dispatching of a helpless and vulnerable victim is the psychological agent needed to place him back into distorted thinking.

Dismemberment

Picquerism is the repeated stabbing and wounding of a person that results in sexual gratification. Accurately, dismemberment may be viewed as a form of picquerism, so the sexual dimension of that activity cannot be ignored. Dismemberment also demonstrates and validates the power and control the killer has over his helpless victim. He is "proving" that his victim is not only nothing, but, by the complete violation of the corpse, "the victim is now little pieces of nothing," as one serial murderer stated (author's files). This unbridled violation of the body, now a corpse, generates some form of gratification for the serial killer, either sexual satisfaction or a psychological enhancement of the ego.

Dismemberment, as might be expected, is most typical of the lust, thrill, and power/control types of serial killer. When visionary serial killers dismember, the sexual component is generally absent; such attacks are more likely to be the result of frenzied compliance with the demands of the killer's perceived demons. Knowledge of the dichotomy of organized nonsocial offenders and disorganized asocial offenders is useful to profilers who are confronted with dismemberment as an element of a crime.

Bondage

The more organized the kill, the more need for bondage. The blitz attack perpetrated by visionary and mission serial killers eliminates the need for bondage, which is used primarily to render the victim helpless and in the control of the serial killer. There are at least three additional motivations for bondage: (1) to hold the victim for torture, (2) to place the victim in a degrading situation, and (3) to hurt or injure the victim. The act of being bound is itself also a form of injury.

Lust, thrill, and power/control serial killers, who connect sexual gratification with personal violence, have a need to see the distress of their struggling victims, and bondage serves this purpose.

Position of the Body

There is also a case to be made that the positioning of the victim's body can provide important information about the serial murderer, but some care must be taken in interpreting the meaning of any positioning. The symbolic positioning of the body (e.g., in a degrading posture) may be a characteristic associated with the mission serial killer or with the lust or thrill killer. The FBI notes that "if the [disorganized asocial] offender has mutilated the body, it may be positioned in a special way that has significance to the offender" ("Classifying Sexual Homicide Crime Scenes," 1985).

Duct Tape

Since the first edition of this book was published, we have made an interesting discovery regarding an apparent relationship between the use of duct tape and the background of an offender. We have talked with several offenders in prison who have used duct tape to bind their victims; they have learned about the efficiency of duct tape for this purpose during time spent inside prison walls. They stated that other offenders instructed them not only in the manner in which the tape should be applied but also the reason for using duct tape rather than another kind of tape or heavy twine. (This method is illustrated in the movie *A Few Good Men*, when a young Marine is forcibly removed from his barracks and bound with camouflage-printed duct tape.) When duct tape is used on a murder victim, it may be an indication that the perpetrator has been in prison at some time or is a past or present member of a special services branch of the military.

Staging

As Douglas and colleagues (1992) defined it, "Staging is when someone purposively alters the crime scene prior to the arrival of police" (p. 251). The deliberate staging of a crime scene may be indicative of a killer who is organized, because it obviously takes some mental ability to realize that there is a need to change the crime scene to divert the investigation of the police. The organized offender may realize that the police will be looking for certain nonphysical evidence that could indicate a certain type of offender with certain social core variables. The disorganized offender may not have the mental ability to alter a crime scene deliberately. In addition, the disorganized offender may truly not understand the investigatory process or the manner in which evidence is gathered and examined. If staging is evident in the crime scene, investigators are wise to look for someone who fits the pattern of the organized offender rather than the disorganized one.

Souvenirs

The immediate reason for a serial killer to take a souvenir from a crime scene is so that he has a reminder of what has transpired. The rational decision to take a souvenir involves the same mental process as might be used by someone collecting souvenirs while on a vacation. It reminds the killer not only of the event, but of what has taken place during that event. The souvenir is also part of the psychological gain realized by the murderer during the kill. What is taken once belonged to the victim, and because of that, it is reminds the serial killer of a personal aspect of the event.

Not all serial killers take souvenirs, and those who do may not take souvenirs after every murder. The killer must make a decision to take a souvenir on a rational basis; in some cases, he may realize that there is little or no opportunity to take a part of the property of the victim without exposing himself to undue risk.

Sometimes when a serial killer takes property belonging to the victim it has less to do with the collection of souvenirs than with the prevention of identification of the victim—a way to hinder the investigation by law enforcement. If the body has been mutilated or somehow altered so that it is difficult to identify the victim, and there are no personal belongings of the victim at the scene, then the serial killer has indeed accomplished one of his purposes. The souvenir, on two levels, strips the victim of his or her identity.

Trophies

In the profiles we have submitted to police departments, we have always made a distinction between souvenirs and trophies. Trophies represent something a person has won, as a bowling trophy or a tennis trophy does. In the case of a serial murder, a trophy is something intrinsic in value; it not only represents something that has been done by the predator but also something that has value of itself. Thus, a trophy is something personal, such as a body part. A souvenir may be only a memento that recalls an experiential high point, whereas a trophy is not only a reminder of the experiential high but a visual reward that serves as an aphrodisiac.

❖ CONCLUSION

The initial step in creating a profile in a serial murder case is the determination that the case under investigation is truly one of serial homicide. This may sound very rudimentary, but as any investigator realizes, sometimes we all have tunnel vision, seeing only what we want to see. Once a homicide is "certified" as part of a serial murder case, the investigators must be prepared for the publicity and other ramifications that come with such a situation.

The methods, gains, and motives of serial murder are unique to each type of killer. If investigators are able to attain some understanding of the psychology of the serial killer and his propensity for violence, if they realize that the serial murderer feels that he is all-powerful and all-knowing, and that it is his birthright to feel this way, they may have a better understanding of the psychopathic serial killer. Knowledge about the nature of differing crime scenes can deepen this understanding. A chaotic or sadistic crime scene, or one in which overkill is apparent, can give investigators valuable information.

In this chapter we have attempted to fulfill two purposes for law enforcement investigators. First, we have introduced a unique typology of serial offenders that offers motives for action and evaluation of the serial killer's mind and a particular model for personal violence. Second, we have outlined some crime scene characteristics that investigators should consider. We will address these characteristics again later in this volume.

In closing, we want to emphasize again that a profile is no substitute for a comprehensive investigation; it is simply one more investigatory aid. A profile is rarely as accurate as depicted in fictional works such as *Red Dragon, Copycat, The Silence of the Lambs*, and other such works. Some authors have been very negative about the value of profiling. In a scathing criticism of the FBI's Behavioral Science Unit's operation, Jenkins (1994) charges that the profiles the FBI has offered in serial murder cases have been largely unproductive. One of the Bureau's own, Paul Lindsey, has been quoted as saying, "I mean, how many serial killer cases has the FBI solved—if any?" (Jenkins, 1994, p. 56). In the ongoing debate, it is our position that profiling should be accepted as the aid to investigation it can be. It will not by itself solve any crime despite the abilities of the profiler. Additionally, no one profile will be 100% accurate. But if several profiles are secured, the investigator may be able to see some commonalities and work with those that may be the most reliable.

❖ REFERENCES

Andrews, D. A., & Bonta, J. (1998). *The psychology of criminal conduct*. Cincinnati: Anderson.

Bauman, E. (1991). *Step into my parlor*. New York: Bonus.

Blackburn, D. (1990). *Human harvest: The Sacramento murder story*. New York: Knightbridge.

Blair, D. (1993). The science of serial murder. *American Journal of Criminal Law, 20*(2), 1–12.

Cahill, T. (1986). *Buried dreams: Inside the mind of a serial killer*. New York: Bantam.

Classifying Sexual Homicide Crime Scenes. (1985). *FBI Law Enforcement Journal, 54*, 12–17.

Douglas, J., Burgess, A. W., Burgess, A. G., & Ressler, R. (1992). *Crime classification manual*. Lexington, MA: Lexington Books.

Drukteinis, A. (1992). Serial murder: The heart of darkness. *Psychiatric Annals, 22,* 532.

Egger, S. (1990). *Serial murder: An elusive phenomenon.* New York: Praeger.

Egger, S. (1998). *Serial murder: An elusive phenomenon.* New York: Praeger.

Fox, J. A., & Levin, J. (1994). *Overkill: Mass murder and serial killing exposed.* New York: Plenum.

Gibney, B. (1990). *The beauty queen killer.* New York: Pinnacle.

Godwin, J. (1978). *Murder USA: The ways we kill each other.* New York: Ballantine.

Harris, T. (1981). *Red dragon.* New York: Putnam.

Hickey, E. (1991). *Serial murderers and their victims.* Pacific Grove, CA: Brooks-Cole.

Hickey, E. (2001). *Serial murderers and their victims.* Pacific Grove, CA: Brooks-Cole.

Holmes, R., & Deburger, J. (1985a). Profiles in terror: The serial murderer. *Federal Probation, 39,* 29–34.

Holmes, R., & Deburger, J. (1985b). *Serial murder.* Newbury Park, CA: Sage.

Holmes, R., & Holmes, S. (1998). *Serial murder* (2nd ed.). Thousand Oaks, CA: Sage.

Holmes, S., & Holmes, R. (2001). *Sex crimes* (2nd ed.). Thousand Oaks, CA: Sage.

Jackman, T., & Cole, T. (1992). *Rites of burial.* New York: Pinnacle.

Jenkins, P. (1994). *Using murder: The social construction of serial homicide.* New York: Aldine de Gruyter.

Kennedy, D., & Nolin, R. (1992). *On a killing day.* New York: Bonus.

Kolarik, G. (1992). *Freed to kill: The true story of the serial killer Larry Eyler.* New York: Avon.

Linedecker, C., & Burt, W. (1990). *Nurses who kill.* New York: Windsor.

Lunde, D. (1976). *Murder and madness.* New York: W. W. Norton.

Michaud, S., & Aynesworth, H. (1983). *The only living witness.* New York: Signet.

Norris, J., & Birnes, W. (1988). *Serial killers: The growing menace.* New York: Dolphin.

O'Brien, D. (1985). *Two of a kind: The hillside stranglers.* New York: Signet.

Sears, D. (1991). *To kill again.* Wilmington, DE: Scholarly Resources.

Stack, A. (1983). *The lust killer.* New York: Signet.

Sullivan, T., & Maiken, P. (1983). *Killer clown.* New York: Pinnacle.

8

Psychological Profiling
and Rape

❖ ❖ ❖

Rape is a crime that has definite cultural definitions. Brownmiller (1975) asserted that rape is "a conscious process of intimidation by which all men keep all women in a state of fear" (p. 115). She further adds

that rape in time of war has long been considered the victor's preroga-
tive; the vanquished surrender yet another form of property. When
women are viewed as chattel, rape confirms their inferior social position.
Conversely, a study of rape in Pennsylvania conducted in the early 1970s
espoused a position of victim precipitation (Amir, 1971). This stance "validated" many of the myths about rape that include women secretly wanting to be raped and that the primary motive for rape is sex. Sadly, as
reported by Edward and MacLeod (1999), these myths may have some
impact on the commission of this most violent crime. Perhaps it is these
myths as well as attitudes that have contributed to rape rates remaining
extremely high (Ewolt, Monson, & Kanghinrichsen-Rohling, 2001). We
do not have space available here to refute the above-mentioned myths
about rape, but we want to stress that rape is a crime of power and violence in which sex is the weapon, and our focus will be on this issue.

❖ DEFINITIONS OF RAPE

Rape may be defined as the crime of having sexual intercourse with
another person forcibly and against his or her will (Kenney & More,
1994, p. 33). Rape is often viewed, mistakenly, as a sexually motivated
act; in reality, it is a violent crime. *Statutory rape* is sexual intercourse
that is unlawful because it involves a person younger than the age of
consent as prescribed by statute (Bennett & Hess, 1994, p. 361). *Forcible
rape* is sexual penetration without a person's consent; this is the crime
with which we are concerned in this chapter.

Although in this chapter we address primarily what may be called
"stranger rape," it should be noted that in recent years the very character of what is viewed as rape has been changing, as the phenomenon
of "date rape" or "acquaintance rape" has received a great deal of
attention (James, West, & Deters, 2000). In some ways, our cultural
view of what constitutes rape may be shifting (Gibbs, 1991). Only with
time will we gain improved perspective on this form of sexual crime
(Dunham & Alpert, 1993, p. 91).

❖ STATISTICS ON RAPE

According to FBI estimates, almost 150,000 rapes were reported in the
United States in 1992 (U.S. Department of Justice, 1993, p. 249). This
figure does not include, of course, rapes that were unreported. The Web
site of Men Against Sexual Assault (sa.rochester.edu/masa/stats.php)

reports that there were 97,460 rapes in 1995; if the reporting rate is 16%, as the site claims, this would mean that there were actually 649,733 rapes that year. Johnson and Sigler (2000) reported that almost 20% of all college women are forced to do something sexual that they do not wish to do. Many researchers believe that most rapes are not reported for a number of reasons, including victims' feelings of shame, victims' beliefs that police will not believe them, victims' fear of reprisals, and victims' lack of faith in the criminal justice system (Palmiotto, 1994, pp. 253, 261). Bachman (1998) reported that the likelihood of reporting a rape on the part of a female victim is greater if the victim sustained physical injuries in addition to the rape and if the offender used a weapon (Bachman, 1998; Pino & Meier, 1999). On the other hand, women who are raped by their husbands, even though they suffer typically multiple assaults, tend to shun the police, social service agencies, and medical aid for their injuries (Bergen, 1998). Pino and Meier reported that many men do not report being raped because it would be a personal affront to their masculinity, while women believe that rape should fit the stereotypical definition of rape. Whatever the reasons to report or not, victimization reports suggest higher rates of rape than the FBI data showed (see U.S. Department of Justice, 1991, p. 6).

Men, too, are sometimes victims of rape, but it is clear that men are raped at much lower rates than are women. One study suggested that males account for 1% of all reported rape victims (Groth & Burgess, 1980, p. 806), and Glick (1995, p. 207) reported that of 141,000 rapes reported in 1992, males were victims in about 8% of the cases. (These statistics do not include men who are raped in prisons.)

The majority of rape victims are young, with those in the age cohort of 16–24 being two to three times more likely than those in other age groups to become victims. Most rape victims are White, but Black females are disproportionally represented among victims in comparison with their numbers in the general population. Rape victims also tend to be single and from the lower socioeconomic class (Schwendinger & Schwendinger, 1983; U.S. Department of Justice, 1988).

Marital rape, which we will not address further in this book because of the nature of the topic, is undoubtedly underreported. Russell (1982) estimated that one husband in seven, on at least one occasion, sexually forces his wife to submit to coitus, oral sex, or anal sex.

Attempted but uncompleted stranger rape typically occurs on the street, in a park or playground, or in a parking lot or parking garage during daylight hours. Completed stranger rape most often occurs in the victim's home in the period from 6:00 P.M. to midnight (U.S. Department of Justice, 1988).

Rape statistics may be very misleading, given that some researchers believe that less than 10% of all rapes are reported. As noted above, there are many reasons for women's reluctance to report having been raped. Especially before rape "shield laws" were in place, women often feared that their own sexual backgrounds could be made an issue during the prosecution of a rape case. Indeed, many rape victims have been subjected to yet another vicious personal attack in the courtroom at the hands of defense attorneys. Perhaps the paramount reason many women are reluctant to report rape is the stigma that is still attached to the status of rape victim; in our society it is still common for members of the public to blame the victim, to believe that the victim somehow invited the attack or cooperated with the rapist.

Of course, every rape should be reported. In recent years there have been some improvements in the rates of reporting, in part because of changes in the laws in many states that have effectively limited the right of accused rapists' defense attorneys to introduce in court the victims' sexual histories, and in part owing to increased sensitivity within law enforcement and improved evidence-gathering methods in cases of alleged rape, perhaps a side effect of the increase in the number of female police officers on many police forces.

There are those who believe that some women make false accusations of rape as a form of revenge against men they wish to punish, but it appears that although this occurs, it is very infrequent. One study found that only approximately 15% of all accusations of rape are unfounded (Palmiotto, 1994, p. 262). But that still leaves 85% that are not unfounded, a truly high and disturbing percentage. Of those who are raped, many victims suffer from posttraumatic stress disorder (Jenkins, Langlais, & Delis, 1998). This stress may become acute when the sexual assault occurs in a marriage and when the abuse is severe and accounts for great psychological and physical outcomes for the victim. Mahoney and Williams (1998) reported that in homes where spousal rape occurs, there is a high degree of anxiety and distrust between the spouse and the abuser as well as between the spouses and the children (Mahoney & Williams, 1998). Thankfully there are centers and shelters for those who suffer such abuse in the home. More women are taking advantage of these havens as well as the social services provided (Moriarty & Earle, 1999).

❖ SELECTED CHARACTERISTICS OF RAPISTS

A cursory examination of the research conducted on rapists in cases of stranger rape yields the following information. Rapists tend to be young, with 80% under the age of 30 and 75% under the age of 25 (Kelly, 1976; Queens Bench Foundation, 1976). Those convicted often come from lower class backgrounds and are members of minority groups (often Black), who choose victims of their own race (Hagan, 1986; Hazelwood & Warren, 1989, p. 185). Many rapists' psychosexual backgrounds include histories of conflict and other trouble with women, as well as marked inability to relate to women personally and sexually (Queens Bench Foundation, 1976, p. 189). Rapists are usually unarmed; in the one case in four when a rapist is armed, the weapon is usually a knife or other sharp instrument (Glick, 1995, p. 206; U.S. Department of Justice, 1988). Most stranger rapists plan their attacks (Amir, 1971), and most have histories of violence. One in three has a prior record for a violent crime, and 25% have been before the court for rape (Queens Bench Foundation, 1976).

It should be emphasized that the above characteristics apply only to perpetrators of stranger rape. A growing amount of data suggests that date or acquaintance rape may be much more common than stranger rape, but that is a topic that is beyond the scope of this volume (R. Tewksbury, personal communication, 1995), as we are concerned here with the violent personal crime of rape as perpetrated by rapists who have not had previous relationships with their victims.

❖ PSYCHOLOGY AND RAPE

If we assume that rape is a crime of violence in which sex is the weapon, we can see that certain psychological elements may be expected to be present, elements similar to those found in other violent personal offenses. In addition to these elements, rapists appear to have three added dimensions to their pattern of violent behavior: power, anger, and sexuality (Groth, Burgess, & Holmstrom, 1977). Further, the following intrapersonal variables have been associated with the rapist personality: deficiencies in heterosocial skill development and abuse of alcohol and often enjoyment of violent pornography (Linz, 1989; Pallone & Hennessy, 1992, pp. 246–247).

The elements of power and anger in rape, combined with the crime's sexual component, lend themselves well to psychological profiling. The investigator will find many factors suitable to the examination and interpretation of a personality that insists upon a violent personal attack, sometimes fatal, to find a release from tension and compulsion (Holmes & Holmes, 1996).

There is no simple way to explain why anyone becomes a rapist. Certainly, not all rapists are alike, and rapists' motives, anticipations, and expectations vary. There has been a great deal of interest shown by researchers regarding the effects of early childhood interaction and later personality development of the rapist in which the relationship between the mother and the rapist has been the major focus. The rapist's relationship with his father has been considered to be less significant. The mother of the rapist is usually described as having been, in the rapist's childhood, rejecting, excessively controlling, dominant, punitive, overprotective, and seductive. The father is usually described as uninvolved, aloof, distant, absent, or passive, but occasionally punitive and cruel. Some researchers suggest that in the case of the sex offender, parental cruelty, inconsistency of discipline, envy, and sexual frustration, as well as overstimulation or seduction, are the principal factors that influence the rapist's sexual personality and criminal behavior (Holmes, 1983; Rada, 1978).

The rapist may have experienced parental seductiveness in childhood, usually from his mother; this may have ranged from covert seductive behaviors to actual sexual involvement. There may be a history of early prolonged bed sharing with a sibling or parent that may have sensitized the rapist unduly to sexual stimulation during childhood. In some cases, rapists have shared beds with their mothers into puberty. Many rapists also have a history of severe physical punishment by dominating, sadistic, and castrating mothers, and mild to moderate social maladjustments of the future rapist may be evidenced in fighting, temper tantrums, truancy, and stealing. Their fathers, if present, may not have lent needed support to their children when it was needed. Thus, a rapist's hostility toward women in general in adulthood may stem from the pain he suffered at the hands of a particular woman, his mother.

Regardless of their etiology, rapists are perceived somewhat differently by men and women in our society. Sanders (1983) pointed out that many men tend to look down on rapists as less than fully masculine:

In effect, they "hit girls" and that is something that real men do not do. This conceptualization of rapists is less flattering than that of their being truly "violent men"—men to be taken seriously, dangerous men not to be trifled with. This perception works well for the rapist in that it often scares their victims into submission. However, it is inaccurate. The greater the resistance of women in rapes, the more likely rapists will run off. In the world of violent men, rapists are considered punks and generally low life. . . . Thus, while rapists loom large as fiends and overpowering monsters to women, they loom small to men, more mice than men. (p. 73)

A study of violent rapists being treated at the Atascadero State Hospital in California reported the following (Queens Bench Foundation, 1976):

- The majority of the rapists demonstrated poor relations with women, lack of self-confidence, and negative self-concepts.

- Of the sample, 51% indicated they were seeking power or dominance over their victims.

- The majority had planned to have sex on the day they committed rape, and 92% said rape was their intention.

- None of the 75 subjects indicated a lack of sexual outlet as a reason for his crime.

❖ TYPOLOGY OF RAPISTS

Many researchers have attempted to classify various kinds of rapists (Amir, 1971; Becker & Abel, 1978; Cohen, Garofalo, Boucher, & Seghorn, 1971; Douglas, Burgess, Burgess, & Ressler, 1992; Knight, Carter, & Prentky, 1989; Knight & Prentky, 1987). The FBI's Behavioral Science Unit has been somewhat successful in its attempt to offer a typology, and Groth and colleagues (1977) designed a taxonomy predicated on the elements of power, rage, and sex. In an especially useful study for our purposes here, Knight and Prentky offer a typology that divides rapists into four categories: power reassurance, anger retaliation, exploitive, and sadistic (see also Bradway, 1990; Douglas et al., 1992).

Power Reassurance Rapist

Power reassurance rapists, also termed *compensatory rapists,* are the least violent and aggressive of the four types. They are also the least socially competent, suffering from extremely low self-esteem and feelings of inadequacy.

The backgrounds of such rapists vary. Knight and Prentky (1987) reported that the overwhelming majority (88%) are from homes where either the mother or father was present. Many have had minor problems in school, and their average education level is 10th grade. The compensatory rapist is most often single and lives with one or both of his parents. He is nonathletic, quiet, and passive; he has few friends and no sex partner. Often he lives in a home where he is dominated by an aggressive and possibly seductive mother. He may spend some time frequenting adult bookstores in his own neighborhood. Because of his limited education level, he is often employed in some type of menial occupation and is viewed as a steady, reliable worker.

The power reassurance rapist may have a variety of sexual aberrations. He may be involved in transvestism, for example, or in promiscuous sexual behavior, exhibitionism, voyeurism, fetishism, or excessive masturbation (Shook, 1990). The possible voyeurism of such rapists is an important element for profilers to keep in mind, as it may lead these rapists to select victims in their own immediate neighborhoods (Kenney & More, 1994). For example, one such rapist with more than a score of victims reportedly stalked his victims by looking in their bedroom windows and then entering their houses through those windows when the opportunities arose (G. Barrett, personal communication, 1995).

Table 8.1 lists the social core variables of the power reassurance rapist. Of course, the variables shown in this table and the others in this chapter are meant as general guidelines; they will not fit perfectly every rapist who may be categorized as a particular type (Knight & Prentky, 1987).

Elements in the Rape Process

The basic purpose of rape for the power reassurance rapist is to elevate his own self-status. The primary aim is sexual domination, in contrast to the generally accepted notion that rape is not primarily a sexual behavior but a means of assault in which sex is secondary. For this rapist, the sex act validates his position of importance. Deep down, he perceives himself to be less masculine and important than other men are. However, by controlling another human being he hopes to make himself believe that he is important, if only temporarily. For this reason, he uses only enough force to control his victim.

Table 8.1   Social Characteristics of the Power Reassurance Rapist

Single	Menial occupation
Lives with parents	Frequents adult bookstores
No sex partner	Voyeur
Nonathletic	Exhibitionist
Quiet, passive	Transvestite
Social loner	Fetishist

This kind of rapist's behavior during the commission of his crime is an expression of his sexual fantasies. For this reason, he is concerned with the physical welfare of his victim and will not usually harm her intentionally. He operates under the assumption that his victim actually enjoys the rape. He may request that his victim "talk dirty" to him, but he will use little profanity himself in his verbal exchanges with his victim. He may politely ask his victim to remove her clothing and will often expose only the body parts necessary for the rape to occur (see Table 8.2).

Table 8.2   Elements in the Power Reassurance Rape

Neighborhood attack	Rapist travels on foot
Rapist believes victim enjoys the rape	Rapist may be impotent
Little use of profanity	Use of weapons of opportunity
Rapist wants victim to "talk dirty"	Increasing violence during rape
Victim asked to remove clothing	Possible later contact of victims
Only body parts essential for the rape to occur are exposed	Possible covering of victim's face
Victim of rapist's age cohort	Rapes continue until rapist apprehended
Victim of rapist's race	Possible collection of souvenirs
Rape committed every 7–15 days	Possible keeping of diary by rapist

CASE STUDY OF CLETUS WILSON: THE BEDROOM RAPIST

In a working class subdivision of Louisville, a serial rapist was hunted. In the past four months he had raped at least 16 women, often mothers with small children, who lived in a subdivision of small frame houses. The women were between the ages of 21 and 25, White, not employed outside the home, whose husbands were working, thus the women were at home alone with their children during the day.

The home was located in the southwestern part of the community. Nearby the subdivision was a small shopping center with a national chain grocery store, a drug store, and several other stores and shops. Within walking distance, the children's schools were all located, thus the area was a popular one for young families.

(Continued)

(Continued)

Cletus Wilson, age 32, was a local chiropractor, his office on Dixie Highway 3.6 miles from the subdivision. He opened his practice slightly before the rapes started. Wilson was married, with two small children, both under 5 years of age. He and his wife were Catholic, both attending church regularly in the eastern part of the county. One child was already enrolled in a parochial school, and the younger was in kindergarten in the same school, both operated by the Archdiocese of Louisville. Dr. Wilson was well respected in his employment and residential community. Little did anyone know that he was the Bedroom Rapist.

Wilson was a power reassurance rapist. His "script" never varied, except for on the last rape, when he was caught. He added one element.

Joan England, 22, had three children and a husband who worked for the Ford Motor Company. At noon, Wilson broke through a screen in the master bedroom. He walked down the hallway into the kitchen where Joan was by the kitchen sink washing breakfast and lunch dishes. He attacked her from the rear and forced her back into the bedroom. There was no weapon, gun, knife, etc.; only his hands were used. Once there, he sat down on the edge of the bed and "asked" her to remove her clothing. When she had completely disrobed, he took down his pants and boxer shorts and raped her. During the rape itself he asked, "Am I any good?" The victim answered to the affirmative, "Yes, you are very good."

He asked a second question: "Am I as good as your husband?"

She answered, "You're better than my husband."

He helped her sit up on the bed, let her put on her blouse, and asked her if she would pray the Our Father with him. She consented. He cried, and she consoled.

We should not find fault with what she had done or what she has said. She said and believed as she should have to escape injury.

Then Dr. Wilson added a new part to his script. He asked that since he was so good, could he come back?

She replied, "Yes."

"When?" he asked.

"How about tomorrow?"

He asked, "What time?"

"Nine?"

Dr. Wilson cancelled his appointments at his office for the next morning and broke into the bedroom through the same window as the day before. As his feet hit the floor, the police arrested him. He had no idea that she would turn him in to the police. After all, she said he was good!

Wilson was found guilty of multiple rapes and is presently serving his time in prison.

If we look at the type of rapist Dr. Wilson is, it appears he fits the profile of the power reassurance rapist. Look at the traits of the power reassurance rapist. Certainly there are some differences. Marital status, location of residence, and employment are all examples of differences. But it is also important to recognize that since we are working with human beings, not all people in the same category are the same, which is something we *must* remember.

The power reassurance rapist tends to choose victims from his own age cohort and within his own race, and he usually rapes within his own neighborhood or close to his place of employment, because he travels on foot. He generally commits his rapes at night, in the period from midnight to 5 A.M. The time between rapes for this offender tends to be from 7 to 15 days. Although his rapes generally begin with relatively little violence, the violence may increase as an attack continues. He will choose a weapon, if he needs one, from the home of his victim. He may also collect souvenirs from the victim's home.

The power reassurance rapist is the only one of the four types of rapists described here who may later contact his victims to inquire about their health, as though he is concerned about the possible ill effects of the rape. This kind of rapist may also be so convinced that his victims enjoyed being raped that he may promise to return, as in the case above.

This kind of rapist may have some kind of sexual dysfunction, such as impotence. In addition, he may keep a diary in which he keeps track of the names of his victims and describes his rapes.

Interviewing Strategy

Like most kinds of rapists, the power reassurance rapist will continue raping until he is caught. Unfortunately, there is no clear-cut best strategy to use in interrogating this type of offender once he has been apprehended. The interviewer should be aware of the basic reason behind this offender's crimes: By raping, he seeks to resolve his self-doubts; he has no real intent to inflict harm on others. Because of this, one strategy that may be useful in interviewing is to appeal to his sense of masculinity. The interviewer might indicate to him that the woman who has been raped in the case under investigation has not suffered "undue" trauma, and that the police realize the rapist had no desire to harm his victim; such a statement could set the stage for a "sympathetic" relationship that might result in the rapist's sharing information, not only about the rape currently under investigation but about other suspected connected rapes.

Because this kind of offender wants to be understood and not condemned, another possible strategy is for the interviewer to appear to empathize with the suspect, assuming the role of a "father confessor."

Anger Retaliation Rapist

Unlike the power reassurance rapist, the anger retaliation rapist has as his general overarching purpose to hurt women. He wants to rape to get even with all women for the injustices, real or imaginary, that he has suffered at the hands of other females in his life. As the list in Table 8.3 makes clear, this violent personal offender is usually very socially competent. Typically, the family situation from which he comes has been anything but pleasant or normal. More than half (56%) of the men in this category were physically abused during childhood by one or both of their parents. Approximately 80% come from families where the parents are divorced; further, some 20% of the men in this group of rapists were adopted children, and 53% have spent time in foster homes. Some 80% have been reared by a single female parent or other single female caregiver. Because of this rapist's experiences with his female significant others (mother, adoptive mother, foster mother, or otherwise), he has adopted a position of negative and hostile feelings toward women in general.

The self-perception of this offender is very important. He sees himself as athletic and masculine, and for this reason he often seeks recreation that centers on contact sports and may also be involved in an action-oriented occupation, such as police work or race car driving. He is likely to be married and, like many rapists, is not assaultive toward his mate. Supporting his macho image, he may also be involved in a variety of extramarital affairs.

This kind of rapist's friends will often report that he has a quick, violent temper. He seems to have an uncontrollable impulse to rape, and his rapes tend to follow precipitating events involving his wife, mother, or some other significant woman in his life. This event can send him into a rage, and rape is the action that follows.

Table 8.3   Social Characteristics of the Anger/Retaliation Rapist

Parents divorced	20% adopted
Ninth-grade education	Does not assault wife
Married	Athletic
Majority physically abusive (56%)	Frequents bars
Socially competent	Likes contact sports
Hates women	Action-oriented occupation

Elements in the Rape Process

As shown in Table 8.4, the anger retaliation rapist tends to rape close to his home. His attacks are sudden, or blitz attacks, which shows that there is little planning in his rapes. For this rapist the rape is not a sexual act; it is primarily an expression of anger. The aggression in the rape is intended to harm the victim.

The aggression manifested in the rape ranges from verbal assault to physical assault to possible murder. The rapist usually uses a great deal of profanity toward his victim, and he will often rip off her clothing and assault her with weapons of opportunity, including his fists and feet.

The anger retaliation rapist has made a vital connection between sexual gratification and his expression of anger and rage. Once he secures his victim within his "comfort zone," he uses profanity for a dual purpose: to heighten his own sexual excitement and to instill fear and terror in the victim. He feels the need to express his anger and rage in many forms. For example, this rapist may rape his victim anally and then force her to perform oral sex upon him immediately afterward. Following oral sex, he may ejaculate in her face in a further attempt to degrade her.

This type of rapist tends to seek women of his own race and in his own age group or slightly older. He stalks his victims close to his home, and he tends to travel by car. Unlike the power reassurance rapist, after this rapist commits an attack he will make no further effort to contact his victim.

Table 8.4   Elements in the Anger/Retaliation Rape

Neighborhood attack	Situation-precipitated attack
Blitz attack	Increasing aggression
Little planning	Rapes committed every 6 months to a year
Intent to harm the victim	Possible ejaculation into the face of the victim
Use of weapons of opportunity	
	Anal and oral sex
Ripping off of victim's clothing	Victim of same age as or older than rapist
	Possible retarded ejaculation
Use of excessive profanity	

Interviewing Strategy

Keeping in mind this rapist's deep hatred of women, it is best to have a male interview the rapist because the rapist believes that women in general have done him great injustices, and he will not cooperate with any female officer in an interview. The interview should also be conducted in a very professional and businesslike manner. One ploy that might be used is for the initial approach to the suspect to be made by a team of officers in which one is male and the other female, with the male officer taking the lead and exerting his dominance over his female counterpart. This symbolic move may convince the rapist that the male officer is the more experienced and powerful of the two, and this may influence the rapist's level of cooperation. In reference to this strategy, we have even heard it suggested at a presentation by the Behavioral Science Unit of the FBI delivered at the Southern Police Institute, the male officer should speak in disparaging terms about the female officer after she has left the interviewing room. We find this a rather radical position, and such a strategy may be considered by many to be unethical under any circumstances.

Power Assertive Rapist

For the power assertive, or exploitive, rapist, rape is an attempt to express virility and personal dominance. This kind of rapist has a sense of superiority simply because he is a man, and he rapes because he believes he is entitled to—this is what men do to women.

For this offender, rape is not only a sex act but an impulsive act of predation. The aggression exhibited in the rape is intended to secure the compliance of the victim. The rapist is indifferent to the comfort or welfare of his victim; she is at his mercy, and she must do what he desires.

Some of the social core variables of the power assertive rapist are shown in Table 8.5. Approximately 70% of these rapists have been reared in single-parent families, and a third of them have spent time in foster homes. Approximately 75% were victims of physical abuse during childhood (Knight & Prentky, 1987). This type of rapist generally has many domestic problems and has often been involved in a series of unhappy marriages. He is very image conscious and tends to be a flashy dresser. He is often a regular at singles bars, and probably most of the other regulars know him as one who is always trying to pick up women. He is loud and boisterous and is continually trying to validate his image as a macho individual.

Table 8.5   Social Characteristics of the Power Assertive Rapist

Raised in single-parent family (69%)	Frequents singles bars
Lived in foster homes (31%)	Macho occupation
Physically abused in childhood (74%)	Domestic problems
High school dropout	Property crime record
Serial marriages	Athletic
Image conscious	Dishonorable discharge from military

This type of offender may be involved in some type of traditionally masculine occupation, such as construction work or police work. A uniform of some kind may be part of his masculine image. He often drives a flashy car, perhaps a sports car or a particular model that is a favorite among his social crowd.

Elements in the Rape Process

As Table 8.6 shows, the power assertive rapist often finds his prey in singles bars, where there is always an ample supply of females from which to select.

The attack of the power assertive rapist consists of a mixture of verbal and physical violence. If resisted, he will physically overpower his victim to get what he desires. This rapist will often tear the clothing off his victim—after all, he believes, she will not need them in the future, so why take care in removing them?

Table 8.6   Elements in the Power Assertive Rape

Rapist cruises singles bars	Retarded ejaculation
Attacks occur from 7 P.M. to 1 A.M.	Rapist has no further contact with victim
Victim's clothing likely to be torn	
20–25 days between rapes	Victim conned or overpowered
Multiple assaults	No attempt by rapist to hide identity
Anal then oral assault	Very brutal attack
Rapist selfish in behavior	Victim of rapist's age group
	Victim of rapist's race

This type of rapist may commit multiple assaults on a particular victim, and his victims are usually of the rapist's age group. Not only will this rapist assault his victim vaginally, he will also often commit anal rape and then demand that she perform fellatio immediately after he withdraws. He may suffer retarded ejaculation, so he may force the victim to perform oral sex on him so that he can become physically aroused enough to rape. As noted above, for this rapist, sex is expressed as an impulsive act of predation.

The power assertive rapist tends to commit rapes in a 20- to 25-day cycle, a time span strangely similar to the length of a menstrual cycle. This contrasts with the tendency of power reassurance rapists to assault within 7- to 15-day cycles and that of anger retaliation rapists to commit new offenses approximately every 6 months to a year.

The power assertive rapist does not rape for sex but as an act of predation. He typically has a steady sex partner, a wife or lover. This rapist feels the need to rape, and his aggression is intended to force the victim's compliance with his demands. The aggression of such rapists tends to escalate as they continue to rape. This kind of rapist may bring his own weapon to the rape situation, a behavior that shows forethought and planning.

The power assertive rapist does not hide his identity from his victims; masks, darkness, or blindfolds are not necessary. He has no intention of ever contacting his victims again.

This rapist will not apologize after the rape, nor will he collect souvenirs and/or keep a diary. He generally makes a conscious determination to rape within his own race.

Interviewing Strategy

The power assertive rapist has little control over his impulses and thus may be considered to be close to the clinical evaluation of having a character disorder. Such persons are commonly termed *sociopaths* or *psychopaths*. This kind of rapist will not respond at all well to a police interview based on assumptions or guesses. Investigators should know the details of the case and be certain of the suspect's involvement, because the power assertive rapist will appreciate a well-prepared case. If the questioning is not conducted effectively and professionally, any chance of gaining information from the rapist may be lost.

It is best for the interviewer to approach the interview session with all the facts in hand: the placement of the suspect at the scene, physical evidence that directly implicates him in the rape (or rapes), and other pertinent information that shows that the interviewer is a professional. What the police should communicate is, "We know you did it, and this is how we are going to prove it." If the interviewer is in error about the facts, or if there is some other reason for the rapist to discount the interviewer's competence as a professional, it is unlikely that any cooperation will be gained from the rapist through any means, including intimidation, pleas for aid, and appeals based on the victim's welfare.

Sadistic Rapist

Of all the types of rapists discussed here, the sadistic rapist is the most dangerous. The aim of this offender in raping is primarily the expression of his sexual-aggressive fantasies. His purpose is to inflict physical and psychological pain on his victims. Many of the rapists who fall into this category have antisocial personalities and are quite aggressive in their everyday lives, especially when criticized or thwarted in their quests for personal satisfaction. This rapist has made a vital connection between aggression and sexual gratification—in other words, he has eroticized aggression and violence.

CASE STUDY: THE FOUR-POSTER RAPIST

In a southern state, five women were raped in their own homes. There were some similarities. All the women belonged to the same country club and all played tennis and golf. They were between the ages of 35 and 42, White, unemployed, and all with college degrees. All were married, and the husbands were all executives. One husband was an Episcopal minister, the pastor of the largest church in this southern city of more than 50,000.

The women were brunettes, less than 5 feet 3 inches tall. They were all athletic, attended the same church, and all had children, some in grammar school, some in high school, and some in college.

The homes of the victims were located in an upper-class, residential, low crime rate area. The homes were multistoried dwellings, but all had the master bedroom on the first floor, visible from the side yard. All the victims had four-poster beds.

Again, in viewing the last rape, a man, well-dressed in a suit, white shirt, and tie, knocked on the front door. One victim, Mary C., came to the door and opened it. The man said he was from the local air-conditioning company, and the husband had allegedly called for an estimate on a new furnace and air-conditioner. Of course there was no call; this was a ruse by this serial rapist.

The victim permitted the man to come into the home. Once inside, he started small talk—e.g., what a beautiful home, what a great job she had done on the

(Continued)

(Continued)

decorations, did she sew, and, oh, did she have a needle and thread? Once she answered she did have a needle and thread, his demeanor suddenly changed. He grabbed her and forced her into the master bedroom.

Once inside the master bedroom, he tore her clothing off until she was completely nude and swore at her with vile and violent words. He anally sodomized her and then orally. After that he vaginally raped her. He slapped her and hit her with his fists. She had a broken nose, two black eyes, and numerous other black and blue marks on her body. She had bite marks on her breasts and neck, shoulders, and buttocks. Her body was covered with scratches. He pulled out small bunches of her hair. After the whole sexual violent episode, he made her stand up next to the bed and pulled the headboard away from the wall and made her stand next to the post on the left side of the bed so that the post itself was between her breasts. With a gun lying on the bed, he asked where the needle and thread was, retrieved it from the nightstand, and threaded the needle. He then sewed her nipples together across the post of the bed.

As he left, he turned to her and told her not to report this to the police. He said he had an informant at the police station who would tell him immediately if a report had been filed.

What kind of rapist would this be? Would he later kill a victim if he had not been apprehended? Match this up with the traits and characteristics of the sadistic killer. How closely would these traits follow this case? What would the profile look like?

Table 8.7 displays the social characteristics associated with the sadistic rapist. As the table shows, some 60% have been reared in single-parent homes. The majority suffered childhood physical abuse, and many come from homes where there has been evidence of sexual deviance (e.g., fathers who were rapists themselves). Many sadistic rapists have histories of such juvenile sexual pathologies as voyeurism, promiscuous sex, and excessive masturbation (Kenney & More, 1994, p. 196).

In his adult life, the typical sadistic rapist is married and is considered to be a "good family man." He often lives in a middle-class residential area where crime rates are low, is viewed as an asset to his community, has a better-than-average education, and is in a white-collar occupation.

This kind of rapist exhibits a compulsive personality, a factor that can be particularly important in the profiling process. He demonstrates his compulsiveness in his personal appearance and in the automobile he drives, which is neat, clean, and kept in good condition.

Table 8.7   Social Characteristics of the Sadistic Rapist

Raised in single-parent home (60%)	Some college education
Parents divorced (60%)	Married
Lived in foster homes (13%)	No arrest record
Physically abused in childhood (63%)	Age range 30–39
Raised in sexually deviant home	Compulsive personality
Middle-class family man	White-collar occupation

This offender is intelligent and probably does not have a police record. He has the ability to escape detection for his offenses, if for no other reason than because he carefully plans his rapes and carries them out within the parameters of his plans. His intelligence, knowledge of police work, antisocial personality, and care in the planning and implementation of his rapes make him especially difficult to apprehend.

Elements in the Rape Process

There is an expressive aim in the rapes of this kind of rapist. The aggression component of the rape is not simply for control; he intends to do personal harm to his victim. If this rapist is not apprehended, he will eventually begin to kill his victims (see Table 8.8).

The sadistic rapist uses his well-maintained automobile to stalk his victims. He takes great care in selecting victims, making certain that he is not seen and taking all precautions necessary to hinder the detection of his crimes and thus his apprehension. He generally takes his victims to a place where he controls the action, his "comfort zone"

Table 8.8   Elements in the Sadistic Rape

Victim stalked	Degrading language
Victim transported	Retarded ejaculation
Use of gags, bonds, handcuffs	Increasing violence
Possible use of blindfold	Rapist has rape kit
Possible triolism	Rapist may eventually kill
Victim's clothing cut	Periods between rapes vary
Elements of ritual	Victims' ages vary

(Holmes & Holmes, 1998, p. 120; Ressler & Shachtman, 1992). Warren, Reboussin, and Hazelwood (1998) suggest that distance plays an important role in the sadistic serial rapists. They report that serial rapists travel on average 3.14 miles to rape. Half of the rapists raped at least once within a half mile of their residence, which may place them at some risk for detection and arrest.

Less to control his victims than to instill terror in them, the sadistic rapist uses gags, duct tape, handcuffs, and other paraphernalia in the commission of his crimes. He may also blindfold his victims, also primarily to increase their fear. He may tell his victims what he plans to do to them, detail by detail, using excessive profanity and degrading language. As he is attacking his victim, he may call her by another name, perhaps his wife's or his mother's.

The sadistic rapist is very ritualistic. Each rape must go according to plan for him to experience the feelings he believes are necessary. He may need for his victims to say certain words to him for him to become aroused. Also, he may insist on oral sex as a prelude to coitus. Like the power assertive rapist, the sadistic rapist may suffer from retarded ejaculation. This rapist often carries in his vehicle a "rape kit" (Ressler & Shachtman, 1992); Ted Bundy, for example, carried a kit that included handcuffs, an ice pick, a ski mask, a mask made of panty hose, rope, black garbage bags, and a tire iron (see Figure 8.1).

As he continues his crimes, the sadistic rapist learns increasingly effective methods to stalk his victims and better ways of disposing of the bodies of those he has killed. For this rapist, murder is secondary. As Ted Bundy remarked during a 1985 interview while he was on death row at Florida State Prison, "A large number of serial killings [are] simply an attempt to silence the victims, a simple but effective means of elimination" (author's files).

The sadistic rapist is often mildly intoxicated and may be a recreational drug user. He feels no remorse for his crimes and will continue to rape until he is caught. It is not unusual for this offender to escalate his violence to the point where the serial rapist becomes a serial killer.

Interviewing Strategy

Unfortunately, there appears to be no one interviewing strategy that is generally effective with this type of rapist. As the Behavioral Science Unit of the FBI notes, this type of offender requires eclectic interviewing techniques. The interviewer must be aware of the many variables and nuances of the particular case, as this offender is highly unlikely to cooperate if he believes that the interviewer is anything less than competent and professional. Any interview of the sadistic rapist

Figure 8.1   Ted Bundy: A Sadistic Rapist's Rape Kit

should be conducted in a businesslike manner, and the interviewer should be sure of the factual details of the case before presenting them to the offender.

Some researchers have suggested strategies for police interviews with suspected rapists in general. Hertica (1991, p. 39) proposes that a suspect be invited to come to the police station for the purpose of clarifying certain aspects of the case. In such a situation, the rapist may be eager to give his side of the story. Hertica also notes that it is useful for the interviewing officer to try to build a rapport with the suspect; this may be aided by the interviewer's demonstrating some form of empathy with the suspect. As we have noted above, however, rapists are not all alike; it may be that these interviewing techniques will work with some but be detrimental with others.

❖ CONCLUSION

Many people view rape as one of the most despicable crimes that may be committed against a human being. The byproducts of rape can include the destruction of the victim's feelings of worth and the victim's internalization of feelings of responsibility for her own victimization. Although recent research on rape has tended to emphasize date or acquaintance rape over stranger rape, and the reported incidence of acquaintance rape has been increasing, the fact is that stranger rape still takes place. We believe that it is important to emphasize this point, in part because many of the kinds of rapists described in this chapter continue to escalate their acts of rape and may move to murder. The investigation and resolution of cases of stranger rape, in which sex is the weapon used in crimes of personal violence, require the concentrated efforts of law enforcement.

❖ REFERENCES

Amir, M. (1971). *Patterns in forcible rape.* Chicago: University of Chicago Press.

Bachman, R. (1998). The factor related to rape reporting behavior and arrest: New evidence from the national crime victimization survey. *Criminal Justice and Behavior, 25*(1), 8–29.

Becker, J., & Abel, G. (1978). Men and the victimization of women. In J. Chapman & M. Gates (Eds.), *Victimization of women.* Beverly Hills, CA: Sage.

Bennett, W., & Hess, K. (1994). *Criminal investigation.* Minneapolis: West.

Bergen, R. (1998). Wife rape. *Violence Against Women, 5*(9), 989–1085.

Bradway, W. (1990, September). Stages of sexual assault. *Law and Order,* 119–124.

Brownmiller, S. (1975). *Against our will: Men, women and rape.* New York: Simon & Schuster.

Cohen, M., Garofalo, M., Boucher, B., & Seghorn, T. (1971). The psychology of rapists. *Seminars in Psychiatry, 3,* 307–327.

Douglas, J., Burgess, A. W., Burgess, A. G., & Ressler, R. (1992). *Crime classification manual.* Lexington, MA: Lexington.

Dunham, R., & Alpert, G. (1993). *Critical issues in policing.* Prospect Hills, IL: Waveland.

Edward, K., & MacLeod, M. (1999). The reality and myth of rape: Implications for the criminal justice system. Expert evidence. *International Journal of Behavioral Sciences in Legal Context, 7*(1), 37–58.

Ewolt, C., Monson, C., & Kanghinrichsen-Rohling, J. (2001). Attributions about rape in a continuum of dissolving marital relations. *Journal of Interpersonal Violence, 15*(11), 1175–1182.

Gibbs, N. (1991, June 3). When is it rape? *Time*, 48–54.

Glick, L. (1995). *Criminology*. Boston: Allyn & Bacon.

Groth, A., & Burgess, A. (1980). Male rape: Offenders and victims. *American Journal of Psychiatry, 137*, 806–810.

Groth, A., Burgess, A., & Holmstrom, L. (1977). Rape, power, anger and sexuality. *American Journal of Psychiatry, 134*, 1239–1243.

Hagan, F. (1986). *Criminology*. Chicago: Nelson-Hall.

Hazelwood, R., & Warren, J. (1989). The serial rapist: His characteristics and victims. *FBI Law Enforcement Bulletin, 58*(2), 18–25.

Hertica, M. (1991, February). Interview sex offenders. *Police Chief*, 39–43.

Holmes, R. (1983). *The sex offender and the criminal justice system*. Springfield: Charles C. Thomas.

Holmes, R., & Holmes, S. (1996). *Profiling violent crimes* (2nd ed.). Thousand Oaks, CA: Sage.

Holmes, R., & Holmes, S. (1998). *Serial murder* (2nd ed.). Thousand Oaks, CA: Sage.

James, W., West, C., & Deters, K. (2000). Youth dating violence. *Adolescence, 35*(139), 455–465.

Jenkins, M., Langlais, P., & Delis, D. (1998). Learning and memory in rape victims with posttraumatic stress disorder. *American Journal of Psychiatry, 155*(2), 278–279.

Johnson, I., & Sigler, R. (2000). Forced sexual intercourse among intimates. *Journal of Family Violence, 15*(1), 95–108.

Kelly, C. (1976). *Uniform crime reports: Crime in the United States*. Washington, DC: U.S. Government Printing Office.

Kenney, J., & More, H. (1994). *Principles of investigation*. Minneapolis: West.

Knight, R., Carter, D., & Prentky, R. (1989). A system for the classification of child molesters. *Journal of Interpersonal Violence, 4*, 3–23.

Knight, R., & Prentky, R. (1987). The developmental antecedents and adult adapatations of rapist subtypes. *Criminal Justice and Behavior, 14*, 403–426.

Linz, D. (1989). Exposure to sexually explicit materials and attitudes toward rape: A comparison of study results. *Journal of Sex Research, 26*, 50–84.

Mahoney, P., & Williams, L. (1998). Sexual assault in marriage: Prevalence, consequences, and treatment of wife rape. In J. Jasinski & L. Williams (Eds.), *Partner violence: A comprehensive review of 20 years of research*. Thousand Oaks, CA: Sage.

Moriarty, L., & Earle, J. (1999). An analysis of service for victims of marital rape: A case study. *Journal of Offender Rehabilitation, 29*(3/4), 171–181.

Pallone, N., & Hennessy, J. (1992). *Criminal behavior: A process psychological analysis*. New Brunswick, NJ: Transaction.

Palmiotto, M. (1994). *Criminal investigation*. Chicago: Nelson Hall.

Pino, N., & Meier, M. (1999). Gender differences in rape reporting. *Sex Roles, 40*(11/12), 979–990.

Queens Bench Foundation. (1976). *The rapist and his crime*. New York: John Wiley.

Rada, T. (1978). Alcoholism and forcible rape. *American Journal of Psychiatry, 32*, 444–446.

Ressler, R., & Shachtman, T. (1992). *Whoever fights monsters*. New York: St. Martin's.

Russell, D. (1982). *Rape in marriage*. New York: MacMillan.

Sanders, W. (1983). *Criminology*. Reading, MA: Addison-Wesley.

Schwendinger, J., & Schwendinger, H. (1983). *Rape and inequality*. Beverly Hills, CA: Sage.

Shook, L. (1990). Sexual glossary. In L. Shook (Ed.), *Investigation of variant sex styles*. Montgomery, AL: Auburn University Press.

U.S. Department of Justice. (1988). *Report to the nation on crime and justice*. Washington, DC: U.S. Government Printing Office.

U.S. Department of Justice. (1991). *Criminal victimization in the United States*. Washington, DC: U.S. Government Printing Office.

U.S. Department of Justice. FBI. (1993). *Uniform crime reports: Crime in the United States, 1992*. Washington, DC: U.S. Government Printing Office.

Warren, J., Reboussin, R., & Hazelwood, R. (1998). Crime scene and distance correlates of serial rape. *Journal of Quantitative Sociology, 14*(1), 35–39.

9

Pedophilia and Psychological Profiling

❖ ❖ ❖

Definition of Terms: Child Molester or Pedophile

Types of Pedophiles
   The Situational Child Molester
   The Preferential Child Molester

Profiling Child Molester Types
   The Sadistic Offender
   The Fixated Offender
   Immature and Regressed Offenders

Common Threads Among Child Molester Types

Conclusion

There is no doubt that the sexual abuse of children is considered a heinous act. This victimization of children is such an unexplainable phenomenon that its etiology and practice is most difficult to explain and understand. Consequently, we view those who prey on children as being truly "perverted" or disturbingly ill. After all, what well person would rape a child? Even more disturbing is an assertion that child sex is being more tolerated in American society as well as being more prevalent (Leo, 1993, p. 37).

Unfortunately, there are those who regard children as sex objects and deserving in some way to be treated as exploited objects, and in fact, it may be that many child abusers believe the children chase the adult until the adult finally consents to sex. This is a most interesting attempt at neutralization, a mental manipulation of behavior and rationalization that negates personal responsibility. Thus under this conceptualization the child is the cause, the prime mover; the molester is the victim, and the predatory pattern of the molester will continue.

❖ DEFINITION OF TERMS:
   CHILD MOLESTER OR PEDOPHILE

There are ambiguities involved in the definition of child molesters and pedophiles. A generic definition of a child molester is an adult who touches or fondles a child for his or her own sexual gratification. However, an accurate definition needs to include age, sex of victim, sex behaviors, etc. The generic definition is very simple and to the point. It is devoid of any intricacies or refinements to aid in the understanding of the dynamics of the child offender or the behaviors that are manifested. While it is a simple definition, it is a starting point. This is not intended to be a criticism of the term or the definition. However, in investigating the child molester/pedophile, it is important to reach a better understanding. We take issue with those in the academic literature that state that "a child molester is simply an individual who engages in illegal sexual activity with children" (Leo, 1993, p. 37). This statement is so broad that it loses any implications for criminal psychological assessment and simply does not accurately describe the etiology of the child sexual offender.

For example, let us examine the word *pedophile*. A pedophile is a "lover of children." The definition is simple, but the understanding of this individual's whims and wants is quite complex. Both of the authors of this text love children. Each of us has had children and believes that our nation's children are our most prized possession. But that, of course, does not mean either of us has a sexual interest in children or would ever exploit them for our own sexual needs. Underlying the definition of the pedophile is a person that not only loves children but also uses them for their own sexual pleasure. The sexual interest the true pedophile has in children ranges from fondling to mutilation and sometimes murder.

But, of course, not all pedophiles wish to harm children; some wish only to hold and fondle the child. To the other extreme, some sadistic pedophiles are only gratified with the death of their captive child. Since their range of behaviors is so wide, and their behaviors are so diverse, if we are to accept the definition of *pedophilia* to be a "lover of children," we can see how difficult, if not impossible, it is to understand them, much less profile their crimes.

Also important is the need to differentiate between the pedophiles and child molesters. While some pedophiles may molest children, in general, child molesters do not share any great love or affection for kids. Many true child molesters, especially the preferential type, have no great love for children. Children are there to abuse and then discard.

For the purposes of this book, we start with the definition of a pedophile as a "*perverse* lover of children." If one accepts our definition of *pedophilia*, this is the first step in the investigation process. Now we need to become more specific. The Diagnostic and Statistical Manual of Mental Disorders of the American Psychiatric Association defines *pedophilia* as "the acts or fantasy of engaging in sexual activity with prepubertal children as a repeatedly preferred or exclusive method of achieving sexual excitement." This is a classic definition that illustrates the action involved (sexual), the age of the child-victim (prepubertal), and an indication of duration (repeatedly or exclusive). But there is another group of pedophiles, termed "hebephiles," who prefer children who are already into puberty. Seldom is this term used. It is indicative of a type of child offender who makes a distinction regarding victimization solely on age (American Psychiatric Association, 2000).

Child molesters, on the other hand, may share many of the same traits as pedophiles and hebephiles; however, they are not diagnosed by *DSM-IV* as having a mental disorder. The difference in being diagnosed and not being diagnosed is, however, small. For the most part, in order to be diagnosed as suffering from pedophilia, one must over a period of 6 months have recurrent, intense sexually arousing fantasies or urges (American Psychiatric Association, 2000). Clearly this diagnosis may not fit all offenders, especially those who are new to this type

CHILD MOLESTATION IN THE CHURCH

July 2001

In Salem, Massachusetts, a former church youth leader and a swim coach pled guilty to multiple counts of molesting children. In court, Christopher Reardon, age 29, admitted to molesting 29 children and pled guilty to 75 charges. A former religion teacher at the St. Agnes Catholic School, he is only one of several child abusers who have become known to the criminal justice system in widespread publicity cases. For example, in Dallas, Texas, the Catholic Church agreed to pay $30 million to 11 former altar boys of a former priest who was then sentenced to life in prison. In nearby Boston, the church allegedly paid millions regarding nearly two dozen molestation cases by a former priest.

Reardon purported that he wanted to plead guilty to the charges so the children would not have to undergo embarrassing testimony in court. He was sentenced to life in prison for eight charges of raping a child, each of which carried a life sentence.

of paraphilia. For many actors in the criminal justice system, and others, this difference is irrelevant. What does appear to be significant, though, is that on the average, child molesters appear to use physical force more often than pedophiles to coerce their victims into their sexual escapades (DeFrancis, 1969).

An added dimension, and one often confusing to law enforcement, is the sex of the offender and the sex of the child-victim as it concerns the issue of homosexuality and heterosexuality. Consider the following scenario. The police go to a home to arrest a man suspected of molesting several young boys. The police are convinced the offender is a homosexual because of the sex of his victims. They arrive at the door and discover he is married and has several children. When talking to the suspect, they find that he self-identifies as heterosexual and views having sex with an adult male as repugnant. The other suspected possibility is that he is gay or bisexual and is in his heterosexual marriage because of special circumstances. The point here is that we should not automatically believe we are looking for a gay male if only young males are victimized. Consider the case of John Gacy, the executed killer of 33 young males in Chicago. Gacy did not consider himself to be homosexual, and he was rankled when this was suggested (author's files). If the focus of the Gacy investigation had been centered solely on the gay community, the resolution would have been impeded.

There is yet another consideration here before we look at other elements to be appraised. There are women who are child molesters and pedophiles. They receive meager attention in the academic literature, and only relatively recently are we beginning to hear about these offenders as the number of female teachers who molest children begins to make national, state, and regional news . Despite the recent attention to these cases, very few incidents are actually reported because these crimes tend to attract less rage from parents, especially when an adolescent male is the victim. Some parents may even condone this behavior as a young boy's "rite of passage."

The majority of American citizens are opposed to those who view children in a sexual manner and who wish to victimize children in a sexual way, and vast resources have been expended in the investigation of individuals and organizations that are intent on the sexual victimization of children. But it is also a truism that those who molest children are different. Just as it is impossible to compare exhibitionists with lust killers, it is also impossible to believe that all pedophiles molest in the same fashion and that they have the same social core variables.

❖ TYPES OF PEDOPHILES

Just as all members of one group are somehow and in some fashion different, pedophiles are different in their behavioral patterns, selection of victims, usage of lures, and propensity toward violence, even fatal violence.

The Situational Child Molester

The first broad category is the situational type. The situational pedophile typically has fewer victims than the preferential type. This child molester does not have a "true sexual interest" in children but will experiment with children when stress is introduced into his life. Also, this type of sexual molester will not only molest children, but he will also abuse the elderly, the impaired, or the sick. Within the situational type, there are several subtypes.

The Regressed Child Molester

The first subtype is the regressed type. This pedophile has a situational occurrence, which impels him to turn to a child as a temporary object for sexual gratification. If one examines the word *regressed*, then it is easily understood that this molester turns to children as substitute sexual partners. There has occurred something in the molester's life that challenges the self-image and results in poor self-esteem. The regressed pedophile is one who has been traditionally involved with adults in normal relationships. Certainly, there are some extant interpersonal problems, but from an outward perspective, there were no great problems in relating with adults in personal as well as sexual relationships. Psychologically, this type of child offender views the child as a pseudo-adult because of some type of situational stress—e.g., breakup in a marriage, poor performance evaluation, or some other life stressor (Burgess et al., 1978). Often, this type of child molester is married and lives with his family, but something happens in his life that propels him into a circumstance where he feels more comfortable in the presence of usually nonjudgmental children, which results in their sexual victimization.

Witness the following case:

I had never thought of molesting children. I was a deacon in my church, a Cub Scout leader, and a youth minister. I had been around children all my life with no intent to harm them. One day, I came home from work and my wife said that there was something she wanted to talk to me about. She said, "Tony, you physically disgust me and I never want you to touch me again!" This really affected me, as you can imagine. In the next 2 weeks, I was coming up for a big promotion and I knew that if I did not get it I would never be promoted before I retired. I [was] 60 years old, and this would have been my last shot. It came down to me and a young fellow at work who was only 30 years old. He got the job.

I was crushed. That weekend, I and the Cub Scout troop went on a camping trip. As usual, there were two people to a pup tent, and there was a young 9-year-old sharing a tent with me. It started raining and thundering and the boy got scared. He asked if he could come over to my side of the tent and climb into my sleeping bag. Well, one thing led to another, and before long, I was fondling him. This led to other young boys, which went on for over a year. (Author's files)

This abuser was discovered when one child related the experiences to other children and finally to the minister of the church. He was arrested and sent to prison. Holmes and Holmes (2001) reported that the regressed type is more apt to sexually abuse children he does not know, and the children are typically victims of opportunity. Also, this type of offender is more apt to sexually abuse females, the above abuser molested young boys simply because they were available. There are other traits that are prevalent in this type of offender. He is generally geographically stable, employed, married, may have some problems with alcohol abuse, and has low self-esteem.

The Sexually Indiscriminate Child Molester

The morally indiscriminate molester is an abuser of all available persons. Children are just another category of victims. The morally indiscriminate offender has a basic motivation toward sexual experimentation: He is a "try-sexual"—that is, willing to try anything. He may be involved in a wide variety of sexual practices including tyndarianism (mate-swapping), bondage and discipline, triolism, and other forms of unusual sexual practices. He may involve his biological children, or children by marriage, in these sexual practices. As one can see, this molester does not have a sexual preference for children; they are simply there for the taking.

The Naive or Inadequate Child Molester

The third subtype is the naive or inadequate child molester. These offenders include those persons who suffer from some form of mental disorder that renders them unable to make the distinction between right and wrong as far as sexual practices with children. The people in the neighborhood will know this molester, and he has a reputation in the community as being "strange," "bizarre," or "senile." They are loners, usually not by choice but because they are not capable of establishing personal relationships with others. This type of offender usually does not physically harm a child, and he is more likely to experiment with children with sexual practices including holding, fondling, kissing, and licking, but not sexual intercourse (Haas & Haas, 1990).

From Table 9.1, it is apparent that with each type of child molester, there are certain traits or characteristics that are unique to that particular molester. The basic trait of victim criteria, for example, will vary from one molester to the other. With the regressed, for example, the simple availability will be the paramount trait in the consideration of who will be molested. With the naive or inadequate, on the other hand, the selection of the victim will depend on the threat potential to the molester himself.

Table 9.1   Situational Child Molesters

Element	Regressed	Sexually Indiscriminate	Inadequate
Basic trait	Poor coping skills	Sexual experimentation	Social misfit
Motivation	Substitution	Boredom	Insecurity and curiosity
Victim criteria	Availability	New and different	Nonthreatening
Method of operation	Coercion	Involve in existing activity	Exploitation of size advantage
Porn collection	Possible	Highly likely	Likely

The Preferential Child Molester

Many cases of severe sexual abuse occur within the situational child molester type, typically by the sexually indiscriminate offender. However, there are different types of child molesters/pedophiles who look at children much differently and perhaps more intensively as providers of pleasure. This group of abusers "prefers" children as the providers of personal and sexual gratification, hence "preferential." There are two common subtypes of the preferential child molester.

The Mysoped Child Molester and Killer

As within the broad category of situational molesters, the preferential type contains several different types of molesters. One type has made the vital connection between sexual gratification and extreme personal violence: the mysoped (Holmes & Holmes, 2001). This type of pedophile is usually male and has made a vital connection between sexual arousal and fatal violence. Typically, the child is a stranger to this aggressive and sadistic child offender. This type of offender may stalk the child, rather than use any form of seduction (the method typical of many pedophiles).

The mysoped will often abduct a child from places where children gather: playgrounds, schools, shopping centers, and other such places. He will usually not attempt to seduce or otherwise induce the child to go with him; he simply takes the child by force. A scenario that includes pain inflicted upon the child, followed by the child's death, follows the abduction.

This type of pedophile has no real sexual interest in children in the traditional sense, although he may sexually abuse them. His interest is primarily rooted in torturing, humiliating, and mutilating his young and vulnerable victims to whom he feels greatly superior. If the victim is a young boy, the child's penis may be cut off and inserted into the child's mouth. Small girls are also brutally assaulted and the physical violence is often directed toward the child's genitals. This sexual sadist often terrorizes the child with some type of weapon, and the crime is premeditated and ritualized.

There are other obvious examples of the mysoped. Westley Dodd, an executed child killer, was considered an aggressive and sadistic child offender. Dodd was considered to be a loner in high school—but honest and dependable according to many of his teachers. The band teacher, for example, remarked that Dodd was quiet, always did what he was told, and was not a behavioral problem. Dr. Al Carlisle, a psychologist from Utah, interviewed Dodd. Dodd stated that he considered himself a humanitarian sociopath. He said that if a child fell off his bicycle, he would be the first one to reach the child and tender aid. But how could he intend to inflict so much pain and suffering on children whom he also loved in the way that he did?

Dodd killed three young boys—two brothers and one 5-year-old child. The last victim was abducted from a public park while his older brother played with some friends. He took the boy home with him and over a period of several hours sexually abused the boy before finally murdering him. He placed the body in the closet, and after he came home from work later that afternoon, he retrieved the corpse and committed anal sex and other forms of sexual abuse before he disposed of the boy's body. The police apprehended Dodd as he attempted to abduct a fourth young boy at a neighborhood theater. He was later executed by hanging (his choice) in Washington State.

Cases of sadistic child offenders are not rare. Albert Fish, the "moon maniac" in the early part of the 20th century, is yet another example. Fish, an elderly grandfatherly type, was finally arrested after years of careful investigation in New York. When arrested, police found body parts that apparently came from various children. Fish took his final victim from her home under the pretense of taking her to a birthday party on Long Island. He transported her to an abandoned area, killed her, and then cooked portions of her body for his own consumption. More than a pedophile and a cannibal, Fish was also involved in infibulation, self-torture of one's sexual body parts. When he was executed in the electric chair at Sing Sing, the autopsy discovered 29 sewing needles implanted in his penis and scrotum (Schechter, 1990).

There are two other types of preferential molesters: the seduction and the introverted molester. The seduction molester entices children by courting them with attention, affection and gifts. This molester is involved in courting the children over an extended period of time and may be involved with several children at the same time. On the other hand, there is the introverted type. These offenders have no real skill or knack at courting children and instead prefer to marry or date women with children whom they will later victimize. These two types of molesters are similar to the fixated molester or pedophile, desiring affection, "a cynical need for affection" (Johnston, French, Schouweiler, & Johnston, 1992, p. 6).

This child offender is not really developed past the point where he, as a child, found children attractive and desirable. In other words, he has become "fixed" at an early stage of psychosexual development (Burgess et al., 1978). The fixated type of child molester's pedophiliac interest started in adolescence; unlike the case of regressed child offenders, there is no precipitating cause in his child abuse. His interest in children is persistent and compulsive. Male victims are the preferred targets of abuse.

The Fixated Child Molester

The fixated child offender has little or no activity with age mates, usually is single, and is considered to be immature and uncomfortable around other adults. This offender is generally thought to be fixated in terms of his psychosocial development at the age of his intended victims. While he may be physically and psychologically more mature than his victims, he believes that the age range of his intended victim holds some allure. It may be at this age that he believes people to be the most innocent and thereby sexually attractive. On the other hand, Burg (1983) found that many pedophiles select children as sexual objects because youths are less demanding, more easily dominated, and less critical of their partners' performance than are adults.

The fixated child offender is not interested in physically harming the child. He, misguidedly, loves children and does not desire to do anything that might harm them. He courts a child, buys the child gifts as a seduction ploy, and slowly becomes intimate with the child.

Oral-genital sex is the norm, and actual intercourse develops only after a significant period of time has passed (Holmes & Holmes, 2001).

❖ PROFILING CHILD MOLESTER TYPES

In examining the various types of child molesters, it is important to remember that each molester is different: victimization ritual, method of selection, and the abduction process (Knight, Carter, & Prentky, 1989; Okami & Goldberg, 1992). To aid in some understanding of the various types of child molesters, we have decided to examine only a few of the child molesters and ones that may be more likely to abuse children and also come into contact with the criminal justice system. We have chosen the following types of abusers: the immature offender, the regressed offender, the sadistic offender, and the fixated offender.

Table 9.2 contains selected elements or traits that are important in the profiling process. These traits are considered to be important when in the process of investigating crimes against children, and the alert investigator must consider some of these items while examining such a case as a child abduction, a molestation of a child, or even the murder of a child.

From the information contained in the Table 9.2, it is readily apparent that there are differences in the various traits that surround the various types of child molesters and pedophiles. Consider the first listed trait, "harms the child." By this we mean is the child

Table 9.2   Typology of Child Molesters

Element	Immature Offender	Regressed Offender	Sadistic Offender	Fixated Offender
Physically harms the child	No	No	Yes	No
Aggressive personality	No	No	Yes	No
Antisocial personality	No	No	Yes	No
Child sexual preference	No	Yes	Yes	Yes
Knows the child	Yes	No	No	Yes
Intercourse occurs	No	Yes	Yes	Yes

abuser physically harmful to the child? We are not certain of the extent of mental and psychological damage that is done to a child by an adult who uses a child for gratuitous pleasure. Children who are victimized by adults often will repeat this abuse on children when they reach their adult years (Holmes, 1983). This is a dismal conclusion, if true, but must be considered important in the investigatory process. Only the sadistic offender is purposely intent on inflicting physical harm to the child. This harm eventually will result in the death of the child. Again, witness the case of Westley Dodd; he was intent on performing exploratory surgery after he killed his abducted, helpless victims.

The Sadistic Offender

Again, the sadistic offender has an aggressive and antisocial personality. He is best considered to be a sociopath. Because of the sociopathy and aggressive personality, he may also possess a criminal record. His personality and temperament may necessitate his involvement with the criminal justice system with crimes such as rape, assault, and a variety of other types of violent crimes.

Unlike the immature or naive offender, the sadistic offender will have a sex preference: usually young boys. The molester and fatal abuser often will mutilate the young victim even to the extent of decapitation and cutting off the penis that is then inserted either into the victim's mouth or anus. This is not to say this offender will not victimize young girls, which is also sometimes the case.

Unlike the other types of child molesters, the sadistic offender is more likely to be geographically transient. He is more likely to hold sporadic employment positions, less likely to form long-lasting personal relationships, and is more likely to move on very quickly after a fatal victimization.

The Fixated Offender

The fixated offender has young boys as his preferred sexual target. Fixated offenders will surround themselves with toys, videogames, sporting equipment, and other types of paraphernalia that is attractive to children. He seems himself as being one of them and often has the same interests as these children do. He will often lurk in chat rooms where children congregate and be able to speak the language spoken by kids who match his ideal victim type. He may self-identify as heterosexual but commit pedophiliac acts with children of his own sex. This he often feels is not an act of homosexuality but rather an expression of love or tutelage for his prey. He is neither aggressive in his hunt or search for children nor in his acts of intimacy. Most of the time, he, like other pedophiles, will only proceed sexually with the child once he garners their consent (which often is not legally possible).

Immature and Regressed Offenders

Immature and regressed offenders are more apt to be geographically stable. There are reasons for this, which are readily apparent. The immature offender is often suffering from various stages of dementia or has a disability that often forces him to live close to family, friends, or his care provider. Similarly, the regressed offender, while not suffering from a form of disability, typically has a family or other job responsibilities within the community in which he lives and is not ready to pick up and move to another jurisdiction. Typically the offending behavior of the regressed offender is a way that the individual has chosen to medicate for the difficult time he is going through at the present time.

❖ COMMON THREADS AMONG CHILD MOLESTER TYPES

As mentioned previously, there simply is no way to provide readers or those in the field of law enforcement a definitive list of characteristics that differentiate between the different types of pedophiles and child molesters. Many of the characteristics discussed cross types and subtypes of offenders. Most all child offenders today will utilize some form of technology, if not to prey on their victims than to stay in constant communication with those who make them feel young and alive. Since most children are both comfortable and adept in the use of technology, so are their predators. As the age of technology advances, two types of child abusers will utilize the computer in their search for child victims most often. These are the sadistic and the fixated types. There are electronic chat rooms; computer bulletin boards advertising sexual proposals; closed (or password protected) forums in which pedophiles exchange fantasies, stories, pictures; and Web sites that cater to nudist themes that many pedophiles use to mask their true interest. Law enforcement officers and other child-protection groups must be familiar with these forums in any attempt to seek out these offenders and bring them to justice.

The possession of child pornography is also a common element across child molester and pedophile types. Remember the role that fantasy plays in their sexual predation. Many offenders will keep pictures of their victims or images of other children that match their ideal victim type close by at all times. Usually the child molester will have these images stored in multiple locations so they can view them at a minute's notice. You will find them in desk drawers, laptop and desktop computers, and wallets as well as in the glove compartment of the pedophile's car. Knowing this, the alert investigator could include this in the search warrant.

Another common element among the child molester/pedophile is the belief that they themselves were once molested as children and that this prior victimization led them to victimize others as a way to cope with their prior victimization (Freeman-Longro, 1986; Groth, 1979; Romano & De Luca, 1997). Research into other areas of criminal victimization obviously shows the linkages. For instance, it is commonly established that children (especially boys) who witness one parent physically abusing their other parent are more likely to mimic that behavior as adults (Strauss, Gelles, & Smith, 1990; Wolfe, Wekerle, Reitzel, & Gough, 1995). And again, male survivors of incest are also more likely to commit incestuous behavior as they mature than are non-incest survivors (Williams & Finkelhor, 1992).

Armed with this knowledge, it is obvious that the background in which the perpetrator grew up is important in the development of this offender. While it would be difficult to work the societal or family demographics into a profile because of an individual's free will, it is an important point to keep in mind when talking to or interrogating potential suspects in an attempt to build rapport.

❖ CONCLUSION

This victimization of children is real and significant. The Texas Office of the Attorney General (2001) reported that 1 young person in 5 has been solicited sexually over the Internet, and 1 in 17 has experienced threats or harassment (Ellison, 2001; Williams, 2001). After researching the trolling habits of adult sexual offenders who prey on children for more than 50 years, we now find that the methods these offenders are using are more dangerous and stealthy than ever before. More effort needs to be directed toward the education of our nation's youth and ultimately their caregivers concerning the dangerousness of these offenders and the methods they use to entice children to meet with them. While most individuals that engage in pedophilia may not intentionally mean to harm children, it is clear that they truly don't understand the psychological damage that can result even from one victimization or near-victimization experience. The victimization of a child or an adult must not be tolerated. The technology of the Internet provides a template for victimizations as well as offering an invaluable source for legitimate gathering of needed knowledge. Free speech must be protected; however, we must be aware of when victimizations occur and what the responsibility of each community is.

❖ REFERENCES

American Psychiatric Association. (2000). *Diagnostic and statistical manual of mental disorders: DSM-IV-TR* (4th ed.). Washington, DC: Author.

Burg, B. (1983). *Sodomy and the perception of evil.* New York: New York University Press.

Burgess, A., Groth, A., & Holmstrom, L. (1978). *Sexual assault of children and adolescents.* Lexington, MA: Lexington Books.

DeFrancis, V. (1969). *Protecting the Child Victim of Sex Crimes Committed by Adults.* Denver, CO: American Humane Association.

Ellison, L. (2001). Cyberstalking: Tackling harassment on the internet. In D. Wall (Ed.), *Crime and the Internet* (pp. 141–151). London: Routledge.

Freeman-Longro, R. E. (1986). The impact of sexual victimization on males. *Child Abuse and Neglect, 10,* 411–414.

Groth, A. N. (1979). Sexual trauma in the life of rapists and child molesters. *Victimology, 4,* 10–16.

Haas, L., & Haas, J. (1990). *Understanding sexuality.* St. Louis: C.V. Mosby.

Holmes, R. (1983). *The sex offender and the criminal justice system.* Springfield, MA: Charles C. Thomas.

Holmes, S., & Holmes, R. (2001). *Sex crimes* (2nd ed.). Thousand Oaks, CA: Sage.

Johnston, S., French, A., Schouweiler, W., & Johnston, F. (1992). Naiveté and need for affection among pedophiles. *Journal of Clinical Psychology, 48,* 620–627.

Knight, R., Carter, D., & Prentky, R. (1989). A system for the classification of child molesters. *Journal of Interpersonal Violence, 4,* 3–23.

Leo, J. (1993, October 11). Pedophiles in the schools. *U.S. News and World Report, 37.*

Okami, P., & Goldberg, A. (1992). Personality correlates of pedophilia: Are they reliable indicators? *Journal of Sex Research, 29,* 297–328.

Romano, E., & De Luca, R. V. (1997). Exploring the relationship between childhood sexual abuse and adult sexual perpetration. *Journal of Family Violence, 12*(1), 85–98.

Schechter, H. (1990). *Deranged.* New York: Pocket Books.

Strauss, M., Gelles R., & Smith, C. (1990). *Physical violence in American families: Risk factors and adaptations to violence in 8,145 families.* New Brunswick, NJ: Transaction.

Texas Office of the Attorney General. (2001). Cybercrimes. *Criminal Law Update, 8*(3), 4–11.

Williams, L., & Finkelhor, D. (1992). *The characteristics of incestuous fathers.* Washington, DC: National Center on Child Abuse and Neglect.

Williams, M. (2001). Language of cybercrime and the Internet. In D. Wall (Ed.), *Crime and the Internet* (pp. 152–166). London: Routledge.

Wolfe, D., Wekerle, C., Reitzel, D., & Gough, R. (1995). Strategies to address violence in the lives of high-risk youth. In E. Peled, P. G. Jaffe, & J. L. Edleson (Eds.), *Ending the cycle of violence: community responses to children of battered women.* Thousand Oaks, CA: Sage.

10

Autoerotic Asphyxiation

❖ ❖ ❖

Evidence of Past Autoerotic Behaviors
Videos and Pictures of Self-Practice
Position of the Knot in Erotic Hanging
Facial Coverings
Anal Insertion
Accessory Symmetry

Conclusion

Perhaps no other sexual behavior is more baffling than that of auto-erotic asphyxiation. What is known is that the person who practices this form of sex play puts oneself in imminent danger of death. Typically we find cases of this kind of eroticism (that which restricts breathing) only when there has been some type of failure on the part of the practitioner resulting in harm and often death. And how many deaths arise from this type of sex play? There is no reliable number to cite here because many are ruled suicides or accidental deaths instead of a death associated with autoeroticism. In some cases cardiac arrest is a consequence of this form of activity. It is not the purpose of this chapter to relate the medical and physiological conditions surrounding the individual involved in autoerotic asphyxiation. The reader may wish to consult other publications for this information. This chapter, however, is intended more for the criminal justice practitioner investigating a suspected case of autoerotic asphyxiation.

Witness the following case.

As the husband caught his ride to work at 8:00 A.M., the wife waved good-bye from their front door. The wife of less than 1 year told the husband that she was not going to work that day and was going "to hang out with my girlfriends." The husband told the police later that he tried to call her a couple of times during the day with no success.

On the ride home, the victim's husband invited the three friends he carpooled with to come into his home and have a beer. The four entered the apartment and the husband called the wife's name, but there was no response. He told the men to help themselves to a beer and he went down the hallway to his bedroom. The wife was not there. On the way back to the kitchen, the husband looked into the bathroom. He saw his wife on her knees, leaning over into the bathtub, filled with six inches of water. She was dead.

The police investigated the case and thought it to be a homicide. The victim's feet were bound by a telephone cord tied around the ankles and bound with a knot. Her wrists were also bound with another telephone cord wrapped around 21 times but not knotted. She was wearing her nightgown and a brown, terrycloth robe, the same robe that she was last seen wearing by the husband and his three friends who picked him up for work that morning. She also had one of her husband's brown knit ties around her neck. Her face was in water, and the medical examiner later ruled that the cause of death was drowning.

Because of an officer's suspicion, this case was submitted for a psychological profile. The profile indicated that further investigation should be made into the apartment itself. What was troubling was that the victim drowned in only 6 inches of water, the necktie around her neck, and the manner in which the telephone cord was wrapped and not tied around the wrists.

The profile indicated that this may have been a case of aqua-eroticism and suggested that the investigators return to the apartment and examine the doors, the doorknobs, and the bedroom for any collateral evidence of this type of sexual paraphilia. The police did find rope burns on the top of the door in the bedroom. Rope fibers were also found on the door knobs on the inside of the closet door. The victim had practiced erotic asphyxiation before, on many occasions, and had placed a rope around her neck (the husband's heavy neck tie around her neck was used to prevent ligature marks), then the rope was placed over the door and tied to the knob on the closet side of the door.

The husband, who was not considered a suspect in the case because he had a perfect alibi, finally admitted that his wife had shared with him her practice of this form of autoeroticism. He added that he had never personally witnessed this. He also stated that he was not aware of any interest in aqua-eroticism, and it was assumed that this was the first time and she failed in her attempt at sexual gratification using water. He suspected that she had tried to expand her sexual repertoire but was hesitant to say anything to the police because her parents were fundamentalist Christians. He believed that the parents would be better suited to handle a suspicion that their daughter had been murdered rather than be a fatal casualty of a sexual act that many consider sinful.

❖ WHAT IS AUTOEROTIC SEXUAL BEHAVIOR?

The strict definition of autoerotic sexual behavior would include sex behaviors done by oneself. While masturbation is naturally included under this topic, we will not include it in our discussion, as we are focusing on autoerotic asphyxiation and like practices.

We have found there are at least four forms of autoeroticism, excluding simple masturbation: autoerotic hanging, aqua-eroticism, chemical eroticism, and a type of self-suffocation, and there is a common theme to all these sexual practices. When someone practices autoerotic asphyxiation, a deficiency of oxygen is realized in the brain, inducing cerebral anoxia. This lessening of oxygen to the brain is done by self-applied suffocation methods, usually with some form of genital self-manipulation. The restriction of blood supply to the brain with some can intensify sensations because it may produce lightheadedness, giddiness, or a sense of euphoria. There may also be a sense of excitation with the realization of the potential danger and the very real possibility of death.

We know little about the various practices of autoerotic behavior regardless of the format it takes. This sexual behavior is done in private and only becomes public when the person commits an error and accidentally dies.

Forms of Autoeroticism

Autoerotic Asphyxiation

For the purposes of this book, we will strictly adhere to this type of autoeroticism as sexual hanging. In this form, different types of bindings are used around the neck. What is important is that the material used—rope, ties, etc.—exerts equal pressure on either side of the neck, on the carotid arteries, to induce cerebral anoxia.

One can practice this form of autoeroticism in a variety of different ways: One could place a part of the rope over a pipe, a beam in a ceiling, or over a door. In one case, a woman placed a rope around her neck with the other end around a doorknob. She knelt with her back to the door, and then she simply leaned forward until she passed out. Her body was found by her parents when they came home from work. In another case, a young man was found dead in the attic of his parents' home. He tied a rope around his neck, then over a beam in the ceiling of the attic, and then around his ankles. He pulled on the rope with his feet but the beam broke. He fell through the drywall and was left hanging only a few feet from the dining room floor, his back broken.

Aqua-Eroticism

The second type of autoeroticism we'll cover is aqua-eroticism. With this form of paraphilia, the practitioner will deliberately place oneself in water to create a drowning possibility but raise one's head out of the water before losing consciousness.

In a case recently, a man placed himself in a sleeping bag alongside the bank of a river. Inside the sleeping bag he had tied his feet and wrapped his hands in duct tape. He had in one hand a pair of scissors. One end of a rope was placed around a small tree on the bank, and the other end was placed around his neck. He was able to crawl and move into the river, and soon the sleeping bag was underwater. The plan was apparently to cut the tape around his wrists before he drowned. Unfortunately the rope broke from the tree on the bank, the man was pushed into the middle of the river, and he was run over by a speedboat and died. His involvement in aqua-eroticism was verified by collateral evidence found in his home: pornography, stories, and pictures and videos.

Chemical Eroticism

There are some cases where a person practices autoeroticism using a chemical, such as Freon, to induce a sense of lightheadedness, a giddy feeling, and other sensory apparitions.

A repairman made a house call to a couple's home where the air-conditioning unit was not working properly. The lady of the house left for a few minutes to go to the grocery. When she got back, she found the repairman dead. He had placed a plastic tube in his mouth from a tankard of Freon and had lowered his pants and underwear and turned on a grinder that vibrated against his penis and scrotum. Apparently he swallowed the Freon too quickly, which then resulted in his death.

In another case of chemical eroticism, a man was dressed in panties and bra with a plastic tube connected to a helium tank running under a plastic baggie over his head. His 16-year-old daughter came home from school to find her father dead on the kitchen floor.

Suffocation

In some cases of autoeroticism, the person will deliberately attempt to suffocate to the point of almost passing out or losing consciousness. Of all the ways of practicing this form of solitary sex, this may be the safest if manual strangulation is used. But in some cases, a partner is chosen with a key word agreed upon ahead of time. This is a risky situation.

Take, for example, the following case. In a southern town, a woman was found dead in her bed. She had a towel around her neck and one hand was on her stomach. The left hand was under her back and she was on the bed, face up. The police were investigating this case as a homicide. Upon further inspection, the police decided to seek a psychological profile. In their investigation, they found some information about sadism and masochism. There was also a swinger's magazine with circles around some names. The profile suggested that this may have been a murder, but the appearance of the towel around the neck and the position of the left hand was thought to be indicative of some form of autoeroticism. The direction of the investigation changed from a murder investigation to one of accidental death. It was learned that the victim had found a date with a man and suggested that he slap her, which he did several times. She then told him a fantasy she had about being strangled. He agreed to strangle her, and they arranged a release word. He started to strangle her but never heard the release word and she died. The man was charged with a lesser charge of murder and was granted probation.

❖ TRAITS AND CHARACTERISTICS OF AUTOEROTICISM PRACTITIONERS

From information contained in various police reports and academic literature from various sources, certain traits and characteristics can be ascertained. How accurate these items are of the total universe of those involved in erotic asphyxiation is unknown. This information is obtained from people who have come to the attention of the criminal justice system usually because of an accidental death. Nonetheless, it is a starting point, and until further information can be obtained by more objective and scientific studies, it is the information we have.

In the course of researching this topic, we have gained some information from the Eulenspiegel Society. This society is located in New York and was founded in 1971. One of its main goals is to support sexual liberation in all formats between and among consenting adults. They sponsor classes for autoerotics as well as other classes that deal with S&M, B&D, group sex, and other topics.

Gender

In autoeroticism, males are the overwhelming practitioners. The exact ratio is unknown, but generally it is accepted that males are the predominant practitioners. Females sometimes practice this form of paraphilia, but the setting and circumstances are different.

Age

From the information available it appears that autoeroticism is predominately a young person's practice. We must be very careful in this assumption because other than scarce stories of self-reports, the cases seen are those in which injury or death is realized. Thus, what may be happening is that as one ages and becomes more experienced in this sexual paraphilia, the chance of error diminishes. The attention to details and what accounts for safety as well as sexual gratification becomes more of a ritualized event and ensures that the practitioner will be safe from a fatal mishap. Thus early in a person's career in autoeroticism, mistakes are likely to be made, resulting in tragic consequences.

Race

In the overwhelming number of cases involving autoeroticism, we have found the practitioners to be of the White race. This not to say that other races do not practice autoeroticism, but in the fatal cases with which we are most familiar, the victims are almost exclusively White. Why this seems to be the case is unknown. It may be that the non-Whites are reported practicing this sexual behavior in the same ratio as the population. Statistics, however, are missing in this analysis.

Social Habits

In interviewing family and friends of those who are fatal victims of autoeroticism, the reports suggest these persons are shy, introverted, and often have few friends and personal associates and have few interests and hobbies. If particularly young and in high school, teachers and counselors report that they were loners despite the teachers' efforts to get the person involved in school activities, including clubs and athletics. The person may also be shy and timid around people of the other sex, lacking social skills to interact adequately.

Ambition

Some involved in this form of sexual paraphilia are described as overachievers. This would be evident in the school situation as well as the workplace setting in an older practitioner. This person will devote attention to detail to almost everything. This is one reason the person will be successful in the school situation as well as in the workplace. This may also be evident in the person's health and appearance. We have found that many of those we have examined were in good physical condition, were neat and clean in personal appearance, and had well-kept homes or other living domiciles.

Economic Status

Many of the practitioners found as a result of a fatal sex act were from middle-class backgrounds. The parents often are professionals in the community, and if the practitioner is a student they are often involved in academic programs. If already in the workplace, they are usually involved in occupations that are professional in nature.

The person may also appear to be an intellectual. Regardless of age, the individual may appear to be conversant on many topics. The list of topics, however, seldom includes the sexual practices of autoeroticism. This is a personal topic, not to be discussed in public or even with most close personal friends.

Religious Orientation

Perhaps ironically, the person is often a churchgoer and is judged to be a religious person by those who attend the same religious services. This dissonance could be a contributing factor to another trait: In many cases, the person has suicidal tendencies. In notes left after a related suicide, police will often find comments about the feelings of guilt, shame, and remorse regarding the autoerotic acts. Not everyone who commits suicide in these situations leaves this form of note, but the ones that have been found have contained such as statements as, "I'm sorry I am this way," or "Please don't tell my parents. Let them think I was just tired of living" (author's files).

❖ AUTOEROTIC SCENE INDICATORS

There are gender differences in the examination of scenes of where an autoerotic fatality has occurred. Women are different from men in their habits of autoeroticism. First, women will often practice the acts in their bedrooms or bathrooms. Seldom will women become involved in autoeroticism outside or in open areas. They will not typically move furniture or use sexual devices or toys, as do many male practitioners.

The following is a general list of items for the investigator to examine when one enters a scene where a suspected autoerotic death has occurred.

Cross-Dressing

Cross-dressing is very prevalent with males involved in autoeroticism. The cross-dressing is said by many just to enhance the experience. This simply mirrors transvestism in the American society. Women do not cross-dress for the same reason as men. For women, the cross-dressing experience is usually a matter of fashion or comfort. However, when men cross-dress, it is usually a sexual matter, at least initially (Holmes & Holmes, 2001). Men who cross-dress will either be in "high drag" (dressed completely in women's clothing) or "low drag" (dressed in a few articles of clothing such as panties and a bra).

Mirrors

In many cases involving erotic hanging, for example, the investigator will find a mirror somewhere within the visual field of the deceased. This may be a full-length mirror, a mirror on the wall, or even a small, hand-held mirror.

What the investigator should do is to assume the position of the deceased. What will likely be seen is a reflection of the individual from the neck down. Why? From this view, the person can imagine it to be anyone he or she wishes it to be. This feeds into the fantasy system of the person. This is especially true when the deceased is involved in cross-dressing.

Pornography

Pornography is present in many cases of autoeroticism, and it will be in the sightline of the person involved. The character of the pornography will reflect the fantasy of the erotic practitioner himself. Few cases in which women are the practitioners involve pornography.

This "pornography" may be an advertisement for women's, or even children's, underwear, something that feeds into the fantasy of the practitioner. In one case of an individual involved in erotic asphyxiation, an advertisement from the newspaper for women's nightgowns and leisure wear was in view. This was for him a form of erotic arousal and one that he used to get himself into a sexual stage of sexual excitation.

Genital Binding

Bindings around the genitals of the male practitioner may be part of the scene. This binding may come in many different formats: Some asphyxiates use rope, some prefer nylon cord, and others use clothing in strips as forms of binding.

Body Marks and Bruising

A close examination of the body of the person involved in this form of sexual practice will oftentimes show at least two forms of marks on the body.

The first mark could be around the neck: burn marks. The burn marks are sometimes concealed by the practitioner by high collars, scarves, or other items of clothing placed around the neck. This is true for both males and females, and it may be that some styles of clothing are better suited for this concealment than others.

The other marks that may become evident are around the wrists. The locations of the bruises become extremely important. For example, in erotic practitioners who have some preference for being tied around the wrists, the bruising is more apt to occur on the anterior side of the wrists, below the palm. When a person may be tied by the wrists against his or her will, the bruising is more likely to occur on the outer wrists below the back of the hand. This indicates a struggle: the person trying forcefully to separate the wrists from each other, thus bruising the wrists below the back of the hand.

There may be other bruising, especially around the ankles.

Diaries and Writings

Diaries and writings often found in the possessions of the practitioner can serve as collateral evidence. These writings will contain descriptions of the fantasies and practices of the person involved in this form of paraphilia. Some contain dates of practice as well as the various methods utilized in the practice of autoeroticism. One person found dead kept a diary of the various manners in which he practiced sexual asphyxia. He also mentioned the times of his sex acts as well as various new things he tried, such as cross-dressing and trying Freon as well as aqua-eroticism.

Bondage

Bondage is a common practice, especially with males. As anticipated, this bondage may take place in traditional places such as the arms and legs. But this bondage may occur in other places as well. For example, in a northern city, a 16-year-old male was found in the attic of his home. His parents called him for dinner, and then went to look for him. He was dead in the attic with a rope around his neck, over a rafter in the ceiling, and then the other end of the rope wrapped around his ankles. There was additional binding around waist. This binding was tubing from the vacuum machine. There was also duct tape around his waist.

Evidence of Past Autoerotic Behaviors

Sex is very ritualistic. What works well and provides sexual gratification and satisfaction will likely be repeated if possible. For example, in a case in the Midwest, a young husband, age 21, accidentally killed himself, hanging from a pole mounted across a doorway from the apartment's kitchen to the living room. The wife and young child had left only an hour earlier to do some grocery shopping. The wife found him dead when they returned from the grocery and called the police. The police found fibers on the bar from previous actions as well as burns on the bar itself. In another case, a 50-year-old man was found in his kitchen by his married daughter who had not heard from him in a week. She opened the door and found him lying on the kitchen floor with a nylon rope around his neck, tied over the door, and then to a door handle. Fibers, rope burns, and other signs of former practice were discovered.

Videos and Pictures of Self-Practice

In a similar practice of keeping diaries and writings as mentioned above, some practitioners will videotape themselves in their sex play.

For example, in Florida a man was discovered by his wife and father-in-law as they opened the garage door. The man had set up a videocamera on a tripod and took a video of himself hanging. It shows him placing the noose around his neck, stepping off a stool, and hanging. In the video, as he tries to step back upon the stool, it is accidentally kicked aside and he is unable to stop his death. The police found several other videos of his sex acts in the crawlspace of his home.

In another case, a man was found dead in his apartment, and the police found three photo albums containing pictures of him in various scenarios of autoeroticism. There were over 500 pictures of him, many in drag. The purpose: to relive the experiences of his sexual paraphilia.

Position of the Knot in Erotic Hanging

In a case of suspected erotic hanging, the investigator should look at the position of the knot. Usually in a true case of erotic hanging, the knot will be in the back of the neck. The purpose of this is to ensure that equal pressure is placed on either side of the neck for sexual pleasure and gratification. This is one of the first items at the scene the investigator should inspect.

If the knot is on the side of the neck, it should be determined if the deceased is right-handed or left-handed. If the person was right-handed and the knot is on the right side of the neck, the death may be the result of a suicide. If the knot is on the left side, this may be an indication of foul play of some type. Of course, if the person is left-handed, the information would be the reversed.

Of course there may be a deliberate placement of the knot on the side of the neck, below the ear, and arranged so the running end goes behind the neck and then around the front of the neck: There will be some air flow through so the person can, with this arrangement and with some effort, open an air path that can lead to a much longer experience. This, however, comes with some practice and experimentation. If a victim is found like this, the investigator will have to rely on other scene evidence to rule a suicide or accidental death. Because of the rapid loss of consciousness, brain damage can occur within 4 minutes, and death within 10–15 minutes. But the heart may stop before this.

Facial Coverings

In many cases of autoeroticism, the face is covered in a variety of fashions. In a previously cited case, the young man who died while his wife and child went to the grocery, the wife's panty hose were placed over his face. In the case where Freon was ingested, the man placed a plastic baggie over his face. This was also true in the case of the man who was found in the river in the sleeping bag.

The purpose of the placement of something over the face is to complement the experience of losing consciousness and for some becomes a part of the ritual of the autoerotic experience.

Anal Insertion

The practitioner inserting objects into the anal opening is a common practice among males. A variety of objects are used, from dildos that are purchased at adult stores, to wine bottles, to the spouts of bleach bottles. One man was freebasing cocaine and placed his head and shoulders in a closet but kept his buttocks and feet outside. He had placed a condom on the handle of a vacuum machine, turned the vacuum on, and inserted the handle into his anus. He died from complications associated with the drugs that prevented him from freeing himself from the hanging apparatus. When found by a relative, the handle was still inserted. Most objects inserted are not as elaborate as the one just mentioned, usually being common items such as bottles, tools, and other household items.

Accessory Symmetry

Perhaps one of the most interesting aspects of physical evidence is that of accessory symmetry: When a person is involved in this form of sexual activity, the accessories used are often part of the fantasy and ritual, and these accessories tend to appear on both sides of the body. For example, if duct tape is used to wrap around the right calf, the left calf of the leg is also decorated. If a belt is placed around the upper right thigh, the upper left leg will also be decorated in the same manner. Why this is done in this manner is unknown, but it is something that appears time and again in the investigation of cases of death by autoeroticism.

❖ CONCLUSION

Perhaps no other sexual behavior is more complex, considered more bizarre, and is so unexplained than autoeroticism. The very manner in which one learns about this paraphilia and the manner in which sex is realized in this activity are also unknown. Even if one is familiar with the practice, the manner in which the act is carried out to the point of sexual gratification is complex. So how does one learn the manner in which to act to achieve gratification? Certainly few of the person's friends and acquaintances practice it, and even the adult bookstores carry little information. What we have found, however, is that on the Internet there are new sites that give instructions as well as precautions if one is wishing to become involved in this potentially dangerous sex behavior. The Eulenspiegel Society offers classes on a variety of different sex practices, including autoeroticism. The classes are offered at the headquarters in New York City, but the society does offer information over the Internet concerning breathing exercises, "buddy sex," and other items of sexual interest to those who may visit the site.

What we have to be aware of with the information in this chapter is that it is gathered from those who have in some way "failed" in their sexual practice. They have died by accident, and we have gathered data from their deaths. Common sense tells us that there are other, perhaps more experienced, autoerotics who have been practicing autoeroticism for years with no complications. What are their traits and characteristics? We may never know, since this is a solitary sexual act and the practice of it is seldom shared with others. Nonetheless, it is important for the investigator to know of the scene indicators to properly evaluate the scene itself, to distinguish a crime from an accident.

❖ REFERENCE

Holmes, S., & Holmes, R. (2001). *Sex crimes* (2nd ed.). Thousand Oaks, CA: Sage.

11

Profiling Satanic and Cult-Related Murders

❖ ❖ ❖

Roots of Satanism

Satanism in the United States

The Satanic Bible
Definitions in Satanism

Types of Personal Involvement in Satanism
Type I
Type II
Type III

General Elements of Satanism
Trinity of Satanism
Human Sacrifice
Hierarchy of Hell
Devices Used in Satanic Rituals
Satanic Masses
Satanic Ceremonies

When the popularity of *Rosemary's Baby* and *The Exorcist* reached pandemic proportions more than three decades ago, the type of consciousness about the occult was stimulated to a height probably unknown since the time of the Salem witch hunts. These two movies made a case for the existence of a pure evil spirit or entity and the existence of a group of followers not too different from us. One consultant and actor in *Rosemary's Baby*, Anton LaVey, a former rock musician, later became the founder of the Church of Satan.

What accounted for this sudden rise in popularity in the occult, beyond the influence of these films, and why today do we see more evidence of Satanism in a greater number of crime scenes? There has to be more to it than the 1960s, with its emphasis on sex, drugs, and rock and roll. Perhaps there was something about the time when we, as a society, were looking around for stability and a complete distinction between right and wrong, good and evil. As crime may be a social cement that helps us with an instant sense of identification of those who are good and those who are not, it may be that the occult is a social invention that arises periodically to provide for some a sense of stability and individuality, creating a definitive sense of "us" and "them." For the youth of our time, the involvement may be a cry for attention, while for the adults it may be an attention to the myths of yesteryear—the time of werewolves, vampires, and the devil. Regardless of the reason some are involved in Satanism and others are not, it is apparent that satanic crimes and activities are once again on the increase.

With the interest at a peak, what we are seeing is a resurgence in the existence, interest, and practice of Satanic or other cult-related crimes (DeYoung, 1998). Regardless, it rests with law enforcement at the initial phase to investigate alleged crimes of occult groups if youth or adults are involved (Bernet & Chang, 1997; Crews, 1996). Despite reports by police and other authors, it appears that Satanists are not as involved in serious crimes as once suspected. Of course, there are some murders committed by dabblers, but these are relatively few. Most crimes committed are those that deal with cemetery desecrations, vandalism, writing of graffiti on public and private property, and other such nonviolent crimes. Nonetheless, we still need to be concerned with their activities, even if their crimes are not as serious as once suspected.

❖ ROOTS OF SATANISM

This interest in Satan as an alternative to Christ did not reach alarming popularity overnight. The roots of Satanism date back to the Old Testament. In addition, the practice and belief in magic, spells, and curses, as well as divination of the future, were found among all primitive people. Demon worship was widely practiced in ancient Egypt and Mesopotamia. Originally not associated with an evil spirit, it was simply a way to manipulate nature and fate.

The Jewish rabbis in the Old Testament condemned the belief in Satan because the devil was part of a non-Jewish religion, and rabbis saw demonology as an attempt to influence the destiny of man rather than accepting the will of God. Toward the time of Christ, the Jewish faith used Satan to protect the ideal of a perfect God. After all, how could a good God create evil? The credible answer was that he did not; Satan was the responsible culprit.

Early Christian theologians believed that Satan, now a "reality," had no control over the followers of Christ, only pagans and apostates. The Gnostics saw the world as being evil and life on earth as a "prison sentence" imposed on them by Yahweh of the Old Testament. Since the world was evil, the one who created it must also be evil. Ergo, Yahweh was evil. The good God must live far away in some distant heaven, and they were in bondage to the evil god, now called the devil, Satan, Lucifer, Papablas, or any other of the multitude of demonic names.

❖ SATANISM IN THE UNITED STATES

The greatest influence on those who find Satanism so attractive must be Aleister Crowley. Raised in a traditional Christian family, Crowley became attracted to the occult while still quite young. Crowley offended many of his own followers who made mud casts of his form and killed him in effigy. What made him so popular and effective were apparently the social conditions of the time, as well as his apparent charismatic authority.

In 1966, Anton LaVey founded the Church of Satan on the satanic feast day of Walpurgisnacht, April 30. Gaining great popularity from LaVey's performing marriages and burial rites, the Church of Satan has grown to a membership that some estimate at 20,000.

As a youthful runaway, LaVey worked in a circus as a carney barker, a cage boy for Clyde Beatty, a hypnotist, and a bump-and-grind organ player for a stripper named Marilyn Monroe. He finally moved to San Francisco, where he was photographer for the San Francisco Police Department. Tiring of the alleged inconsistencies of traditional Christianity, LaVey founded a new religion predicated partly on the premise that "the strong shall inherit the earth."

❖ THE SATANIC BIBLE

The writings of LaVey provide the faithful with a written dogma and liturgy of the Church of Satan. *The Satanic Bible*, available in paperback, has sold thousands of copies. It illustrates rituals, rites, holy days, and lists the nine "statements" of the devil, as seen in Table 11.1.

Table 11.1   LaVey's Nine Statements of the Devil

1. Satan represents indulgence, instead of abstinence!
2. Satan represents vital existence, instead of spiritual pipe dreams!
3. Satan represents undefiled wisdom instead of hypocritical self-deceit!
4. Satan represents kindness to those who deserve it, instead of love wasted on ingrates!
5. Satan represents vengeance, instead of turning the other cheek!
6. Satan represents responsibility, instead of concern for the psychic vampires!
7. Satan represents man as just another animal, sometimes better, more often worse, than those who walk on all fours, who because of his divine and intellectual development has become the most vicious of all!
8. Satan represents all of the so-called sins, as they lead to physical, mental or emotional gratification!
9. Satan has been the best friend the church has ever had, as he has kept it in business all these years!

The basic teachings of LaVey concern a worship of the trinity of the devil: Lucifer, Satan, and the devil. The Church of Satan is actually a human potential movement. Each member is encouraged to actualize his or her own potential. The type of actualization can be reached through magic, spells, rituals, and incantations to the demonic trinity.

The Satanic Bible includes an "Invocation Employed Towards the Conjuration of Lust," "Invocation Employed Towards the Conjuration of Destruction," "Invocation Employed Towards the Conjuration of Compassion," a list of holy days, chapters on the black mass and rituals, as well as a chapter entitled "On the Choice of a Human Sacrifice."

LaVey passed away in 1997 and is succeeded in power and office by his daughter.

Definitions in Satanism

To understand satanic worship and rituals, it is necessary to understand the terms used. The words in Table 11.2 are fairly commonly used in satanic worship and rituals.

Table 11.2   Words, Rituals, and Rites of Satanists

Antichrist:	Enemy of Christ
Archfiend:	A chief or foremost fiend (Satan)
Black Magic:	Basically the same as sorcery
Black Mass:	A ritual of the Church of Satan, which is a mockery of the Roman Catholic Mass
Circle:	A declaration of sacred ground
Cove:	An assembly of thirteen witches
Equinox:	First day of autumn or spring
ESBAT:	Coven meeting
Fire:	Symbolizes Satan
Goat:	Satan appears in the form of a goat
Hectate:	Goddess of the Lower Region and patroness of witchcraft
Incubus:	A male demon that copulates with human females
Lilith:	Adam's first wife and later the wife of Lucifer
Lucifer:	The archangel cast from heaven for leading a revolt of angels. He is the "father" of the trinity of the devil.
Mass:	A ceremony
Necromancy:	The art of controlling the spirits of the dead
Pentacle:	Five-pointed star
Pentagram:	A five-pointed star that is used as a barrier against evil. The pentagram with one point upward repels evil, but a reversed pentagram, with two points upward, is a symbol of the devil and attracts sinister forces. In this case, the two points represent the horns of the goat, which is the symbol of the devil.
Sabbath:	Holy days and celebrations, of which there are eight in a year; assemblies of witches in honor of the Archfiend
Satan:	A member, the "son," of the trinity of the devil
Solstice:	First day of summer or winter
Sorcerer:	Male witch
Sorcery:	The use of supernatural power over others through the assistance of evil spirits
Succubus:	A female demon that copulates with human males
Talisman:	An object believed to hold magical powers
Voodoo:	A form of primitive sorcery that was organized in Africa and is generally associated with fetishes (dolls, etc.)

(Continued)

Table 11.2 (Continued)

Walpurgisnacht:	The eve of May Day believed in medieval Europe to be the occasion of a witch's sabbath
Witch:	Female witch
Witchcraft:	The process of using the forces of the unseen world through potions, incantations, or ceremonies for the purpose of controlling or changing conditions or situations

Dates of significance:	
February 2:	Candlemas
March 20:	Spring equinox
April 30:	Walpurgisnacht
June 21:	Summer solstice
October 31:	Halloween
November 1:	Festival of Hectate
December 21:	Winter solstice

Numbers of significance:	
1:	Equates with primal chaos
3:	Triple repetitions, effective in incantations
5:	Symbolizes justice
7:	Possesses mystic implications
13:	Number of members in a coven
4×4:	The devil's own number
$7 + 9$:	Multiples of these possess thaumaturgical potency

❖ TYPES OF PERSONAL INVOLVEMENT IN SATANISM

As in any religious movement, some members are more involved and indoctrinated into the liturgy and rituals than others. In personal interviews with two high priests and several coven members of satanic cults, three types of personal affiliation were revealed. Table 11.3 graphically delineates these types of involvement and participation.

Table 11.3 Organizational Elements and Types of Personal Involvement With Satanic and Devil Worship

Type I	
Large membership	Fiscal organization maintenance
Stable membership	Long-term membership
Formalized rituals	Lateral sect transfer
Ecclesiastical hierarchy	Human and animal sacrifice
Recognized authority membership	Converted and familial
Official holy days	
Type II	
Limited membership	Transient membership
Informal rituals and liturgy	No ecclesiastical hierarchy
Personal authority	No holy days
Total fiscal commitment	Moderate-term membership
No lateral religious transfer	Human and animal sacrifice
Converted membership	
Type III	
Individual and solitary membership	No rituals
No ecclesiastical authority	No external authority
No holy days	No fiscal maintenance
No lateral religious transfer	Human and animal sacrifice
Self-styled membership	

Type I

The first type resembles religious affiliation with any church. Members are similar to other, more traditional church members, with an affinity for worship, familiarity with church ritual and liturgy, and recognition of church hierarchy and bureaucratic lines of authority. Regular attendance of church-related functions, observance of feast days, and organizational maintenance through contributions by members are all characteristics of this type of membership. There are many instances where children are born into this religious affiliation. There may be movement of membership from one satanic "denomination" to another. Unlike the more traditional religions, there is no evidence of a "baptism." *The Satanic Bible* does state that for a person to be baptized, the liquid used is salt water, but in reality, it appears that if one wishes to become a member in the Church of Satan, for example, one needs only to complete application and mail in the required fee (see Figure 11.1 on p. 211).

We must stress that there is no firm evidence that organized churches are responsible for crimes such as homicide, forced suicides, child abuse, or other types of serious crimes. They may be responsible for some simulated animal sacrifices, and if one would examine *The Satanic Bible,* there are sections that demand the true believer not break the law in certain areas, including the human sacrifice of adults and children. However, there may be small, splinter groups that are led by those who demand obedience to a set of rules that may be contrary to the Church of Satan, the Temple of Set, or other churches of this ilk.

Type II

The second type of personal affiliation is membership in a cult, satanic or not. A cult is composed of persons who are bound together by the acceptance of a leader, a less sophisticated system of beliefs, and a less formal ritual. The charismatic quality of the leader is essential since the leader will obviously lend direction to the cult's activity. The membership in the cult is modally short termed and will depend largely on the persona of the leader.

There are some excellent examples of cults, which have existed in America in the last few decades. The Manson Family is probably the most infamous example of a cult, in this case based in no small part on the charismatic authority of Manson himself. Terry (1999) put forth a theory that David Berkowitz was involved in the same satanic cult as Manson, even though they belonged to the cult at different times. There is no firm evidence to support this claim by Terry. And in fact, in talking with a serial killer in prison in California who knows Manson, he said the cult leader denied any involvement with the Process Church in New York at the time of the Son of Sam killings or any other time.

Another cult that has recently come to the attention of the American public is the Heaven's Gate cult headed by Marshall Applewhite and Bonnie Nettles. They convinced their small group of followers that they were living in a foreign body, a pod, that was awaiting space transportation to another planet, their home. Each member of the cult (38 others) committed suicide with the belief that they were to be transported to their true home. This was not a criminal cult, a cult such as the Manson Family. Another cult was headed by David Koresch, whose members were killed in a fatal confrontation with American law enforcement agents in Texas. Koresch was apparently a strong personality who convinced many people to leave their homes, families, jobs, and other social and personal ties to follow him. In another case, in a southwestern state, police are finding bodies wrapped in aluminum foil in the desert. The intelligence the police have gathered suggests that all the people are members of a cult that share similar beliefs as the Heaven's Gate group. They differ in one respect at least. They believe that when they die of natural causes, their bodies are placed in a pod of foil and after a while the corpse is destroyed by the sun and the weather, and the group believes that the essence has been taken by the space beings and transported back to their home planet. From all indications, these groups were not criminal or satanic groups, although other cults may be.

Henry Lucas admitted to membership in a devil cult, along with Ottis Toole, his alleged accomplice to multiple murders in various states. Both convicted serial killers, Lucas said he was also involved in the kidnapping of small children and paid several thousands of dollars to deliver the children for human sacrifice or prostitution; others were sold to wealthy Mexicans (author's files). This story was never verified. And Lucas died in prison without admitting further details. Lucas at one time admitted to more than 300 murders across the United States. He went with police officers and told them stories that were sufficient for them to close scores of unsolved murders. It may be that Henry suffered from some type of mental or emotional disorder that compelled him to confess to crimes he did not commit so he would have some time in the social spotlight.

Type III

The third tier of participation is on a personal, self-styled type. The organization may take a content format of Satanism, Gothic lifestyle, or other type of cult membership. This involvement may be either on an individual dimension or in a small group. Ritualism is quite limited, if not nonexistent.

The younger person is more inclined to participate in this measure of Satanism. The member has little knowledge of the liturgy of Satanism and may be quite heavily involved in animal sacrifice, especially small dogs and cats.

There are few members of any one particular self-styled aggregate. With no liturgy or religious hierarchy, the participant sets himself up as the authority and proceeds to "worship the devil" as he deems appropriate. There is no need for fiscal organizational maintenance; there is no tithing or collections. There are no buildings, schools, churches, or a religious bureaucracy to financially subsidize. This "Satanist" is a loner with little knowledge of the Satanic oath, Satanic prayers, hierarchy of hell, or the personalities of the trinity of the devil.

Richard Ramirez, the Night Stalker, was a self-styled Satanist. On his left palm he displayed a tattoo of a pentagram, and as he walked out of the court at his arraignment, he shouted, "Hail Satan." One Satanist related during an interview that he was personally offended that people would put Ramirez into the same category as a Church of Satan member (author's files).

It is easily evident that not all people who practice Satanism truly believe the same and practice the same liturgy. It is also true that some believers are more immersed in Satanism than others without an awareness of the nuances of membership and doctrine. These occult members, sometimes referred to as "dabblers," create their own form of the occult. They may set up a small and simple set of dogma, ceremonies, and rituals. They may also sacrifice small animals, such as dogs and cats.

Ricky Kasso was a high school student who declared to anyone who would listen that he was a self-styled Satanist. He practiced the drinking of blood and other types of rituals and ceremonies of a Satanic dogma. Eventually, he stabbed one young student to death, and for several days he brought other high school students to the site where he dumped the young boy's body. Finally, one student informed on him and Ricky was arrested. The night he was arrested and placed in jail, he hanged himself with his T-shirt. He committed the ultimate sacrifice for his satanic belief. Thankfully, there are few like this young person.

❖ GENERAL ELEMENTS OF SATANISM

Within Satanism, there are many belief elements that are prevalent. First, most Satanists acknowledge the existence of God. After all, they profess, there could be no Satan without God. Just as every person has a good side and a bad side, there are interesting parallels when one examines the belief system of the satanic church.

Figure 11.1   Application for the Church of Satan

Church of Satan
Central Administrative Offi ce
P.O. Box 499, Radio City Station, New York, NY 10101-0499
www.churchofsatan.com

If this form was not provided by the Church of Satan or downloaded from www.churchofsatan.com, it may be invalid.

APPLICATION FOR ACTIVE MEMBERSHIP

Provide accurate answers to all questions to the best of your ability. All data is held in strict confidence. False answers are grounds for immediate termination of membership.

PART I

Complete Legal Name: _____

Mailing Address: _____

Telephone: _____

Email: _____ (required if you wish to be included on the E-Bulletin list)

Sex: _____ Date of Birth: _____

Place of Birth: _____

Height: _____ Weight: _____ Color of Eyes: _____ Color of Hair: _____

Marital Status: _____

Name, Birthdate, and Birthplace of Spouse (if married): _____

Number of Children/Ages: _____

Previous Religious Affiliations and Offices: _____

_____

Nationality: _____ Ethnic Background: _____ Current Citizenship: _____

Educational Background and Degrees: _____

Present Occupation: _____

Special Interests, Talents, Abilities: _____

_____

Hobbies or Collections:

_____

I am interested in participating in Special Interest Groups (Internet access required): _____ Yes _____ No

I am interested in participating in contact with local Active Members: _____ Yes _____ No

I am interested in serving as a contact point or media representative in my area: _____ Yes _____ No

PLEASE ENCLOSE A RECENT PHOTOGRAPH WITH THIS MEMBERSHIP APPLICATION

(Continued)

Figure 11.1 (Continued)

PART II Provide typed answers to all of the following questions on additional sheets of paper.

1.   What are your impressions of *The Satanic Bible?*

2.   What do you expect to accomplish through membership in the Church of Satan?

3.   If you were granted three wishes, what would they be?

4.   What is your attitude toward animals? If you have any pets describe them. What is your ideal?

5.   Are you satisfied with your sex life? Describe your ideal of a physically attractive sex partner.

6.   What is your life's goal, and what steps have you taken to attain it?

7.   Do you find any of our tenets objectionable? If so, which and why?

8.   How many years would you like to live?

9.   What are your musical tastes? Provide examples.

10. Cite four motion pictures you consider your favorites, and why.

11. What are your food preferences?

12. Cite four books you consider favorites, and why.

13. If you own an automobile, describe it. What is your ideal automobile?

14. As a child, what were your favorite pastimes? What was your disposition?

15. Of which country other than the one in which you now reside would you prefer being a resident?

16. In what type of dwelling do you live? Describe your ideal home.

17. Describe your political philosophy.

18. What is your personal definition of magic?

19. Do you feel oppressed or persecuted in any way? If so, explain.

20. Are you self-sufficient or are you most productive in a group?

21. Do you make friends easily if you so choose?

22. What is more important to you, self-satisfaction or approval from others?

23. Would you rather influence or be influenced?

24. Do you feel you have leadership abilities?

25. Do you consider yourself a good judge of character?

26. In what organizations do you hold membership?

27. Have you possessed or used illegal drugs or been convicted of a crime? If so, explain in full.

28. Describe a significant experience in your life bordering on what you would consider the paranormal or demonic, if any.

29. What forms of entertainment do you prefer?

30. Tell one of your favorite jokes.

31. Have you served in the armed forces? If so, provide pertinent data.

32. How long did it take you to join the Church of Satan?

33. Are you a smoker? If so, to what extent.

34. Have you accomplished anything important or significant? If so, what?

35. Which parent do you admire most and why?

36. Do you drink alcoholic beverages? If so, to what extent? State preferences.

37. Do you have any tangible services or resources which you would care to contribute?

38. Are you free to travel? To what extent?

39. Define Satan.

40. Provide your signature attesting to the above, and enclose photograph.

FOR OFFICE USE ONLY

Initial Application Processing Date _____

Photograph Enclosed _____

Trinity of Satanism

Consider, initially, the trinity of Satan. As Christians firmly believe in God the Father, God the Son, and God the Holy Spirit, the Satanists believe in Lucifer, Satan, and the devil. They are three different parts of one being.

Lucifer

Lucifer holds the position of the primary godhead and the ruler of hell. He is the god of power and can give power to his followers or take the power from them. Lucifer has more power than Satan, who has more power than the devil. Lucifer, functioning in the same role as God the Father, has never been personally seen. He can, it is believed, take any form, animal or human. He is the Leader of Hell, the Worker of Evil, and the Ruler of Evil. Lucifer, once the shining angel of God, was cast out of heaven with his wife, Lilith. They later had one son, Mendes. Lucifer demands human and animal sacrifices.

Satan

The second personality of the trinity of the devil belongs to Satan. His parallel in the Christian Trinity is God the Son. Satan is the son of Lucifer, not a son in the same sense as Mendes but in the same sense as Jesus is the Son of God the Father. Satan is the leader of the "wasteland," the spiritual realm that surrounds the earth. He is called upon by devoted Satanists for special favors.

The Devil

The main purpose for the devil is to serve as a liaison between the people and Satan. As may be a characteristic of any bureaucracy, there are lines of communication. This is evidently true also in the godhead of the devil. Satan communicates with Lucifer, and the devil communicates with Satan. The particular role of the devil is to tempt people to do the work of Lucifer and Satan. He pulls people into hell.

Human Sacrifice

Human sacrifice takes two forms: blood or burning. A blood sacrifice is usually reserved for those whose souls will be relinquished to Lucifer. This soul, which has been "martyred," will someday be reincarnated into the "wasteland" that is earth and later occupy a revered place in hell.

A blood sacrifice occurs in several of the ceremonies of Satanism. The sacrificial victim is usually cut from the upper part of the chest to above the pubic bone. The heart is often removed and, mixed with blood, urine, and feces, becomes an anthropophagous mixture. This victim's soul will go directly to Lucifer, who will make a determination as to when it will be reunited with its body in a next life.

A burning sacrifice is considered to be a killing of vengeance or destruction. This type of human execution is reserved for those who have done something against the coven or church, and as such, they deserve to be killed. Other persons may be killed who are not Satanists. With Type I members, human sacrifices have been witnessed by some members at a secret ritual or ceremony.

A victim burned to death can never be reincarnated, a vital concern to the Satanist. Moreover, the soul from the sacrificed goes directly to Lucifer, making him stronger with each burned victim and each blood victim.

How often are there sacrifices? Fortunately the answer is very few. But when one does occur, it is important to know about the doctrine and dogma if one is to understand the full picture of the crime. For example, in Michigan, a young female, age 16, was killed allegedly by two young men, one a juvenile. Her face was skinned, her left finger was cut off, and there were several tattoos on her body, including the 666 symbol. An alert investigator knowing the contents of *The Satanic Bible* would immediately know the significance of the crime scene elements.

Hierarchy of Hell

Some Satanists believe that the earth on which we all live is surrounded by a spiritual "wasteland." Satan commands the wasteland, and the devil serves as a liaison between hell, earth, and the wasteland. But earth is also hell. There is a "free agency" to choose between right and wrong. A person could live life and be good and plentiful, survive this life, and after death, go to heaven. If one does not live life according to certain orthodox principles, that person would go to hell.

Many Satanists believe in reincarnation. If the member does what Lucifer, Satan, and the devil command, when physically dead, the member will be reincarnated. One will never move downward in class in the next life. A high priest, for example, would not come back in the next life as simply a coven member. He would come back as at least a high priest. But the members of the Church of Satan believe there is only one "high priest," and that person is the high priest of the Church of Satan.

Hell is like the heaven Christians envision. In other words, hell is where good Satanists will receive all of their wishes. Lusts will be satisfied, and in hell will reside Lucifer, Satan, the devil, demons (Satanists' answer to the Christian's angels), and humans. Interestingly enough, there are two classes of humans in hell: faithful Satanists, and fallen Satanists and sinful Christians. The faithful Satanists will receive all of their demands, and the servants will be the sinful Christians and fallen Satanists.

Devices Used in Satanic Rituals

In any form of religion, whether it is Christianity, Judaism, or Satanism, there are rituals and ceremonies. This can even be evident in the self-styled Satanist. A ceremony is typically a unique happening, which is intended to mark an important event. A ritual is more. It is repetitive, traditional, and has a certain prescribed set of behaviors that is intended to symbolize and reinforce a system of beliefs. Satanic rituals certainly fit into this operational definition.

Table 11.4 lists the devices necessary for satanic rituals (LaVey, 1969, pp. 134–139).

Table 11.4   Religious Elements in Satanic and Devil Worship Rituals and Ceremonies

Vestments	Altar
Phallus	Candles
Bell	Chalice
Elixir	Sword
Symbol of Baphomet	Gong

Vestments

Cowled or hooded black robes are to be worn by male participants. Females are to wear sexually appealing apparel for the purpose of arousing and intensifying the adrenal or bioelectrical energy of the males.

Altar

The purpose of the altar is to serve as a focal point. A nude woman is used on the altar because the female is the natural passive receptor and represents the earth mother. The altar is to be 3 to 4 feet high and 5½ to 6 feet long. The altar will face west, and the feet of the altar will face south.

Symbol of Baphomet

In Satanism, the pentagram is inverted to perfectly accommodate the head of the goat, its head representing duality and the other three points inverted to symbolize the Trinity denied. This Symbol of Baphomet is placed on the wall above the altar.

Candles

The candles represent the light of Lucifer. Only black and white candles are used, and never more than one white candle can be used. As many black candles as needed can be used to illuminate the ritual chamber. One black candle is placed to the left of the altar, and the white candle is placed to the right of the altar.

Bell

The bell is used to mark both the beginning and the end of the ritual. The high priest rings the bell nine times, turning counterclockwise.

This is done at the beginning of the ritual to clear and purify the air, and at the end to intensify the workings and indicate finality.

Chalice

The chalice should be made of silver, glass, or crockery but not of gold. Gold is traditionally identified with Christianity. Therefore, everything that is identified with Christianity is to be avoided. The contents of the chalice are to be drunk first by the priest.

Elixir

A stimulating fluid is used, but wine is not necessary. The elixir is to be ingested immediately following the Invocation to Satan.

Sword

The sword is the symbol of force and is held pointing toward the Symbol of Baphomet by the priest. If a sword is not available, a long knife, cane, or something similar can be used.

Phallus

The phallus is held in both hands and shaken twice toward each cardinal point of the compass. The phallus may be made of wood, clay, or plaster.

Gong

The gong is used to call upon the forces of darkness.

Satanic Masses

Satanic masses are offered several times during the course of the year. There are several days of the week that are appropriate for a particular service: Thursdays, Fridays, and Saturdays. Thursdays are especially appropriate for witches.

With each mass, there is an accompanying ritual. Colors, prayers, chants, words, meditation, and drugs may accompany each type of mass.

Initiation Mass

This mass is offered when new members are accepted into the satanic group, either in Type I or Type II. The new member will participate in the mass as an acolyte, and once the new member has passed through the rite of initiation, he is sworn to secrecy.

Gnostic Mass

This type of satanic mass is frequently open to satanic members who have shown an interest in joining the satanic group. Demons are called upon to intercede and convince interested nonmembers to join.

Mass of Angels

The manifest purpose of this mass is to seek power from Lucifer to protect the high priest from demonic powers. On the eve of this mass, a black cock is killed, and the heart, eyes, and tongue are cut out and become a potion for the participants to share.

Mass for the Dead

The purpose of this mass is to petition Lucifer to free the celebrant from the fear of hell and to make the demons obey. A lamb will be sacrificed, its throat cut, and the heart, eyes, and tongue removed and ground into powder and then buried with the lamb.

The Black Mass

This is probably the most bizarre and famous of all satanic masses. A parody and a mockery of the Roman Catholic Mass, this ritual is done for evil purposes only.

During the Black Mass, a sacrament by the satanic worshipers, men wear black robes and women wear black sexually erotic dress. The Black Mass is presided over by a priest, who celebrates this mass to recall a spirit, to gain power, or to ask for insight into the future.

A west-facing altar is used, and a nude female lies upon the altar with her head facing south and her feet facing north. The males in the grotto all have sexual intercourse with the woman, and each member, male or female, then inserts a bread wafer into her vagina, which is then ingested.

In *The Satanic Bible*, LaVey (1969) denies the practice of the Black Mass. But the members of Type I who were interviewed admitted the existence of such a ceremony. Additionally, they said that there were no sacrifices of any type. It was mainly a sexual ceremony.

Satanic Ceremonies

Night of the Beast

Unlike the Black Mass, which lasts all night, the Night of the Beast is a three-week ceremony. The ceremony commences at the third full moon of the year with the purpose of replenishing power and gaining new power to foresee the future. It is a great time of happiness, and strangely emotionally similar to the Christians' Christmas. At this time, the newly indoctrinated Satanists are invited to participate in the oath to Satan with the new member making a pact with Satan to give his or her soul to Lucifer. Second, the inductee will learn the principles of black magic. Third, the initiate will learn the vocabulary of Satan, and last, he or she will participate in simulated human sacrifice.

The celebration of the Night of the Beast is the opportunity for a high priest to suffer symbolic martyrdom, his soul dispatched to Lucifer for his uses and reincarnated at some future time. It is also an opportunity for parish members to assume the position of priest, as someone will be needed to fill the now vacant position.

The ceremony begins with the slaughter of a goat. A cloven-hoofed animal is necessary for this ceremony because of its symbolism of Satan. The goat will be slaughtered and hung on an inverted cross, which has been suspended over the altar. Thirteen priests will march counterclockwise around an inverted pentagram, which has been drawn near the altar. As the priests walk slowly in procession, the hope of each is that a drop of blood from the goat will fall upon him. This is taken as a sign that Lucifer has selected this minister as his chosen one; he is to be symbolically martyred.

Once this drop of blood from the goat has fallen upon a high priest, he will be "martyred" midway through the Night of the Beast ceremony. (When we speak of other sacrifices, we are stating that the murders are simulated.) His wife, if a believer, will be "killed" as well. If he is single, or if his wife is not a member of the church, a woman must be chosen from the grotto. There are grotto women who have been specially trained and educated, much like nuns. One will be chosen by the priests to join the "sacrificed" male victim.

The male is always sacrificed first. His abdomen is "opened" from below the throat to the pubic bone. His heart is cut out because this is the life source. The eyes are also removed because the eyes are to see the future. The blood is drained and the blood, heart, eyes, and urine are all mixed with wine into a potion, which the members of the church will drink. The procedure is repeated for the chosen woman, and again for the closing night's ceremony.

The Night of the Beast is presided over by an "Overlord." This person was once a priest, but because of his "martyrdom" in a past life, has been elevated to the present status of Overlord, or "bishop." As with many other satanic rituals and ceremonies, including the Black Mass, there is no evidence that this ceremony occurs with any great frequency.

The Passover

Every 6 months, in February and August, the Passover Rite is celebrated. The purpose of this ceremony is to reaffirm the Satanists' belief
in the dead and hell. This rite lasts only one night, and there will be two
"human sacrifices": a high priest and his wife, or "Bride of Lucifer."

The May Day Rite

This occurs on May 1. The general purpose of this ceremony is to
celebrate the beginning of the new year and also to celebrate the new
life of Satanism. There is both what we believe to be symbolic animal
and human sacrifice, a high priest and a woman. As with the Passover,
the rite is presided over by 13 priests, and the participants are the
Overlord, the coven members, and, according to belief, demons.

❖ CRIME SCENE ELEMENTS

In satanic killings, in any of the three dimensions of personal involvement, certain elements may be present. The extent of the evidence will
vary according to the type of personal involvement in satanic ritualism
and personal affinity. There is less evidence left at the scene of a satanic
killing than there is in a devil worship murder perpetrated by a self-
styled Satanist. The latter is less careful of the crime and the crime
scene. Conversely, the coven of an organized satanic cult will be very
careful in the covering of the scene itself.

Circle of Salt

In a Type I affiliation, and in fewer scenes of Type II and Type III,
there may be two circles of salt that will surround the ritual scene. The
investigator would be aware that the circles of salt, or any amount of
salt found at a suspected ritualistic crime scene, would be a sign that a
satanic sect or a devil worship cult had been involved. There also may
be bowls of salt of different colors around the altar.

The colors of salt, as well as banners and other symbols, all have
expressive meanings. Table 11.5 lists the meanings of the various colors.

Candles

Candles play an important role in the satanic ritual. As stated earlier, black and white candles are to be used by satanic sect members.

Table 11.5   Significant Colors in Satanic and Devil Worship Rituals and Ceremonies

Black	Darkness, evil, devil, night, Satanism, occult
Blue	Tears, water, sadness, pornography
Green	Vegetation, restful, nature, soothing
Orange	Personal aura
Purple	Summons spirits, summons spirits of destruction
Red	Blood, life, energy
White	Cleanliness, purity, innocence
Yellow	Perfection, wealth, glory, power

Never more than one white candle is used. Therefore, wax drippings found at the ritualistic crime scene may serve as an index of satanic involvement. If candle wax is found in colors other than black or white, then it can be assumed that the participants are Type II or Type III worshipers.

Mockery of Christian Symbols

The inverted cross is a sign of satanic or devil worship rituals. Often the inverted cross is made of stone and hung above the altar. An animal may be sacrificed above the altar, and blood may be found on the ground below the cross and altar.

Christian symbols may be desecrated. Statues, crosses, crucifixes, chalices, and other symbols associated with Christianity may all be broken and in pieces.

Satanic Symbols

Drawings of the inverted pentagram or a hexagram may be present. The pentagram or hexagram is always enclosed by a circle, which serves as a protective device from harm and danger from the demons.

In addition there are other satanic symbols, as exemplified in Figure 11.2.

The satanic alphabet may also be present, with the letters drawn upon the ground to spell a prayer, statement, or warning. The satanic number of the beast, 666, may also be present, but this is so well known that accepting this as an unimpeachable indication of direct satanic involvement may be in error. Also, the swastika, older than the Nazi Party itself, is primarily a symbol of satanic worship. If the swastika is present alone without any other visible satanic symbols, the inference of satanic involvement will be diminished.

Blood

Because of the emphasis by Type I participants on blood sacrifice, both human and animal blood may be present at the ritual scene. If, however, everything occurs as ritualistically planned, there will be

Figure 11.2   Satanic and Devil Worship Symbols

AC/DC	Anti-Christ, Devil Child
S	Satan-Stoner
MARKOS	Abracadabra
FFF	Anti-Christ
666	Anti-Christ
NATAS	Satan Reversed
6,9,13, XIII	Occult Numbers
⌐卐	Swastika
⊕ (pentagram)	Pentagram, White Magic
⊕ (inverted pentagram)	Pentagram, Sign of Occult
☽	Lucifer, Morning Star
•	Ank

little blood found of either type, human or animal. The blood is drained from the victim and mixed with certain body parts, urine, and feces, and made into a potion thought to have magical powers for satanic purposes.

Of course, when burning is the method of execution used, blood most likely will be missing. The reason for burning, however, must be kept in mind for the various types of satanic involvement.

Bodies

If a group does practice human sacrifice, and we encourage the reader to remember this seldom happens, bodies will usually not be found at the ritual scene. This is especially true if evidence at the crime scene reflects Type I participation. If the method of murder involves bloodletting, the body is going to be moved and hidden so that at some future time, the soul will be reunited with the body at Lucifer's command. The burned body, however, will often be left at the scene after the artifacts of the ritual have been carefully removed.

A body found at a crime scene where death has been caused by evisceration and cutting is not the result of a satanic sect; rather, it is a cult or self-styled killing. Positioning of the body, foreign objects inserted into body orifices, or bodies found where parts of the body have been removed will all reflect Type II or Type III involvement.

With a bloodletting sacrifice, the body typically will be cut from the pubic area to the upper chest. The heart, parts of the intestines, and other parts of the body will be removed, as well as the eyes. The body will be mutilated as a result of this action. There may be fecal matter smeared over the body, and the body may also be anointed with oils and incense.

With a satanic sect, however, it is unlikely that the body will be found at the kill site. If discovered, its recovery will probably be more by accident than through investigation.

Animals

Small animals, such as dogs, cats, frogs, and rabbits are all favorite targets of sacrifice for Type III satanic cults or devil worship. Perhaps one reason for this choice of animal is the lack of sophistication or knowledge of the dogmatically correct animals of sacrifice.

Sect members will make every effort to secure the "proper" animal to offer Lucifer, who demands blood. Usually, the goat is the desired animal of sacrifice. If this animal is not available, another cloven-hoofed animal can be substituted. If, however, the animal is a dog, cat, or other "inappropriate" sacrifice, this might indicate a younger perpetrator or one who has been involved in the group a relatively short period of time.

❖ SANTERIA AND OCCULT CRIMES

Santeria, "saint worship," has been a part of the American culture for some 400 years. Originally brought over to the United States by the slaves from Africa, and particularly from the beliefs of the Yoruba and Bantu people of southern Nigeria, Senegal, and Guinea, it was "hidden" within the religion of the Roman Catholic Church of many of the slave masters in the early colonies. Imported from Cuba and some other Caribbean islands, it was brought into the United States by the natives of these islands.

Santeria is basically "white magic." It is a multidimensional religion with a supreme god and a series of orishas, or spiritual beings or saints, similar in sight to Roman Catholicism. It has a hidden history in this country because of its intended clandestine practice by the slaves and current adherents as well as some confusion with other like religions of other practitioners.

SANTERIA TERMINOLOGY

- Ebos—spell
- La Regla Lucumi—the formal name for Santeria, the Way of the Saints
- Lwas—the seven African powers of the Vodoun tradition
- Olofi—the supreme god of Santeria
- Orishas—saints of the Santeria and Vodoun
- Orixa—the seven African powers of the Macumba tradition
- Palo Mayombe—the criminal side of Santeria
- Santera—priestess of the Santeria
- Santero—priest of the Santeria
- Vodoun—a form of Santeria originating in Haiti
- Yoruba—West African area, the originating site of Santeria and Vodoun

The Belief System of Santeria

Santeria is a vibrant religion, bursting with songs, dances, and prayers. The prayers and spells are used for good marriages, good health, and to find a job or receive money and many other gifts that would make life easier and happier.

There is one supreme god in Santeria, Olofin. This is the god of creation and one who is unattainable by humans. There are intermediaries, the orishas, that humans must go through so their prayers and supplications can reach Olofin. This god of creation is the most powerful and one who is depicted as Jesus Christ or the dove of the Holy Spirit. There are no gifts offered to Olofin, no colors represented at altars, and no animal sacrifices. Additionally, there are no herbs or ornaments. Since Olofin is unattainable, none of these is necessary.

The orishas are needed by the faithful. Each has a special need, special offerings each finds pleasant, and special prayers unique to themselves. And there is a symbiotic relationship between the faithful and the orishas. If sacrifices and gifts are not made to the saints, the saints will diminish in importance and viability.

Who are these orishas? What do they command? What prayers are said?

THE ORISHAS

Ellegua

- *Saint synchronization*—The Holy Child

- *Colors*—Red and black. If there is a necklace, it is made up of three red beads and then three black beads. After three black beads, a red bead alternates with a black bead three times.

- *Days of the week to pray to Ellegua*—Mondays and the third day of each month.

- *Propitiations*—Small goats and roosters. No chickens. Will eat until satisfied with enough ingestion of blood. Favorite fruit is sugar cane. Also loves rum and water.

- *Spiritual icons*—Ellegua is never without a garabato, the shepherd's hook.

- *Spiritual purpose*—Ellegua is the keeper of the highways and the gates. As the keeper of the highways and the gates, one must get "approval" from Ellegua before one can pray to the other saints. He is also known as the "trickster." He loves to play, and sometimes you will see children's tops, marbles, and kits at an altar. He protects the home and is seen as an oval-shaped head made of stone or cement with cowrie shells for eyes.

(Continued)

(Continued)

Chango

- *Saint synchronization*—St. Barbara

- *Colors*—His colors are red and white. The collar is made up of six red beads followed by six white beads. Then a red bead alternates with a white bead six times. It is then repeated until the desired length is obtained.

- *Days of the week to pray to Chango*—Friday and Saturday. Often a large party is held on the feast of St. Barbara, December 4.

- *Propitiations*—Roosters, small sheep, pigs, goats, deer, rabbits, and oxen. A horse may be necessary to remove a curse or to protect from death. Chango drinks red wine, craves corn meal, okra, apples, and cactus fruit.

- *Spiritual icons*—Chango is often depicted as a sword, an ax, a dagger, and a spear. Chango is often also depicted as a warrior with a hatchet in one hand and a sword in the other.

- *Spiritual purpose*—Chango is seen most often as the major power of the orishas. He is the warrior, needed in times to defend oneself and to cause action against another.

Babalu-aye

- *Saint synchronization*—St. Lazarus

- *Colors*—White with blue streaks. The collar is composed of white beads with blue streaks made to the desired lengths.

- *Days of the week to pray to Babalu-aye*—Sunday is the most proper day to pray to Babalu-aye. Wednesday also permitted.

- *Propitiations*—Spotted roosters, goats, chickens, snakes, quail, hens, and wild pigs. Babalu-aye also prefers cigars, coconut butter, and water from a pond. He also likes stale bread and milk, dry wine, and peanuts.

- *Spiritual icons*—Babalu-aye is always seen as a man with crutches and two dogs. Sometimes Babalu-aye will be seen with a broom used to sweep away the evil spells.

- *Spiritual purpose*—Babalu-aye is the patron against illness and disease. One would pray to this orisha if affected by a disease, especially smallpox.

Oya

- *Saint synchronization*—St. Theresa

- *Colors*—Black and white. The collar is made up of nine black beads and nine white beads. Sometimes brown beads are seen or maroon beads are substituted.

- *Days of the week to pray to Oya*—Friday is the day of worship for Oya.
- *Propitiations*—Chickens and guinea hens. Infrequently female goats are substituted. Her favorite fruit is the apple, and she loves to drink rain water.
- *Spiritual icons*—Oya wears a nine-pointed crown with nine charms. Other times there may be a pick, a hoe, a lightning bolt. Also present on occasion Oya may wear nine copper bracelets.
- *Spiritual purpose*—Once the wife of Chango, she rules over the winds and the whirlwinds. She also controls the gates of the cemeteries and also the dead. Oya is also considered to be a fierce warrior.

Oshun

- *Saint synchronization*—Our Lady of Charity
- *Colors*—Coral and amber. The collar is made up of yellow and red beads. If the practitioner has money, the collar is made of five amber beads followed by five coral beads.
- *Days of the week to pray to Oshun*—Saturday is the day of worship for Oshun.
- *Propitiations*—White chickens, female goats, neutered goats, female pigs, and rabbits. She likes tea made from the water of the river and loves honey on her food. Her favorite fruit is the apple, and she loves to drink rain water.
- *Spiritual icons*—Oshun wears a crown of gold. Also, she prefers fans made of peacock feathers and is often seen with two oars, a bell, and five bracelets.
- *Spiritual purpose*—She rules over the water of the world. She also represents the blood of the human body and is the patron saint of culture and the fine arts.

Obatala

- *Saint synchronization*—Our Lady of Mercy
- *Colors*—His color is white. The collar is made up of all white beads.
- *Days of the week to pray to Obatala*—Sunday is the day of worship for Obatala. Thursday is also permitted.
- *Propitiations*—White chickens, female goats, white canaries. Water comes from the rain and will not drink alcohol.
- *Spiritual icons*—Obatala's icon must of a white metal or silver. In one hand he holds a crown. Also, there may be the sun, four wristlets, a walking stick with a clenched fist, a half moon, and a coiled snake or two ivory eggs.
- *Spiritual purpose*—Obatala is the servant of Olofi. He is the patron saint of all those who are born with some form of deformity, especially albinos, since his color is white.

(Continued)

(Continued)

Yemaya

- *Saint synchronization*—Our Lady of Regla, the patron saint of Havana's port

- *Colors*—Her colors are white and blue. The collar is made up of seven white beads followed by seven blue beads. The sequence is followed until the desired length is accomplished.

- *Days of the week to pray to Yemaya*—Saturday is the day of worship for Yemaya. Friday is also permitted.

- *Propitiations*—Goats, lamb, roosters, fish, and pigeons are all permitted. Yemaya loves watermelon and banana chips, and all food should be spread with sugar cane molasses. Her drink is seawater.

- *Spiritual icons*—Yemaya's icons are made of lead and they include an anchor, a key, the sun, a half moon, a ray coming from the hand, the head of a shovel, a conch shell, and a sea shell.

- *Spiritual purpose*—Yemaya is thought to be the mother of all riches and is viewed as the god of mercy since she never betrays her children.

Dogma of the Orisha

The orishas are perhaps better seen as intermediaries between the Olifi (Olorun) and the faithful. Offerings are placed on an altar by the faithful anyplace in the house and there may be as many altars as desired or needed. This is very dissimilar to the satanic altar that must be placed in a certain direction.

Once an offering is placed on the altar, the offering may not be removed—it must be removed by the saint or by a household critter (if one is not a believer). If a small animal is placed on the altar, it cannot be removed until it has been eaten or removed, in the belief of the believer, by the saint to whom it was offered.

It is not the intent of this section to give a complete digest of the belief and dogma of Santeria. It is only that one must be careful in looking at a scene where it may be a scene of Santeria worship. By examining the colors, offerings, etc., one could get an idea about the purpose of the propitiation, the saint(s) being prayed to, and the problem manifested to the faithful by the saints being prayed to and the offerings placed.

Animal sacrifice is reserved for only the most serious reasons. Most of the time, the offerings are coins, candy, fruit, and candles.

Palo Mayombe

As noted above, Santeria is considered "white magic." But there is a dark and evil side, a criminal side, to Santeria that is called Palo Mayombe. In Palo Mayombe the saints remain the same, but there is a malevolent side to the orishas. To reduce it to perhaps a more understandable level, the saints are amoral. They will do the wishes of the practitioners if the offering is pleasing. The orishas need the sacrifices to survive and will cease to exist if no one prays to them and no sacrifices are offered.

To illustrate Palo Mayombe, there is no better case than the murder of a young American, Mark Kilroy, who was kidnapped in Texas and taken across the Rio Grande to Matamoros, Mexico, where he was sacrificed by Jesus Constanso and his followers. Kilroy's heart was cut out of his body when he was still alive, and body parts were boiled in a giant kettle, a naganga, and all the members of the sect ate a part of the mixture to give them spiritual power. When the Mexican and American legal authorities surrounded the farm, Constanso and his girlfriend had escaped and fled to Mexico City. The others fled the burning house and were captured by the authorities. Constanso was later killed by his own bodyguard, and his girlfriend was captured and sent to prison in Mexico.

The Crime Scene

What are some items of the crime scene evidence that might be present at the scene? If there is a body, organs may be missing. The heart, eyes, brain, and other parts that have special significance to the orisha may be missing. Also, if the body is still present, long bones may be missing. *The short bones, fingers, toes, etc., will be missing if it is a Satanic site.* A naganga may be present. Also, the color of the sacrifices must also be considered—for example, red and white beads will denote a certain orisha while all white beads will denote another. The blood of a certain color rooster will tell the investigator which saint is being prayed to and what the reason for the prayer is.

There are other items to consider. For example, an altar may be placed in any part of the dwelling, and there may be multiple altars. Also, there may be multiple white candles on the altar, while on the Satanic altar there can be only one white candle.

❖ CONCLUSION

As in any crime scene, there is a mixture of profiling elements. It would be safe to assume, however, that the preponderance of satanic elements indicates a type of participation in Satanism or in the occult. This participatory involvement, which entails to some degree a belief system and knowledge component, will reflect not only the amount of worship liturgy but also the method and selection of the total satanic ritual.

Table 11.6 describes the elements in sacrificial rituals and personal involvement, whether it is through sects, cults, or self-styled devil worship. As one can envision from this table, there are fundamental differences in goals, motives, rationalizations, methods, and drives, according to the type of ritualistic offender. If there is a body found at a crime scene with fecal matter spread upon the corpse, and if satanic pentagrams and numbers are present, one would suspect a devil worship killing. If this proves to be the case, a young offender with a limited amount of active involvement in an official satanic church would be suspected. After all, a bloodletting victim is a martyred "saint" for the church, and his or her body would be cared for in the appropriate, revered fashion. In other words, it would not simply be left at the scene. If this were done, then Lucifer would not reunite the soul with the body at a future time.

A burned body would be deliberately placed at a site that would accelerate its discovery. A victim burned by a sect sends a message to other sect members that this member has violated the confidentiality of the sect. The sect will not tolerate a member's disobedience, and the burning execution not only conveys this message but will also negate any potential for reincarnation.

A careful examination of the crime scene will yield some information regarding the type of participation. It is proposed that a sect-related crime will be committed by a person who has been in the

Table 11.6   Elements in Satanic and Devil Worship Ritualistic Killings

Ritual Elements	Satanic Sects	Devil Worship Cults	Self-Styled Devil Worship
Animal sacrifice	Yes	Yes	Yes
Human sacrifice	Yes	Yes	Yes
Victims	Members	Strangers	Strangers
Blood sacrifice	Yes	Yes	Yes
Burn sacrifice	Yes	No	No
Executioner	Priest	Leader	Self-stylist

community for some time, is intelligent, and has been a member of the sect for some time. On the other hand, a ritualistic crime perpetrated by a self-styled devil worshiper will offer a profile of a younger perpetrator, maybe a transient, and probably less educated and lower in the socioeconomic scale. Also, the self-styled and cult offender are more of a danger to society because their victims are almost entirely strangers. They will kill not for worship purposes but because of their quest for power.

The elimination of a person's life can never be taken lightly. An investigation must take into account all parameters. Because there has been mutilation, anthropophagy, or any other bizarre act that would, on the surface, indicate a ritualistic crime, further investigation may indeed yield a different result.

❖ REFERENCES

Bernet, W., & Chang, D. (1997). The differential diagnosis of ritual abuse allegations. *Journal of Forensic Sciences, 42*(1), 32–38.

Crews, G. (1996). Adolescent Satanists: A sensible law enforcement approach. *Journal of Police and Criminal Psychology, 11*(1), 13–18.

DeYoung, M. (1998). Another look at moral panics: The case of satanic day care centers. *Deviant Behavior, 19*(3), 257–278.

LaVey, A. (1969). *The Satanic bible.* New York: Avon.

Terry, M. (1999). *The ultimate evil.* New York: Barnes and Noble Books.

12

Geography, Profiling, and Predatory Criminals

❖ ❖ ❖

This chapter was co-written by Kim Rossmo.

P sychological profiling has been used as an investigative tool for a relatively short period of time, and it would be untrue to say that profiling has been universally accepted by the law enforcement community, but the procedure is becoming increasingly accepted by police officers. It is still vital to practice the time-proven methods of successful investigation: careful preservation of the crime scene, meticulous collection of physical evidence, thorough interviewing of all witnesses, and so on. However the investigator must also be aware of the latest scientific techniques, such as DNA fingerprinting and linguistic profiling, to maximize the chances of successful case resolution. One such novel investigative approach within the profiling field is the analysis of geographic patterns in an effort to determine the location of the offender's residence.

What sort of role does geography play in the criminal profiling process? This is still unclear, and the question deserves a great deal of research and study. Up to now the importance of geography has not been stressed, but there are many indications that the analysis of criminal mobility and an understanding of the geographical characteristics of crime scenes hold significant promise for the advancement of investigative profiling.

❖ THE ELEMENTS OF GEOGRAPHIC PROFILING

Distance

Distance means different things to different people, and we are sometimes surprised at the sundry attitudes displayed by people living in various parts of the country. A colleague from Utah, Dr. Al Carlisle, thinks little of driving several hundred miles, interviewing someone, and then driving home the same day. In another part of the country, a distance of 100 miles might necessitate an overnight stay at a local hotel before the return trip the next day. So distance is a relative concept, and its perception depends on a variety of different elements (Douglas, Burgess, Burgess, & Ressler, 1992) (see Table 12.1). And so it is with criminals, each having different perceptions of distance, and their behavior is reflected in these convictions.

Method of Transportation

One's perception of distance will be influenced by mode of transportation. For example, if a killer has to walk or depend on public

Table 12.1   Elements in the Perception of Distance

Method of transportation
Attractiveness of origins, destinations, and travel ways
Familiarity of roads and highways
Number and types of barriers
Alternative routes
Actual distance

transportation, his range of activities will be more constricted than if he has a vehicle. One murderer, whose case we profiled, traveled by city bus because he had neither a driver's license nor an automobile. He killed and assaulted within the immediate area of his home, and his range of travel was restricted to within his own neighborhood. The hunting area was immediate to his personal activities and was determined not only by his daily actions but also by his personality. He was a "disorganized" personality who saw visions and heard voices. His restricted comfort zone was defined by his daily activities, limited by the range and mode of his travels, and by his own personal inadequacies.

Attractiveness of Origins, Destinations, and Travel Ways

As we all know there are certain roads and highways that we prefer to travel, for reasons that vary from person to person. It may be that there are fewer regulated stops along one route than along another. It may be that a road is particularly attractive. There is an expressway in Kentucky, for example, that wanders through the thoroughbred horse farms. There is also a highway that cuts through a strip mining area, characterized by huge, gaping holes in the earth. Which of these is preferable, based only on the criterion of visual attractiveness?

Of course there are other factors that will enter into the decision of which route to choose. The origin and the destination must also be considered. These exert, respectively, "push" and "pull" factors on the individual. What is the exact nature and character of such forces in a given case? This is the answer only the individual offender knows— but the alert investigator must be able to get into the mind of the criminal, just as Will Graham did in *Red Dragon*.

Familiarity of Roads and Highways

We are all, to one degree or another, creatures of habit. We will repeat those things that are familiar and comfortable to us. Some families take their vacations in the same places year after year. There are obvious reasons for this. Familiarity brings comfort. The routes of travel become memorized, and road maps are no longer needed. Landmarks are easily recognized and anticipated as a means of validating the route traveled.

As one gets to know the roads and highways along with topological elements and landmarks, familiarity leads to comfort and reassurance. This affects the subjective perception of distance and can affect where an offender cruises for victims or searches for places to dispose of bodies. The more familiar the offender is with a highway or road, the more locations he will be aware of that will serve his criminal purposes.

Number and Types of Barriers

There are geographical barriers and boundaries that affect our chosen methods of travel. These include such things as rivers, freeways, railroad tracks, jurisdictional and state lines, and national borders. An offender facing such decisions as whether to cross a river in the hunt for victims must weigh certain factors. How much of a barrier is the river? What is the distance to the nearest bridge? Is he comfortable enough, psychologically, to operate on the other side of the river? Is there a county or state line involved, and, if so, what are the advantages and disadvantages and the various legal issues involved? The investigator must take into account such possible considerations of offenders when examining the geographical landscape surrounding the crime areas.

Alternative Routes

If there are only a few major roads in a community, an offender will quickly become aware of not only the avenues of travel but also of the possibilities for criminal behavior held by each. When several arterial routes exist in a community, however, there are additional elements to consider. Which road is the most direct one? Which is the most pleasant to travel? Which has the lowest risk of detection? These are all important considerations. The existence of multiple routes of travel will enhance the capability of the offender to find, and flee, desirable locations.

Actual Distance

Finally, and not surprisingly, the actual distance between two points, as measured objectively as opposed to subjectively, also has an influence on the perception of distance and therefore on criminal behavior.

Mental Maps

Everyone possesses a "mental map." This is a cognitive image of our spatial surroundings that has been built up over time by our daily activities and experiences. Most of these activities occur in the areas around our home, workplace, recreation sites, shopping districts, and the like, causing these neighborhoods to become known and familiar. Connecting our centers of activity are various routes such as paths, streets, bridges, and highways; separating them are various physical and psychological barriers, such as buildings, rivers, ravines, brush, and lakes.

Based on this spatial information, we choose paths that we use during our daily routine travels. Our activity sites, familiar areas, travel routes, and barriers, all influence the development of our mental maps (Holmes & Holmes, 1998) (see Table 12.2).

Since mental maps are affected by activity sites, we should remember that for the experienced criminal, such locations could include court houses, prisons and jails, criminal justice agencies, areas of prostitution, previous crime sites, and the like. It may be that we should return to an examination of the "concentric zone theory" of years past to develop some theory of the relationship between criminal profiling and geography; but perhaps it is just as effective to consider our thoughts regarding our own mental maps and spatial behavior.

Table 12.2   Elements of a Spatial Mental Image

Location of residence
Location of friends' homes
Work location
Location of recreational outlets (pool halls, bars, parks)
Paths—routes of travel (streets, railroad tracks, paths)
Nodes—focused centers of activity (intersections, subway stations, plazas)
Landmarks—geographic reference points (mountains, towers, billboards)

Criminals and Mobility

One of the main items of interest to us in the examination of the Ted Bundy case, in addition to the number of victims he admitted to having killed over a 17-year murder career, was the manner in which he drove the highways of our nation. In *Serial Murder* (Holmes & Deburger, 1985), the authors termed Bundy a "geographical transient serial murderer." This meant that he killed first in one area and then moved to another area and killed again. In an interview, Bundy stated that "this person we are talking about [himself]" may have killed in as many as nine states (author's files). Only the night before his death did he admit to a tenth state, Idaho!

The highway system makes it possible for a predator to travel long distances, not only in the search for potential victims but also in an effort to confuse law enforcement. Additionally, expanded road networks have opened up opportunities for the disposal of bodies. In the case of the Hillside Stranglers in California (O'Brien, 1985), most of the victims' bodies were dumped close to the freeway, allowing the killers to be back on the road within seconds.

It is important to ask such questions as why the killer decided to search that particular neighborhood for a victim, choose that particular area to dump the body, and pick that particular route to travel. What were the geographical characteristics that made those victim selection areas, body disposal locations, and routes of travel so attractive? We should not consider these choices to be the mere result of accident.

Consider the following case of a serial rapist who admitted, after his arrest, to more than 30 rapes. The attacks commenced when his wife refused to engage in sexual relations because she was fearful of pregnancy. Her refusal, he later admitted, launched him into a mental state in which he both feared and hated women. To ventilate his hatred and to help control his fear, he repeatedly raped but with little overt violence. From the model of personal violence discussed earlier in this book, we can see that he progressed from the "distorted thinking" stage to "the fall."

The serial rapes of this offender took on an interesting geographical pattern. The first rape occurred on the direct route from his home to work. It was less than one block from his commuting path to the apartment of the victim. He admitted to police that he often left home early to search for suitable victims along the route he traveled to work. The next few victims were attacked farther away. After moving to a new address he began to explore other directions, but again, he never traveled more than a block from the main thoroughfare. This rapist is best categorized as a power reassurance rapist with many personal traits of the disorganized (asocial) personality type (Knight & Prentky, 1987). He felt most comfortable in his travels along routes that were familiar and where he felt personally secure.

We have evaluated more than 800 murder cases and have found some interesting results regarding crime travel distances. When cases of serial offenders, rapists, murderers, and child abusers are plotted, we have noted that offender mobility and crime site geography are not only important but are also predictable.

As the neophyte criminal progresses in the "industry of offending," he gains experience that leads to increases in both comfort and confidence levels. With this increasing sense of comfort and confidence comes an expansion in predatory spatial activity, increasing travel distance and enlarging the victim search area. When an offender starts to hunt, the first few acts are usually situated relatively close to the locations of either his home or work site. As initial successes lead to increased confidence, the offender becomes more willing to prey farther and farther from home.

If the investigator is convinced that the crimes have been committed by a serial offender, special consideration should be given to those locations connected to the first few crimes. If it appears that the crimes are the responsibility of a single person, and if the site pattern is spreading, then it may be that the locations of the earliest crimes are close to the home or workplace of the offender: the offender's "comfort zone." Obviously, this has important implications for the successful investigative resolution of a crime series.

Geography and Victim Selection

Crimes suitable for geographic analysis are those in which the offender exhibits some kind of spatial decision-making process. The most obvious of these involve crimes of a predatory nature where the criminal hunts for his victims, choosing the neighborhoods in which he plans to seek out suitable targets. Not only must the perpetrator pick the areas in which he will look for his victims, but he must also determine where he will dump or bury the body, what routes he will travel, and the mode of transportation he will use. The degree of offender movement or travel varies, depending on the type and characteristics of the perpetrator (Hickey, 1991). Serial crimes are the easiest to profile geographically, as each different crime site contains new spatial information, providing the profiler with multiple sources of data. Serial murder, serial rape, and serial arson are the most common offenses profiled in this manner, but the principles can be applied to a variety of other crimes.

Many geographic profilers speak of a series of geographic zones, derived from the Brantingham and Brantingham (1981) model of target selection, within which an offender is most likely to commit his or her crimes. The areas of "home," "work," and "shopping and entertainment" constitute comfort zones that allow predatory offenders to cruise and commit their crimes under a psychological blanket of protection. Bundy created cemeteries in places such as Taylor Mountain and Lake Sammamish State Park. The dump sites were close to the Washington State highway system, situated in areas that he was familiar with and that conveyed a sense of psychological comfort.

The predator has a zone of behavioral activity, an activity space that contains both activity sites and the connecting paths between them (see Figure 12.1). The rapist discussed above had activity sites situated within his home and work neighborhoods and shopping and entertainment areas. His connecting routes were the main streets, which ran from one activity site to another.

Rossmo (1995b) notes that geography plays an important role in the offender's selection of "suitable victims." What defines a suitable victim? Why is it that some predators will let one potential victim pass and wait for another? It has to be more than the physical characteristics of the victim; there has to be a "click" within the mind of the predator that alerts him to a sense of "rightness" for attack.

When a criminal selects a target, there must be a suitability for victimization, which may have something to do with the "rightness of the place." Is the area appropriate for predation? Does it contain sufficient

Figure 12.1   Offender Activity Space

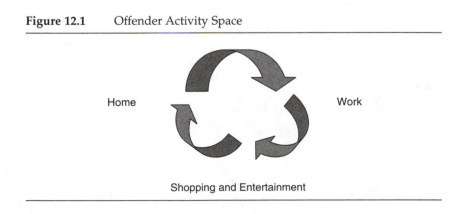

Home   Work

Shopping and Entertainment

and suitable victims? Is it familiar? Does it possess a feeling of comfort? Is the risk of apprehension low? Are there escape routes? As the offender considers these factors, so must the profiler.

❖ THE NATURE OF GEOGRAPHIC PROFILING

A geographical analysis is only one potential source for information and strategies in the successful investigation of a crime series. There are many others (see Table 12.3). Certain of the above-mentioned elements are well known to police and citizens alike, and we are all alerted to the possibilities of similar crimes being committed by the identification of modus operandi or signatures. As discussed earlier, the method of operation may change but the signature will remain the same (Rossmo, 1995a).

When a series of crimes show similarities that suggest that they were committed by the same offender, police agencies now have a variety of investigative options at their disposal. Traditional investigative techniques will always be the mainstay of all detective work. In addition, linkage analysis can identify links between similar crimes committed in different jurisdictions. Such analyses are usually performed at the state or national level through the use of computerized systems such as the Federal Bureau of Investigation Violent Criminal Apprehension Program (VICAP), the Royal Canadian Mounted Police Violent Crime Linkage Analysis System (VICLAS), the New York State Police Homicide Assessment and Lead Tracking Project (HALT), or the Washington State Attorney General Office Homicide Investigation Tracking System (HITS).

Table 12.3   Elements to Consider in Geographic Profiling

Crime location type
Arterial roads and highways
Physical and psychological boundaries
Land use
Neighborhood demographics
Routine activities of victims
Displacement

Not only can linkage analysis systems locate possible suspects from records of similar past offenses, but they also provide, through the identification of similar crimes, maximum information for psychological and geographic profiling efforts. The development of both psychological and geographical profiles, used in a complementary fashion, will hopefully lead to new investigative strategies that can be employed to help solve the crime series.

Geographic Profiling: Nature and Considerations

There is no one method that will identify an unknown offender, so it is beneficial to consider the various elements as complementary to each other. This is especially true when one considers the impact of geography on criminal profiling (see Table 12.3).

Crime Location Type

What determines a crime site location? This depends on the particular offense and the perpetrator's MO. Many violent crimes involve different locations. Table 12.4 lists the various types of crime sites that might be connected to an offense of murder or rape (Rossmo, 1995b). The geographic pattern of these crime sites will be influenced by the mode of travel available to the criminal. An offender who walks, for example, will have a more constricted hunting area than one who has access to a vehicle.

The location where the offender first contacts the victim is termed the *encounter site*. This may be in a bar, a street or park, a red light district, or any other location where the victim and the offender share physical and psychological space. The *attack site* is the location where the offender first attacks the victim. It is often the same as the encounter location. In such cases, it may be that the offender lives relatively close

Table 12.4   Types of Crime Locations

Encounter site
Attack site
Crime site
Victim disposal site
Vehicle dump site

to this position. Two different locations suggest that the personality of the offender may be more developed, indicating a capability for a growth in the range of travel in the search for victims. In other words, this type of offender is more likely to be the "organized personality."

The *crime site* is the location of the actual crime—the murder or rape scene in this case. The *victim disposal site* is the location where the offender dumps or releases the victim. If the victim disposal location is different from the encounter, attack, or crime locations, then we would suspect that the offender has a more organized personality; not only would he be capable of elaborate planning, but he would also be willing to travel greater distances. If all the crime locations are the same, then we have reason to believe that the offender is more disorganized. This type of personality is most comfortable in familiar (i.e., nearer) neighborhoods. Since the more organized offender usually travels longer distances to stalk, attack, or dispose of his victims, it is more likely that this type of offender lives farther from the initial contact site (G. Barret, personal communication, 1990). The same argument can be applied to the other types of crime locations. It should be stressed that often these different crime sites are in the same location. Every case has to be viewed separately because each crime is unique, even if the offender and his signature are the same.

Arterial Roads and Highways

In any area, people have preferences for the roads that they travel. These preferred routes depend on a variety of things. There may be, for example, one road more pleasant to the view than another. Some people travel by car or public transportation, others by bicycle or on foot. Choice of street may depend on the number of stop signs or stop lights that one might encounter along the way, or by the directness of the route traveled. It is safe to say that no one road, despite how planners have laid out the thoroughfare, will be the favorite way to travel.

Camelback Road is one of the main routes between Phoenix and Scottsdale, Arizona. Along this street are numerous businesses, new and used car dealers, restaurants, and stop lights. Asking for directions while there on a speaking engagement, we were told that the best way to get "there" from "here" was another road, less traveled, less direct, but with little to detract the view of the driver and passenger, and with not as pleasant a topology. Which is the better way? It depends. What does one desire? The quickest way? The most visually appealing? The answer will depend not only on the person but on the circumstances and the purpose of the travel. Would a person travel one road to work and a different one to commit a crime? The answer depends on the personality, circumstances, or personal organization of the offender.

Physical and Psychological Boundaries

Physical and psychological barriers and boundaries also exist in our travels. Rivers and railroad tracks act as physical barriers to travel. In some cases the barriers cannot be physically crossed, while in others it depends more on the choice of the traveler. Such choices may not be initially comprehensible to us, from our perspective as investigators, but it makes sense from the criminal's standpoint. People often feel uncomfortable in unfamiliar areas, such as neighborhoods of different socioeconomic or racial composition. The hunting patterns of offenders may therefore be distorted by such influences.

Land Use

The dominant land use in those areas surrounding, and between, the crime locations is important in a geographical analysis. What is the zoning in those areas—residential, commercial, industrial, or parkland? Are there major nearby attractions such as shopping centers, bars, entertainment sites, parks, office towers, or factories? Are there important transportation sites within those areas, such as train stations, bus routes, freeways, jogging paths, or subway stops? The way that the surrounding areas are utilized can provide vital information—in effect, geographic clues—that may significantly assist in the crime series investigation.

Neighborhood Demographics

Related to land use information is demographic and census data. What are the characteristics of those populations that reside in the neighborhoods of the crime sites? Information on sex ratios, racial composition, age breakdowns, occupational groups, socioeconomic status, crime rates, and other demographic variables is important in any profiling process.

Routine Activities of Victims

The behavior, travels, and habits of the victims are critical elements in the profiling process. These are especially important in any geographical analysis. Certain inferences can be drawn if the body dump site in a murder case is found in a location that would not be expected considering the victim's normal range of behaviors and interests. It may be assumed, in such a case, that the location of the dump site has more significance to the offender than to the victim. It is also important to consider the manner in which the body was dumped or displayed, as that information may give us some indication of the characteristics of the offender.

Displacement

Spatial patterning may change as the offender progresses through his crime series, maturing and gaining confidence and learning how to expand his hunting areas. But there is also an additional factor that can affect the location of crime sites. Geographic displacement occurs when the offender moves the locations of his criminal activities (e.g., victim hunting areas, body dump sites) in response to some action taken on the part of the criminal justice system. Patrol saturation efforts by the police in targeted neighborhoods are the most common cause of displacement. Inappropriate media disclosures have also led to changes in MO, and often geography, by the organized offender. Profilers must be aware of, and take into the consideration, the possible influences of these types of factors.

Investigators may ask, "Now what?" We would suggest that profilers should be aware of the geography of relevant areas. Plot the crime locations on a map. Look for patterns. Are there industries, residential areas, or shopping and entertainment centers along the routes between the crime sites? This may seem to be an old-fashioned approach, but what is new is the manner in which the areas of activity and their relationships are viewed.

❖ COMPUTERIZED GEOGRAPHICAL ANALYSES

At a recent national criminal justice conference, speakers discussed psychological profiling, geographic profiling, and other new scientific advances in this area. Rossmo noted that there now exists a computerized program called CGT (Criminal Geographic Targeting), which assesses spatial characteristics of crimes. He described the computerized analysis as a strategy for information management in cases of serial major crimes. The underlying mathematical process involves the scanning of every point in the offender's hunting area, and then the assigning of probabilities based on the distances from the point to each of the crime sites (Rossmo, 1995b). The result is presented in a manner similar to a topographic map of a mountain range, with the high points representing the most likely areas for the location of the offender's residence.

Most major crime cases that are serial in nature suffer from the problem of information overload. Often thousands of tips will be received and hundreds of suspects developed, placing tremendous demands on limited police resources. One of the major values of profiling is that it can provide a means for prioritizing leads and suspects. As many of our sources of information are address based, geographic profiling is particularly useful for strategic information management.

Since the CGT process produces a map that shows probability of offender residence by area, it can be employed as the basis for a variety of investigative strategies, the use of which depends on the specific details of the case. Some of these strategies include the following:

- Patrol saturation and static stakeouts
- Door-to-door canvassing, grid, and area searches
- Suspect prioritization
- Computerized searches of police information and record systems
- Searches of outside agency databases
- Task force tip prioritization
- Zip/postal code prioritization

In one series case, a child was abducted from near her home, murdered, and her body dumped in the outskirts of the city. Investigators had only a brief description of the suspect vehicle from a young playmate of the victim. A geographic profile was constructed using the CGT program, and the prioritized zip/postal codes were used, in conjunction with the vehicle description, in an off-line database search of Department of Motor Vehicles owner registration records. The end result was that thousands of potential suspect vehicles were narrowed down to only a few dozen, greatly facilitating the investigative process.

Rossmo (1995a) stated that the typical construction of a geographic profile involves the following process:

1. A thorough perusal of the case file, including investigation reports, witness statements, autopsy reports, and psychological profile (if available)

2. Detailed examination of crime scene and area photographs

3. Interviews with lead investigators and crime analysts

4. Visits, when possible, to each of the crime sites

5. Analysis of demographic data and neighborhood crime statistics

6. Study of street, land use, and transit maps

7. Computerized analysis (if appropriate)

8. Interim and final report writing

In this whole process, which takes on average about 2 weeks to complete, the computerized analysis involves less than 5% of the total time, and its use requires judicious decision making on the part of the profiler. So while computers play an important role, their function should be placed in the proper perspective. We must always remember that profiling is still more of an art than a science. It is only viable when the human element comes into play. This is what provides profiles with their richness. A computer system, regardless of its sophistication, cannot include all the multitude of details involved in a given case or comprehend the complete range of potential human behavior. While the development of computerized profiling programs involving expert systems has been discussed, their widespread availability is some years away. For now, we still need humans who are schooled in the disciplines of criminology, sociology, psychology, geography, and psychiatry. And a little luck.

❖ CONCLUSION

The role of geography has been ignored too often in the profiling process. This chapter has examined some of the general principles of geographic profiling and crime scene assessment. Much of the material has been gleaned from the research and experiences of Rossmo and others who have worked in this area. Some of the insights have been gained by the authors through the process of profiling cases for police departments across the nation. By blending all this information, a plan has been presented that allows for a consideration of the role of geography and topology in the profiling process. It is critical, however, to retain the human factor in our understanding of the influence of geography. Then, and only then, can we be successful.

❖ REFERENCES

Brantingham, P., & Brantingham, P. (Eds.). (1981). *Environmental criminology*. Beverly Hills, CA: Sage.

Douglas, J., Burgess, A. W., Burgess, A. G., & Ressler, R. (1992). *Crime classification manual*. Lexington, MA: Lexington Books.

Hickey, E. (1991). *Serial murderers and their victims*. Pacific Grove, CA: Brooks-Cole.

Holmes, R., & Deburger, J. (1985). *Serial murder*. Newbury Park, CA: Sage.

Holmes, R., & Holmes, S. (1998). *Serial murder* (2nd ed.). Thousand Oaks, CA: Sage.

Knight, R., & Prentky, R. (1987). The developmental antecedents and adult adaptations of rapist subtypes. *Criminal Justice and Behavior, 14,* 403–426.

O'Brien, D. (1985). *Two of a kind: The hillside stranglers*. New York: Signet.

Rossmo, D. (1995a). Place, space, and police investigations: Hunting serial violent criminals. In J. Eck & D. Weisburd (Eds.), *Crime and place* (Vol. 4). Monsey, NY: Criminal Justice Press.

Rossmo, D. (1995b). Targeting victims: Serial killers and the urban environment. In T. O'Reilly-Flemming & S. Egger (Eds.), *Serial and mass murder: Theory, research and policy*. Toronto: University of Toronto Press.

13

Jack the Ripper

A Case for Psychological Profiling

❖　❖　❖

From August through November 1888, the East End of London, especially the Whitechapel section, was living in a state of fear and foreboding. They feared an unknown killer who called himself "Jack the Ripper." First called the "Leather Apron" killer by the police and the press, the killer sent a letter to the media identifying himself as Jack. This name of this unknown murderer has become famous, or infamous, in the annals of serial crime and serial murder.

This was a time when interest in crime was at an all-time high. Only a year had passed since the first novel by Sir Arthur Conan Doyle depicting the crime resolution efforts of Sherlock Holmes was published. And while Mr. Holmes and his companion, Dr. Watson, were able to resolve the most bizarre crimes within the confines of the pages of the book, these murders by Jack the Ripper are unsolved even into the 21st century.

After the murder of the first victim, Polly Nichols, the subsequent killings became more famous when the name of Jack the Ripper became known. Then, even the West Enders of London became a part of the frightened populace. This was unusual because London was a divided city: The West End was a society of wealth, taste, and power. Their children were attended to by nannies. They went to plays and operas and partook of all the good things offered in the capital city of England. They were the chosen people. Their queen, Victoria, ruled for their benefits and they benefited greatly in comparison to those who existed in the East End of London.

Nine hundred thousand people lived in the East End of London. Many were homeless. Within the East End was an area called Whitechapel. It was an island within a ghetto largely ignored by the powerbrokers of the government and business leaders. Overcrowding, unemployment, disease, and other social maladies affected hundreds and thousands of people. Women were particularly affected. Many had to turn to prostitution for food and shelter for themselves and many times their fatherless children. A man could purchase the services of a woman for the price of a loaf of bread. Because conditions were so bad no one thought the worse of the women who had to resort to the streets for subsistence.

With such deplorable conditions existing for such a large number of people and someone terrorizing the streets of Whitechapel, the citizens of London were becoming more and more alarmed. The women of the West End wrote a letter to the queen asking for protection from Jack before he came into their own section and started killing the affluent women of London.

In general, a pandemic fear enveloped the city of London. Five women, and perhaps at least three more, had been murdered, and, while there were possible suspects, no arrests were forthcoming.

In this chapter we will examine the case of Jack the Ripper. We will introduce five victims with as much information as we could obtain about their backgrounds, habits, behaviors, etc., to provide a victimology report. We will also offer forensic information about the murders, including geoforensic information and certain information concerning viable suspects in the Jack the Ripper case. The last section of this chapter deals with the development of your own profile of the identity of Jack the Ripper. Thus, the manifest purpose of this chapter is to allow the reader to have one's skills enhanced, predicated upon the emerging knowledge of the profiling process.

❖ VICTIM: MARY ANN "POLLY" NICHOLS

Personal History

There is some disagreement concerning the actual number of victims of Jack the Ripper. What we have decided to do is to deal with

Table 13.1   Known Victims of Jack the Ripper

Name	Age	Date Killed	Comments
Mary Ann Nichols, aka "Polly"	43	August 31, 1888	First of the five victims; throat slashed, stabbed in the stomach, and vertebrae were exposed
Annie Chapman, aka "Dark Annie"	47	September 8, 1888	Organs removed from the body
Elizabeth Stride	45	September 30, 1888	Killing was interrupted, and he tried to take her ear with him
Catharine Eddowes	46	September 30, 1888	Same day as Stride killing, only a few minutes later; victim suffered savage mutilation, kidney removed
Mary Jane Kelly	25	November 9, 1888	Killed in her apartment, intestines removed, heart taken, skins and body parts placed on a table next to her bed

the five victims usually mentioned as Jack's likely victims. The first is Polly Nichols.

Polly was born Mary Ann Walker on August 26, 1845, in Shoe Lane in London. She was christened in 1851, and at the time of her death she was 43.

Polly was 5 feet 2 inches tall, with brown eyes, dark complexion, and brown hair slightly turning gray. She had five front teeth missing at the time of her death. Her teeth were also slightly discolored, which was common among the poor. She also had a small scar on her forehead, perhaps the result of an accident as a child. People described her as small and clean. She was also an alcoholic.

Polly's father, Edward Walker, was a blacksmith. The mother's name was Caroline. Polly married William Nichols in 1864; she was 18. Together they had five children: Edward, Percy, Alice, Eliza, and Henry. The couple did not have a happy marriage and separated many times, perhaps as many as six, during their 24-year marriage. She separated from William in 1881 for the last time. Later her husband learned that Polly was making her living as a prostitute. He stopped paying her child support, but some believe that she was living with other men during the time of the final separation until the time of her death. Polly and at least one of the children accused William of having an affair that led to their final separation.

Criminal Background

Polly had a lengthy police record, but all were for minor offenses, such as drunkenness, disorderly conduct, and prostitution.

Residences and Locations

At the time of her death Polly lived with four women in a lodging house at 18 Thrawl Street. Thrawl Street was south of and parallel to Flower and Dean Street in London's East End. One roommate, Emily (or Ellen) Holland, also had a minor record of prostitution. Polly moved from this public lodging house to another one nearby. In this domicile, men and women were allowed to share the same rooms and the same beds! In a high rate of crime area in Whitechapel, it was one-quarter mile from Thrawl Street, so she moved only a slight distance from the previous public lodging house. In this new house, the rooms were small, dark, and dank. The area was rampant with disease, squalor, crime, and despair. Many roomers spent one night at a time, earning enough money during the day to pay their nightly fee for lodging.

The Night of the Killing

The following information was gleaned from various sources concerning the chronology of the night of Polly Nichols's death (Douglas, Burgess, Burgess, & Ressler, 1992; Evans & Skinner, 2000; Harrison, 1993; Paley, 1996; Rumbelow, 1988).

Buck's Row was a narrow street with few well-kept houses. Most were shabby, dirty, and in need of gross repair. On one side of the street were homes and public lodging houses; on the other were businesses and warehouses. The street in this block where Polly's body would be found was illuminated by one street light.

Polly's body was found across from a warehouse in a gateway to a stable. The people who lived next door to the stable and across the street reported that they woke up several times during the night but heard nothing.

Medical Report

The physician reported that Polly had five teeth missing and a slight tear in her tongue. On the left side of her throat was a circular

Table 13.2   Last Known Sighting of Polly Nichols

Time	Comments
11:00 P.M.	Polly is seen seeking dates for prostitution.
1:30 A.M.	She is asked to leave a public lodging house because she had no money for a bed. As she was leaving, she told the manager that she would be back soon so the manager would save the bed for her. The fee that she demanded for an act of prostitution was 2 or 3 pence, the price of a loaf of bread. She also made some remarks about her new black bonnet.
2:30 A.M.	Ms. Holland, who stated to the police that Polly was very drunk and staggered along the walls of the buildings as she walked down the street, sees her.
3:15 A.M.	The local bobbie was walking his beat on Buck's Row and saw nothing unusual. This same information was reported by another beat officer at about the same time.
3:45 A.M.	Polly Nichols's body is found by a man on his way to work.
3:50 A.M.	A local physician arrives at the crime scene and pronounces Polly dead.

Table 13.3   Clothing Worn by Polly Nichols on the Night of Her Death

A black straw bonnet

An aulster of reddish brown

A brown Lindsey frock

White flannel chest cloth

Black ribbed wool stockings

Two petticoats

Brown stays

Man's elastic side boats

A white handkerchief

bruise, and she had a similar bruise on the left side of her face. On the left side of the neck was a 4-inch incision and about an inch below this another of 3 inches. Another below the right jaw severed all the tissues down to the vertebrae. This incision was about 8 inches long. No blood was found on the body. There were several incisions across the abdomen. The physical exam also found that there were three or four similar cuts running down the abdomen on the right side. The knife was reported to be sharp and all the wounds made by the same knife.

❖ VICTIM: ANNIE CHAPMAN

Personal History

Not much is known of Annie Chapman's early life; however, as Annie became an adult, she married but left her husband and two children to become a prostitute and street vendor, selling flowers and her own crochet. She lived in public housing, earning her daily doss from her work and her acts of prostitution. For about 4 years after she left her husband, she received support from him. The husband had custody of their two children, one in school in France and the other in a mental hospital. The support stopped when her husband died in 1886.

People report that "Dark Annie" was a hostile person and would often get involved in physical altercations with other women. This was especially true when she drank. Oddly, she drank only on Saturdays.

The people on Hanbury Street in Whitechapel knew her well. She was described as a stout woman, about 5 feet tall, with light brown wavy hair, blue eyes, a dark complexion, and a flat nose. She was not in good health at the time of her murder, suffering from a disease of the lungs and brain. She could have also had TB and syphilis. Her illness was considered terminal.

Criminal Background

Little is known of Dark Annie's criminal background. She did not have the extensive criminal background of Polly Nichols, but there is no doubt that she did have an arrest record because of her penchant for fighting while intoxicated. Records, as far as we can determine, are scarce.

Residences and Locations

Annie Chapman lived for the last 6 years of her life in Whitechapel. At one time she lived in a rear room adjacent to Mary Kelly, the last known victim of Jack the Ripper. Records do not show many exact addresses, but she resided several times at 35 Dorset Street, 30 Dorset Street, and on Hanbury Street. All the known addresses were public lodging addresses, including the addresses on Dorset Street, Crossingham's Lodging House. She lived with several men during this 6-year period. At one time she called herself Annie Sievey or Siffey.

The Night of the Killing

Most likely, Annie had been out drinking the night of her death. She was removed by the lodging house manager because she did not have enough money for her doss. As she left she said, as had Polly Nichols, that she would be back as soon as she made enough money for a room that evening.

John Davis found the body as he left his own apartment in the rear of 29 Hanbury Street and began his walk to work. He discovered the body in the rear yard of the three-story lodging house. She was laying on her back with her face turned to the right. Her intestine was over her right shoulder and her stomach was sliced open. Her left arm was resting on her left breast. There were two rings on the ground next to her, and both rings had been torn from her fingers. Additionally, there were coins placed at the victim's feet. The right hand was by the right side, and the legs were drawn up and the knees were turned outward. The feet were pointed toward a wooden shed. The hands were raised with

Table 13.4   Last Known Sightings of Annie Chapman

Time	Comments
11:30 P.M.	Left Crossingham's Lodging House to earn money
5:00 A.M.	Seen at 29 Hanbury Street
5:30 A.M.	Seen talking with a man at 29 Hanbury Street
5:45 A.M.	Body discovered by John Davis

the palms upward. There was no evidence of a struggle, and no clothing was found ripped or torn.

"God placed me here on earth to kill all whores."

—Jack the Ripper

Mr. Davis alerted law enforcement officials, who responded in less than 5 minutes. The rear yard was dark, and there was no intent on the part of the killer to hide the body.

Medical Report

The medical information received via the examination of Annie Chapman was sparse. The police physician stated that in essence Ms. Chapman was disemboweled; her uterus was removed from the scene, as was one kidney. The abdomen was laid open and the intestines were lifted out and placed over her right shoulder. The intestines were severed. Parts of the pelvis, the uterus, and the upper part of the vagina were removed. Also, two-thirds of the bladder was removed.

The physician offered that the knife used was very sharp and that it was approximately 6 to 8 inches long. Additional medical information was missing. As in the case of many modern serial killers and investigations of them, turf issues were prevalent and information was not shared. However, because this was a publicized case, 16 influential local businessmen formed the Whitechapel Vigilance Committee. It was the committee's responsibility to patrol the area at night and immediately report to the local law enforcement officials any problems. Nothing is written concerning how effective the committee was. Regardless, the killings continued.

❖ VICTIM: ELIZABETH STRIDE

Personal History

The third victim of Jack the Ripper was Elizabeth Stride, nee Gustafsdotter, born on November 27, 1843, in Sweden. She was baptized a Roman Catholic when she was less than 1 month old. Her father was Gustaf Ericsson and her mother was Beatta Carlsdotter.

Stride was 45 when she was murdered by Jack the Ripper. She was reported to be 5 feet 5 inches tall, with brown hair, light gray eyes, and a pale complexion. She had no teeth in her lower jaw.

The roomers and friends of Stride called her friendly, outgoing and good-hearted, and she would work when she could find a job. She was not well educated but could read. However, some reported that she was a drunkard and spent some time in various workhouses in London. She was also reported to use foul language when she was intoxicated.

She was a registered prostitute but also made some money from sewing and housekeeping. She was treated several times for venereal disease in 1865 in Sweden. In 1866 she moved to London as an unmarried woman. Living with several men before her marriage, she wed John Thomas Stride in 1868. Mr. Stride was a carpenter, and he died in 1884. His nephew, Walter Frederich Stride, was a member of the Metropolitan Police Department in London and identified Elizabeth's body. Somewhat of a storyteller, Elizabeth Stride reported that her husband and child had been killed in a shipwreck and she too had almost been killed. This turned out not to be true, because records have revealed that Mr. Stride died in 1884.

From 1882 to the time of her death, Elizabeth lived in common lodging houses in the East End of London. She lived with several men but perhaps spent more time with Michael Kidney than any other man, about 5 months.

The local churches knew Stride because they would often feed her and give her clothing. Kidney reported that when she started drinking she would disappear for several days or weeks at a time. She would prostitute herself many times an evening to earn money for a night at one of the lodgings, especially in Whitechapel.

Criminal Background

Elizabeth Stride did not have an extensive criminal record. Her record was as follows:

Table 13.5   Criminal Record of Elizabeth Stride

Date	Location/Offense
March 21, 1887	Poplar Workhouse
September, 1888	Arrested for disorderly conduct, spent night in jail

Residences and Locations

Elizabeth Stride was reported to live with many different men from the time she arrived in London until the time of her death. Most of the housings were rented by the night, and the residents were often prostitutes who were also alcoholics and many probably mentally ill. From various sources it appeared that she lived close to Ten Bells, a local tavern, and around 32 Flower and Dean, Commercial Street, and Hanbury Street.

The description of the area was not unlike those of Polly Nichols's residences: shabby and dirty, public lodgings, businesses, and warehouses on one block followed by a combination of similar buildings in the next block.

Things were better when Elizabeth and John married. They moved into their own residence in another part of London, lived above their own business, a coffee shop. This arrangement lasted until 1882 when she left her husband and started to live in public lodgings and turn to prostitution for her own survival. After her husband's death, she moved in with Michael Kidney, but that arrangement was stressful and she would stay with him only for short periods of time over a period of about 5 months.

The Night of the Killing

September 30, 1888, would be the last day in the life of Elizabeth Stride. Various people would admit seeing Stride several times during the evening. She was last seen after midnight in the company of a man described by two different witnesses as being about 5 feet 7 inches tall, with dark hair and a small mustache. He was wearing a long black coat that a reached his heels. She had already made sufficient money to buy her a night's lodging in a public house, and one witness stated that he thought he overheard her tell the man that she was not interested in having another sexual date. This was after midnight.

At 1:00 A.M., Louis Diemschultz was driving his horse and cart into Dutfield's Yard. The horse refused to enter the premises, and the man sensed that there was something wrong but could see nothing because the area was very dark. His whip, as he probed the area, came into contact with a body. He thought that the person was drunk and passed out. He went into the neighborhood club and sought help, and two men came to aid him. The three found Stride's body, her throat cut. There were no other mutilations found at that time.

There was some thought that Diemschultz frightened Jack off by his sudden arrival at the crime scene, but Diemschultz himself thought perhaps the killer was still at the scene when he left for help. The reason for this? He said the horse was still acting oddly and the body was very warm as he touched her.

Medical Report

The physician's report stated that the body was found lying with the face turned toward the wall and the feet toward the street. The left arm was extended. The right arm was over the abdomen, and the back of the hand and wrists had blood on them. The body and face were warm when first examined, but the hands were cold. The throat had been cut parallel to the left jaw, and the throat had a deep gash in it. The cut in the neck was 6 inches in length and started 2½ inches below the jaw. The cut was very clean, and the physician thought that the killer had great strength. There was a superficial cut on her right side. There was mud on the left side of the face and mud matted in her hair.

Table 13.6   Clothing Worn by Elizabeth Stride on Night of Her Death

Long black coat jacket, fur trimmed around the bottom
Black skirt
Dark brown velveteen bodice
Black crepe bonnet
Checked neck scarf knotted on the left side
Two light serge petticoats
One white chemise
White stockings
Spring sided boots

The police offered an opinion apart from the medical report. There was some physical evidence that the killer had tried to cut off her head but was unable to do so, because of being interrupted.

Other than injuries suffered at the hands of Jack the Ripper, there were no other significant health concerns.

❖ VICTIM: CATHARINE EDDOWES

Personal History

Catharine Eddowes was also known as Kate Kelly. Born in 1842, she was 46 when she died. She was 5 feet tall, with hazel eyes and dark auburn hair. She had a tattoo on her left arm, "TC." Her father, George, was a tin plate worker, and her mother was a homemaker. Catharine had two sisters, Elizabeth and Eliza. After the father went on strike, the family walked to London in 1848. Forty years later, Catharine would be dead, murdered at the hands of Jack the Ripper.

At the age of 21, Catharine lived with an older man, causing some turmoil within the family. She gave birth to a child and decided to go back home, but her family rejected her. She returned to her former common-law husband. They had two more children before she left him again. She then married another man, and this union produced one child. She lived with this husband for only a short period of time, which was marked with periods of separation. Returning to London after working in the fields of England on temporary agricultural work, she started living in several public lodgings. She mentioned to one manager of a housing unit that she was hoping that she could get some of the reward for catching Jack the Ripper.

Criminal Background

Catharine was arrested one time for drunk and disorderly conduct. This was on September 29, 1888, the day before her death. She was released from jail at 1:00 A.M. People who knew her said that she was a relatively sober person and easy to get along with but could get angry easily if she had something to drink.

Residences and Locations

Catharine lived in several public lodgings in Whitechapel. One was Cooney's Lodging House. As with the other victims of Jack the Ripper Catharine would stay at various public lodging houses but seemed to be more geographically mobile than the other women. She had left her family several years earlier, traveled mostly with female friends to the countryside, especially during the harvest time and planting months to earn money for her sustenance and residences.

The Night of the Killing

Several people who knew Eddowes saw her during the late night and early morning hours of September 29 and 30, 1888.

The body was found in a square in front of three empty cottages. The entrance to Mitre Square is a broad entrance. When the police responded to the call, they found Catharine Eddowes's body on its back, the head turned to the left. The arms were by the side of the body, and the palms were up and the fingers slightly bent. The abdomen was exposed, and the left leg was extended in a straight line. The throat was cut. The intestines were severed and placed over her right shoulder. The right ear was also cut. The police report continued with the mention that the body was still warm. No blood was found on the abdomen—no small feat, we would suspect—and no blood was found below the middle of the body. As clothing was taken from the body after it arrived for a physical examination, an ear fell from it. The colon was separated and placed in a lump next to her.

Medical Report

The police surgeon examined the body in the late afternoon. The report stated that the body was still not quite cold. A bruise was found on the back of her left hand, but there were no bruises found on the scalp, the back of the body, or the elbows. There was a great deal of

Table 13.7   Last Known Sightings of Catherine Eddowes

Time	Comments
8:00 A.M.	Returns to Cooney's Lodging House, sees Mary Kelly
9:00 A.M.	Pawns a pair of shoes
10:00 A.M.	Seen eating breakfast with Mary Kelly
2:00 P.M.	Leaves Mary Kelly to make some money for lodging
8:00 P.M.	Seen drunk and doing imitations of a fire engine
8:50 P.M.	Arrested for drunk and disorderly conduct
1:00 A.M.	Released from jail
1:35 A.M.	Seen by two men in the company of another man
1:45 A.M.	Eddowes's body found in Mitre Square

mutilation found on the face. There was a cut through the lower left eyelid and the right upper eyelid. A deep cut was found in the nasal bone, and the tip of the nose was cut off. Another cut was found at a right angle on the mouth, and on each side of the cheek there was a triangular cut about an inch and a half long.

The throat was cut with a slash of about 7 inches. Also, another cut was found by her left ear. The larynx was severed to the bone, and the killer took the kidney and uterus from the crime scene. The liver was also cut, and the womb was cut horizontally and parts taken by Jack the Ripper. It was the opinion of the police surgeon that the throat was first slashed and the other attacks then took place. Interestingly, the surgeon stated that he did not think the wounds were self-inflicted!

At the time of her death, the victim was wearing and in possession of the following:

Table 13.8   Clothing Worn and Items in Possession by Catherine Eddowes on Night of Her Death

Black straw bonnet trimmed in green and black velvet
Black cloth jacket
Large metal buttons
Dark green skirt
Man's white vest
Brown bodice
Gray stuffed petticoat
A very old green alpaca (worn as an undergarment)
A white calico chemise
A pair of men's lace-up boots
Gauze used as a neckerchief
1 white handkerchief
1 blue striped bed ticking pocket
2 short black clay pipes
1 tin box containing tea
1 tin box containing sugar
1 tin matchbox, empty
12 pieces of white rag
1 piece of coarse, white linen

(Continued)

Table 13.8 (Continued)

---

1 piece of red flannel with pins and needles

6 pieces of soap

1 small-tooth comb

1 white-handled table knife

1 metal spoon

1 red leather cigarette case

1 ball of hemp

Several buttons and a thimble

A printed handbill

1 red mitten

❖ VICTIM: MARY KELLY

Personal History

Mary Jane Kelly was 25 years old at the time of her death. She was 5 feet 7 inches tall, with blond hair and blue eyes. The reports stated she was pretty but stout. She was called attractive, neat, and clean, and she always wore a clean white apron. She was also judged to be a quiet, polite, and industrious person, except when she drank. She then became loud and in some cases belligerent.

Kelly was born in Limerick, Ireland, one of several children born into the middle-class family of John and Catherine Kelly. Educated for her day, Mary was also judged to be intelligent, possessed good reading skills, and was an artist with some promise.

At 16, she married for the first time and is thought to have had one child from this marriage. Her husband was killed in an explosion at work. After spending some time with relatives in various parts of Wales and England, Mary went to London in 1884. She was thought to have lived in a convent with Catholic nuns when she first arrived. She secured other employment as a maid, housekeeper, and had been a nursemaid for an illegitimate child of the Duke of Lawrence, a suspect in the Jack the Ripper case. Later she became a prostitute in a high-class brothel in London.

Mary lived with several men after she arrived in London. The last was Joseph Barnett. He stated that she lived with other men before she moved in with him. They apparently had a good relationship except when both were drinking. Both would become loud and disturbing to others.

Criminal Background

Mary Jane Kelly had no extensive criminal background. She had perhaps one arrest for being drunk and disorderly in a public place. She received a fine from the Thames Magistrate Court on September 19, 1888.

Residences and Locations

When Mary Kelly came to London, she first lived at the Providence Row Convent on Crisp Street in London. She stayed there only a short period of time. She became a prostitute, and her addresses changed with some rapidity.

The room on Miller's Court was small, approximately 12 feet by 12 feet. Inside the room were two small tables, a small bed, a pail, and a washstand. The windows that faced the outside had two broken panes covered with stuffed clothing.

The Night of the Killing

Mary Kelly was 3 months pregnant at the time of her death on November 9, 1888. Several citizens of Whitechapel saw her on the night of her death and in the early morning hours.

When the police arrived, Mary Kelly's body was found in her bed. The body was nude and the head was turned to the left. The right arm was slightly moved from the side of the body, elbow bent. The left arm was crossed over the abdomen. Her clothing was found neatly folded on a chair, and the boots were in front of the small fireplace. The legs

Table 13.9   Last Known Sightings of Mary Kelly

Time	Comments
8:00 P.M.	Joseph Barnett leaves the room to go to his own abode
11:00 P.M.	Seen at the Britannica Bar drinking with another woman
11:45 P.M.	Mary Ann Cox sees Kelly talking with a man
12:30 A.M.	A neighbor is disturbed by Kelly's singing
1:00 A.M.	A neighbor sees the lights on in Kelly's room
2:00 A.M.	A neighbor meets Kelly on the street; she seeks money
3:00 A.M.	Same neighbor sees her in the company of a man
4:00 A.M.	A roomer hears a cry from Kelly's room
5:45 A.M.	Someone reports that a man left Kelly's room
10:45 A.M.	Kelly's body is discovered by the lodging's manager

were spread apart, the left thigh at right angles to her body and the right askew. The surfaces of the abdomen and thighs were removed. The breasts were cut off, the arms mutilated, and the face was also mutilated beyond recognition. The nose, cheeks, eyebrows, and ears were partially removed. The lips were cut several times. The neck was cut down to the vertebrae. The heart was removed and was not found at the crime scene. Additionally, some of her skin was placed on a table next to the bed.

Neighbors reported that when she was seen earlier that night, she was in the company of a man who wore a long dark coat, dark felt hat, dark jacket, and trousers, boots, linen shirt collar, and gloves, and had a mustache. He was estimated to be about 35 years of age and about 5 feet 7 inches tall.

Medical Report

Medical reports stated that the face was covered with a sheet at the time of the killing. One breast was found by her right foot, and the killer placed a kidney under her head. The liver was situated between her feet. The thighs were on a table next to the bed with the skin already mentioned.

The arms and hands had defensive wounds on them, and there were also abrasions on the back of the hands. The thorax was opened; the lower part of one lung was ripped and torn off. The cause of death was the cutting of the carotid artery.

❖ WHO WAS JACK THE RIPPER?

This is a question that has, at least at this time, no definitive answer (see Table 13.10). Competent minds for the last century have pondered this question, and still the case of Jack the Ripper has not been resolved.

In examining the suspects in the Jack the Ripper case, various profiles have been offered. For example, a profile by Paley (1996) offered the following:

Jack the Ripper was a white male, 28–36 years of age, who lived or worked in the Whitechapel area, and probably worked at a sort of job in which he could vicariously experience his destructive fantasies, such as a butcher. He would have come from a family with a weak, passive or absent father, and would have probably suffered from some sort of physical disability, such as a speech impediment. He would have displayed a strong dislike to prostitutes, and during

Table 13.10   Selected Suspects in the Jack the Ripper Killings

Dr. Thomas Cream	Cream was at one time considered a viable suspect. Later information revealed that he was hanged in 1892 but was in prison in the United States at the time of the Jack the Ripper killings.
Jill the Ripper	Sir Arthur Conan Doyle, creator of Sherlock Holmes, believes that Jack the Ripper was a woman. One reason for this belief was that he thought she was a nurse and had medical knowledge to remove the body parts taken by the killer.
George Chapman	He was hanged in 1903 for the murders of his wives by poison. There is no evidence that ties him to the murders of Jack the Ripper. But just as he was about to swing from the gallows, he shouted, "I am Jack . . ."
Dr. Roslyn Donston	A surgeon in a hospital two blocks from the murder scene of Polly Nichols. He was also known to associate with prostitutes, and one news clipping identified him as Jack the Ripper. No evidence supported this accusation.
Prince Edward Albert	The Duke of Clarence and the grandson of Queen Victoria. There was a theory that the royal household was covering up the prince's involvement in the murders. He died in 1892 of syphilis or the flu.
Montague Druitt	School teacher, barrister, drug user, Druitt was strongly considered to be Jack the Ripper. He allegedly committed suicide by jumping into the Thames River.
James Maybrick	Maybrick is a new suspect because of the alleged "Jack the Ripper Diary." He was a cotton broker, moving about England from Liverpool to London and doing business in the Whitechapel area. He appears to be a main suspect in many people's minds.
Dr. Francis Tumblety	An Irish American outlaw, he was in London at the time of the murders. He left London in 1888 after being arrested. He escaped custody.
Aaron Kosminski	A Polish Jew and a resident of Whitechapel, he was known to be a person who was insane and held great hatred for women. He spent his final years in an insane asylum, where he died.

the course of the investigation, he would have been interviewed by the authorities, and consequently overlooked or eliminated as a suspect. His ordinary, neat and orderly appearance would not have fitted the prevailing impression of the Ripper as being an odd or somehow ghoulish-looking man. (pp. 3–4)

John Douglas, a former agent with the FBI, offered his profile of Jack the Ripper in his book, *The Cases That Haunt Us* (2000). Similar to the one cited above, Douglas said that Jack the Ripper was a White male, 28–36 years of age, who lived or worked in or near the Whitechapel area. His parents were dysfunctional; the mother was domineering, sexually promiscuous, and possibly an alcoholic. The father was passive or absent. As a child, Jack was a loner and also a fire-setter who was cruel to animals. As he grew into adulthood, he craved power and domination over others. He worked as a butcher, mortician helper, a hospital worker, or a morgue attendant. An asocial personality, he dressed well to show his wealth and social status. He carried a weapon because he was paranoid. He had been married in the past and infected with a sexually transmitted disease. Outwardly he appeared to be quiet, shy, obedient, and neat in appearance. He also frequented the local pubs in Whitechapel.

But what do you think? We have provided you with information not only in this chapter but also earlier in the text to help you examine this case and develop your own and personal profile of this famous unresolved murder case. Apply the information that you have learned from the previous chapters and the details of the case from this chapter to do so.

❖ CONCLUSION

The case of Jack the Ripper has fascinated criminologists and other interested persons throughout the world for the last century. Despite the case being closed by the local police, Web sites, books, articles, conferences, and seminars have been offered for public consumption in attempts to discover the identity of Jack. None has been successful. One of the latest endeavors has been the publication of the diary of Jack the Ripper in the book *The Diary of Jack the Ripper: The Discovery, the Investigation, the Debate* (Harrison, 1993). In this book, an alleged diary of James Maybrick, the cotton dealer with ties to London, Liverpool, and the United States is suggested as Jack's. Serious debate is now dedicated to the authenticity of this diary. If the diary is authentic, the case of Jack the Ripper may be closed.

Regardless, the serial killings motivated by a perverse sense of sex will continue to be of interest to us who are interested in human behavior and homicide.

❖ REFERENCES

Douglas, J., Burgess, A. W., Burgess, A. G., & Ressler, R. (1992). *Crime classification manual*. Lexington, MA: Lexington Books.

Evans, S., & Skinner, K. (2000). *The ultimate Jack the Ripper companion: An illustrated encyclopedia*. New York: Carrol and Graf.

Harrison, S. (1993). *The diary of Jack the Ripper*. New York: Hyperion.

Paley, B. (1996). *Jack the Ripper: The simple truth*. London: Headline.

Rumbelow, D. (1988). *The complete Jack the Ripper*. New York: Penguin.

14

Lizzie Borden

❖ ❖ ❖

Lizzie Borden took an axe
And gave her mother forty whacks;
When she saw what she had done
She gave her father forty-one!

On August 4, 1892, it was hot in Fall River, Massachusetts, unusually hot for summer in the small town in southeastern Massachusetts. This town was not used to crime, a population of more than 80,000, its industry a mixture of rolling mills, shipping, and manufacturing.

It was not a "sleepy" town with huge elm trees reaching across the streets, one from the other to touch and provide shade for the men and women. It was an industry town, certain to grow. But as history tells us, it would never catch Boston, a larger city within 50 miles, its growth stunted by the other larger cities' magnificent growth and attention to business.

The industrial history of Fall River began in 1811 when Colonel Joseph Durfee and several investors built the first cotton mill. Two years later Troy Mill was built. Fall River and the town's population began to grow. By 1830, the town had a population of over 4,000. This growing trend continued and, by 1872, more new mills and corporations were started.

The abundance of work available in the mills drew people looking for work. They arrived in such vast numbers that by 1900 Fall River had the highest percentage of foreign-born residents of any city in the entire country. These immigrants gave Fall River a great diversity.

A man new to the area, Andrew Borden was a successful businessman. He married his first wife, Sarah Morse, when he was only 23. He moved into his home at 92 Second Street and would later purchase the house in 1871. He would die in that same house 47 years after he first moved in with Sarah. Lizzie Borden was born in 1860; her sister, Emma Borden, was born several years earlier. There was another sister who died as an infant. The mother of Lizzie and Emma died in 1863. Andrew Borden remarried to Abby Gray 2 years later. She, too, died in that house on Second Street.

But let us review the major actors in this popular historical unsolved murder case.

❖ KEY PEOPLE IN THE LIZZIE BORDEN CASE

Lizzie Borden

Lizzie Borden was born on July 19, 1860. Lizzie's mother died when she was 2 years old, and she told many people that she was very

Figure 14.1   Lizzie Borden

close to her father, Andrew. Lizzie had an older sister with whom she lived for almost a decade after the parents' deaths. Lizzie never married, and after her parents' deaths she and her sister sold the family home and moved to a new home, Woodcroft, in a better section of the city. Friends often remarked that Lizzie had always been upset with her father because he had refused to move to a better section of town despite having the money and means to do so.

Lizzie was 32 when the murders occurred. She died of natural causes in 1927 at the age of 67. She left an estate of more than $200,000, which was given to animal-humane societies. She was buried in Oak Grove Cemetery in Fall River with her sister and the other members of the Borden family, including the sister who died in infancy.

Emma Borden

Emma Borden was born on March 1, 1851. She was 8 years older than her sister, Lizzie. She was 12 years old when her mother, Sarah,

Figure 14.2   The Gravestone of Lizzie Borden

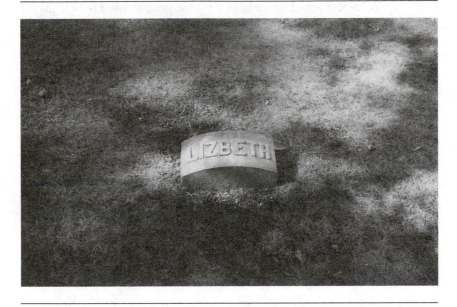

died. Emma Borden was never married, and history tells us that she was never employed. She lived with her parents, then Lizzie, and by herself in the early 1900s until she and Lizzie had a falling out over Lizzie's emerging lifestyle. She bought her own home with a portion of her inheritance from the family estate.

At the time of the murders, Emma Borden had gone to visit friends in a small town about 15 miles away from the Borden household. She came home late at night after being informed that her father and step-mother had been brutally and viciously killed with an ax. She was never considered to be a suspect in this case. Emma Borden remained a silent person in the murder investigation. At one time, some suspected that she was an accomplice of Lizzie, but this was never verified.

At the time of Lizzie's death, Emma Borden, who lived then in New Hampshire, fell and broke her hip. She eventually died within 2 weeks of Lizzie's death.

Andrew Borden

Andrew Jackson Borden, age 69 at the time of his death, was a wealthy man in Fall River. He was the president of the local bank, held several other business interests, was the director of three mills in town, and also owned various real estate properties. He was given to expensive tastes, but he walked to work in the downtown area of Fall River. From reports, it appears that both daughters wanted to live in a more prestigious part of the town, but Mr. Borden would have none of that. He was a self-made man. He started his career as a carpenter, then became a fishmonger, and then a partner in a casket company.

He was twice married, and Lizzie's mother was his first wife. Two years after his first wife passed away, Mr. Borden married his second wife, Abby. They were married for 27 years. Mr. Borden was thought to be a good father, attentive to his children and concerned of their welfare. He worked every day, some say 14 hours a day including weekends, but when he was home he was a devoted family man.

Abby Borden

Andrew Borden's second wife was Abby Borden. When they married, Abby was 37 years old. By the social custom of the time, she was considered to be an old maid.

There was no evidence to suggest that she was a battering or abusive stepmother, but the records suggest that she was a person who did not have a close relationship with her two stepdaughters. Several years after Abby married the father, both children decided to call her Mrs. Borden and kept calling that name until the time of her death.

Mrs. Borden was killed in the upstairs guest bedroom, on her knees and forearms, bludgeoned 18 times (not 40 as the song suggests). The autopsy will enumerate the wounds, the locations, and the significant other data pertinent to the reconstruction of the murder itself.

Bridget Sullivan

Bridget Sullivan was the maid. She moved from Ireland to the United States in 1883. Somewhere in her mid-20s when the murders occurred, she had worked in the Borden household for about 6 years.

Ms. Sullivan did many chores around the Borden home. These included cooking, washing, and general housecleaning, although Mrs. Borden helped with that particular chore. Emma and Lizzie cleaned their own rooms in the house.

Figure 14.3   The Gravestone of Andrew Borden

What was the relationship between Bridget Sullivan and the murders? Probably none. Some have suggested that she was a paid accomplice of Lizzie, but this has never been proven. What we do know is that she testified at the murder trial, and all viewers believed she was telling the truth about Lizzie calling out that her mother (Abby Borden) had been killed.

John Morse

John Morse was the brother of Andrew Borden's first wife. He and Mr. Borden were considered to be close friends. He was at first also considered to be a prime suspect in the murder case. Some people tried to make something out of him coming to town on the day before the murders, but he often came to town to look after his business interests. However, he was not at home at the time of the murders. He left the Borden home after eating breakfast with Mr. and Mrs. Borden and went to town. Several people in town verified his presence in town at the times of the murders, and he was never charged in this case.

After the murders and the trial, Mr. Morse moved to Illinois and then to Iowa, where he lived as a horse breeder.

Hosea M. Knowlton

Mr. Knowlton was the prosecutor in the Borden case. He was the district or commonwealth attorney for the previous 14 years. He had an outstanding reputation in local and state politics and served as a state representative and senator.

William Moody

Mr. Moody was second chair prosecutor in the Lizzie Borden case. He was considered to be an up and rising attorney, although he was also the youngest of all the lawyers involved in the murder case.

George Robinson

Mr. Robinson was the lead defense attorney for Lizzie Borden. He was a former governor in Massachusetts and a well-known, statewide politician. Although he was assisted by another attorney, Andrew Jennings, he was the principal litigator in the murder case. He was 59 years of age at the time of the trial.

❖ THE MURDERS

On the hot summer day in August, 1892, the maid, Bridget Sullivan, was the first to awake. From her apartment on the third floor of the home, she descended the steps to the kitchen, where she started breakfast. Mrs. Borden arrived about 30 minutes later and Andrew Borden came into the kitchen 5 minutes after her. Mr. Borden had carried a slop jar from the couples' bedroom and took it outside beyond the barn to dispose of its contents. The house had no inside plumbing and no electricity.

Bridget fixed breakfast for Mr. and Mrs. Borden. As she was serving them, she noted the presence of John Morse, the brother of Mrs. Borden. He sat down at the kitchen table and they all ate a breakfast of mutton, mutton broth, johnnycakes, coffee, and cookies.

Bridget Sullivan recalls that after breakfast, John Morse and Andrew Borden both left the house. Morse went into town to visit with some relatives. Andrew Borden left to supervise the remodeling of a large business structure that he recently purchased. At about that same time, Lizzie Borden came into the kitchen for breakfast but said that she was not too hungry and wanted some coffee and cookies. Bridget

Figure 14.4   The Home at 92 Second Street Where the Murders Took Place

was ill that morning and went outside into the backyard to vomit. When she came back inside, Mrs. Borden said that she wanted the windows cleaned both inside and out on the first floor. Sullivan stated that she was slightly miffed with Abby Borden since she did not appear to be concerned with the way Bridget was feeling.

Despite her illness Bridget started her chores. The maid said that was the last time she would see Mrs. Borden alive. Ms. Sullivan went to get rags to wash windows. According to testimony of Emma Borden, both sisters left the home. Lizzie came home only after a short period of time and was back by about 9:15. Emma Borden visited friends 15 miles away. She would be contacted by telegram later that day when her parents were found dead. However, she did not rush home, instead coming home late that evening, despite knowing her parents had been murdered. Later, Bridget Sullivan would find Mrs. Borden first in the guest bedroom, where Mr. Morse had spent the night, and then Mr. Borden on the sofa on the first floor.

The maid then testified:

Then I washed the parlor windows on the south side of the house—the Kelly side. This was away from the screen door. Before I started washing, Mrs. Kelly's girl appeared and I was talking to

Figure 14.5   The Sofa Where Andrew Borden's Body Was Found

her at the fence. Then I washed the parlor windows; the two front windows. Between times I went to the barn and got some water. I washed the dining room windows and one parlor window on the side. I went to the barn for water twice while I was on the south side of the house, went 'round by the rear and went three or four times more while I was working in front or on the other side of the house. Then I went past the screen door to the barn. During all that time I did not see anybody come to the house. (court testimony, June 7, 1893, public domain)

She continued with her testimony to the court, adding that she later heard Lizzie Borden in the house on the second floor. Then Mr. Borden came in the home, went into the dining room, and finally went into the lounge.

Miss Lizzie came downstairs and came through the front entry into the dining room. . . . I heard her ask her father if he had any mail . . . but I heard her tell her father that Mrs. Borden had left a note and had gone out. (ibid.)

After finishing the windows, Bridget Sullivan took a nap. She stated that it was 11:15 A.M. Lizzie Borden awakened her, stating that someone had killed her father.

Adelaide Churchill, a widow and a next door neighbor of the Borden's, testified that she had returned from an early morning shopping trip to the town market. When she got home, she saw Bridget Sullivan running over to Dr. Bowen's home and she then went into the house and looked out the window in her kitchen. She then saw Lizzie standing inside the screen door at the side of her house, and Lizzie asked her to come over because someone had killed her father. When she arrived, she saw Lizzie sitting on the chair. The following testimony was given by Ms. Churchill, depicting the events after her arrival at the Borden house. She stated to Lizzie:

"Where is your father?" She said, "In the sitting room." And I said, "Where were you when it happened?" and she said, "I went to the barn to get a piece of iron." I said, "Where is your mother?" She said, "I don't know; she had got a note from someone who is sick but I don't know but she is killed too, for I thought I heard her come in." She said, "Father must have an enemy, for we have all been sick, and we think the milk has been poisoned. . . ." (court testimony, June 8, 1893, public domain)

Ms. Churchill continued with her testimony and said,

Miss Russell [another neighbor] came soon afterwards, and Lizzie said she wished someone would try to find Mrs. Borden. So Bridget and I started. She led the way, and as I went upstairs, I turned my head to the left, and when I got up so my eyes were level with the front hall, I could see across the floor of the spare room. At the far side, I saw something that looked like the form of a person. I turned and went back. I don't know what I did. I went into the dining room and made some noise or other, and Mrs. Russell said, "Is there another?" I said, "Yes, she is up there." (ibid.)

❖ THE CRIME SCENE

The Borden home was located in town. It was a three-story frame home. The first floor contained a front lobby, the kitchen, and a front room, a sitting room, and a dining area. The second floor held the bedrooms of Mr. and Mrs. Borden, Lizzie and Emma Borden, and a guest bedroom, where John Morse spent the night before the murder. This was also the room where Mrs. Borden was found dead on the floor between the bed and dresser. Mr. and Mrs. Borden's bedroom was accessible only by the stairway that ran off the kitchen. The other two bedrooms were accessible by the stairway in the front of the home.

On the third floor was the bedroom of Bridget Sullivan, the housekeeper.

The Autopsies

Autopsies were done on both victims. The reports are far different in respect to what is contained in today's autopsy reports. The autopsies

Table 14.1   Timeline of the Murders, August 4, 1892

6:00 A.M.	Bridget Sullivan leaves her room to go to the kitchen to fix breakfast.
7:00 A.M.	Andrew and Abby Borden come downstairs for breakfast.
	John Morse leaves the guest bedroom to go to the kitchen for breakfast.
8:15 A.M.	Lizzie comes down to the kitchen for breakfast.
8:45 A.M.	John Morse leaves the home to go to town to visit friends; Mr. Borden locks the doors.
9:00 A.M.	Mrs. Borden is killed.
9:15 A.M.	Andrew Borden leaves home to walk to town, 5 minutes away.
9:30 A.M.	Andrew Borden gets back home.
9:45 A.M.	Andrew Borden goes into the sitting room to take a nap on the sofa.
11:10 A.M.	Lizzie calls for Bridget Sullivan to tell her Mr. Borden is dead.
	Lizzie does not come into the sitting room; sees her father from a distance.
11:15 A.M.	Dr. Bowen, a neighbor, comes to the house to discover Mr. Borden.
11:20 A.M.	The police are called.
11:30 A.M.	Morse comes back to the Borden house.
11:45 A.M.	Dr. Dolan, the medical examiner, comes to the house.
1:00 P.M.	Mr. Borden is taken to the morgue.

Table 14.2   Dateline for the Lizzie Borden Murder Case

December 25, 1845	Mr. Andrew Borden marries Sarah Morse, mother of Lizzie and Emma Borden.
March 1, 1851	Emma Borden is born.
July 19, 1860	Lizzie Borden is born.
March 26, 1863	Sarah Borden dies.
June 6, 1865	Mr. Borden marries Abby Gray.
1889	Bridget Sullivan starts to work for the Borden family.
August 3, 1892	Lizzie tries to buy some poison from a local drug store.
August 3, 1892	John Morse arrives at the Borden home.
August 4, 1892	The murders of Andrew Borden and Abby Borden.
August 9–11, 1892	An inquest is held to consider the murders.
August 11, 1892	Lizzie Borden is arrested for the murders.
August 23, 1892	Preliminary hearing finds probable cause.
November 31, 1892	Grand jury indicts Lizzie Borden.
June 5, 1893	Lizzie Borden murder trial opens.
June 20, 1892	Jury finds Lizzie Borden "not guilty."
June 1, 1927	Lizzie Borden dies at age 67.
June 13, 1927	Emma Borden dies.

done by the medical examiner, W. A. Dolan, described injuries, but unlike autopsy reports of today, they did not offer a definite cause of death.

Autopsy of Andrew J. Borden

Record of autopsy held at Oak Grove Cemetery on the body of Andrew J. Borden. Autopsy performed by W. A. Dolan, Medical Examiner, assisted by Dr. F. W. Draper. Witnesses F. W. Draper of Boston and John W. Leary of Fall River. Clerk E. E. Crone of Fall River. Time of Autopsy 11.15 A.M. August 11, 1892, one week after death.

Body that of a man well nourished. Age seventy years. 5 feet 11 inches in height. No stiffness of death on account of decomposition, which was far advanced. Inguinal hernia on right side.

Abdomen had already been opened. Artificial teeth in upper jaw. There were no marks of violence on body, but on the left side of head and face there were numerous incised wounds and one contused wound penetrating into the brain.

The wounds beginning at the nose and to the left were as follows:

Incised wound 4 inches long beginning at lower border of left nasal bone and reaching to lower edge of lower jaw, cutting through nose, upper lip, lower lip, and slightly into bone of upper and lower jaw.

Began at internal angle of eye and extended to one and 3/8 inches of lower edge of jaw, beginning 4 and ½ inches in length, cutting through the tissues and into the bone.

Began at lower border of lower eyelid cutting through the tissues and into the cheekbone, 2 inches long and one and 3/8 inches deep.

Began two inches above upper eyelid ½ inches external to wound three, thence downward and outward through middle of left eyebrow through the eyeball cutting it completely in halves, and excising a piece of the skull one and ½ inches in length by ½ inch in width. Length of wound 4 and ½ inches.

Began on level of same wound superficial scalp wound downward and outward 2 inches long.

Parallel with this ¼ inch long, downward and outward.

Began ½ inch below No. 5, 3 inches in length downward and outward, penetrating cavity of skull. On top of skull was a transverse fracture of 4 and ½ inches in length.

Began directly above No. 7 and one inch in length downward and outward.

Directly posterior to No. 8 beginning at ear and extending 4 inches long, 2 inches in width, crushing bone and carry bone into brain. Also crushing from without in.

Directly behind this and above it, and running downwards backward 2 inches long superficially.

The general direction of all these wounds is parallel to each other.

HEAD. Right half of top of skull removed. Brain found to be completely decomposed; and in fluid condition.

CHEST. Chest and abdomen opened by one incision extending from neck to pubis. Right lung glued to ribs in front. Left lung normal. Heart normal.

ABDOMEN. Spleen normal, kidney normal, liver and bladder normal. Stomach and portion of liver has been removed. Lower part of large bowel filled with solid formed feces. Feces also in lower part of small bowel. (Public Record, Coroner's Office, Fall River, Massachusetts.)

Autopsy of Abby D. Borden

Record of autopsy on body of Abby D. Borden, aged 64 years. Thursday August 11, 1892. At 12:35 P.M. One week after death.

The autopsy was performed by W. A. Dolan, Medical Examiner, assisted by Dr. F. W. Draper, and witnessed by F. W. Draper of Boston, and J. H. Leary of Fall River. Clerk of Autopsy D. E. Come of Fall River.

Body that of a female very well nourished and fleshy 64 years of age. 5 feet 3 inches in height. No stiffness of death, owing to decomposition, which was far advanced. Abdomen had already been opened. Artificial teeth in upper jaw. No marks of violence on front of body. On back of body was

FIRST an incised wound 2 and ½ inches in depth. The lower angle of the wound was over his [sic] spine and four inches below the junction of neck with body, and extending thence upward and outward to the left. On the forehead and bridge of the nose were three contused wounds. Those on the forehead being oval, lengthwise with the body.

SECOND The contusion on bridge of nose was one inch in width.

THIRD On the forehead one was one inch above left eyebrow, one and ¼ inches long by 3/8 inch in width, and the other one and

¼ inches above the eyebrow, and one and ½ inches long by ¼ inch wide. On the head there were 18 distinct wounds, incising and crushing, and all but four were on the right side. Counting from left to right with the face downwards, the wounds were as follows:

Was a glancing scalp two inches in length by one and ½ inches in width, situated 3 inches above left ear hole, cut from above downwards and did not penetrate the skull.

Was exactly on top of the skull one inch long, and penetrating through the skull.

Was 2 and ¼ inches long above occipital protuberance and one and ½ inches long.

Was parallel to No. 4 and one and ½ inches long.

Was just above and parallel to No. 5, and one and ¼ inches in length.

Was just above and parallel to No. 5, and one and ¼ inches long. On top of skull was a traverse fracture two inches in length, a continuation of a penetrating wound.

Was 2 inches long and two inches behind ear hole crushing and carrying bone into the brain.

Was 2 and ½ inches long.

Was 2 and ¾ inches long.

Was one and ¾ inches long.

Was ½ inch long.

Was 2 and ¼ inches long.

Was one and ¾ inches long.

Was 2 and ½ inches long.

Reached from middle line of head towards the ear 5 inches long.

Was one inch long.

Was ½ inch long.

Was 3 and ½ inches long.

These wounds on the right side were parallel, the direction being mostly from in front backwards.

HEAD. There was a hole in the right side of the skull 4 and ½ to 5 and ¼ inches, through which the brain evacuated in fluid condition being entirely decomposed.

CHEST. The chest and abdomen was opening by one incision from chin to pubis.

LUNGS. Bound down behind but normal.

HEART. Normal.

ABDOMEN. Stomach and part of the bowel had been removed. Spleen and intestines were normal. Womb was the seat of a small fibroid tumor on anterior surface. Fallopian tubes and ovaries normal. Lower bowel empty. Upper portion of small bowel containing undigested food. (Public Record, Coroner's Office, Fall River, Massachusetts.)

❖ ADDITIONAL THOUGHTS

The case of Lizzie Borden has never been solved. Some believe that Lizzie did not kill her father and stepmother, and the court found Lizzie not guilty. There were no additional murders of this ilk in Fall River after that time. Only a short time after Lizzie was found not guilty, she and Emma Borden moved out of the house and into their own home in a better part of town.

There was no physical evidence to connect Lizzie Borden with the murders, but there was a question raised by the prosecutor about a dress that Lizzie burned in the kitchen several days after the murders. She stated that the dress was dirty and stained and she could not get it clean. So she decided to burn it. There was some confusion in court about the existence of the dress, its color, and the character of the

Figure 14.6   Indictment of Lizzie Borden for Murder: December 2, 1892

Indictment

Commonwealth

vs.

Lizzie Andrew Borden

MURDER

Commonwealth of Massachusetts

BRISTOL SS. At the Superior Court begun and holden at Taunton within and for said county of Bristol, on the first Monday of November, in the year of our Lord one thousand eight hundred and ninety-two.

The jurors for the said commonwealth , on their oath present, - That Lizzie Andrew Borden of Fall River in the County of Bristol, at Fall River in the County of Bristol, on the fourth day of August in the year eighteen hundred and ninety-two, in and upon one Andrew Jackson Borden, feloniously, willfully and of her malice aforethought, an assault did make, and with a certain weapon, to wit, a sharp cutting instrument, the name and amore particular description of which is to the jurors unknown, her, the said Abby Durfee Borden, feloniously, willfully , and of her malice aforethought, did strike out, cut, beat and bruise in and upon the head of her, the said Abby Durfee Borden, giving to her, the said Abby Durfee Borden, divers to wit, twenty mortal wounds, of which said mortal wounds the said Abby Durfee Borden then and there instantly died.

And so the jurors aforesaid, upon their oaths aforesaid, do say that the said Lizzie Andrew Borden the said Abby Durfee Borden in manner and in form aforesaid then and there feloniously, willfully, and of her malice aforethought did kill and murder against the peace of the said Commonwealth and contrary to the form of the statute in such case made and provided.

A True bill

HOSEA M. KNOWLTON,   HENRY A. BODMAN,

District Attorney.   Foreman of the Grand Jury.

---

stain. Nonetheless, it was never ascertained if the dress had blood-stains on it.

Lizzie Borden claimed in court that she was innocent and did not kill her father or stepmother. Moreover, she added that she knew of no one who would have done such an act.

But there were other suspects.

Suspect 1

Several months before the murders, someone had broken into the Borden home. Some things were taken, including a small amount of money. For this reason, Mr. Borden decided to keep all the doors locked even during the day when someone was home. The doors inside the home were also kept locked. The burglar was never caught, but some believed that this person came back once again and was confronted by someone at home. Who was home at this time? Lizzie, Bridget Sullivan, and Mr. and Mrs. Borden. There was no sign of a break-in, but this theory still has some believers. Gross (1963) offers a novel theory that the murders were committed by Lizzie Borden and Bridget Sullivan. He further adds that Sullivan was paid money to go back to Ireland, which she never did. There was also a discussion of a death bed confession by Bridget Sullivan, which has never been verified.

Mr. John Morse

Mr. Morse also is considered a viable candidate. He was a frequent visitor to the Borden home and knew its layout. He always stayed in the guest room on the second floor of the home and next to the bedroom of Lizzie.

What could have been the motive for Morse killing the Bordens? Some believe that it was money. There was some thought that Morse's business ventures were not going as well as he would have liked and an influx of money would have been beneficial to his business enterprises. There is no real evidence that Morse was the killer. His whereabouts at the time of the murders was verified by a relative whom he was visiting in town, but it was only 5–10 minutes away on foot. Morse was seen getting back to the Borden home at 11:30 A.M., the morning of the murders.

Emma Borden

The sister of Lizzie was at one time considered a suspect. Many believed that Emma and Lizzie had planned the killings together. It was believed that Emma Borden was not the actual killer, and it was verified that she was 15 miles away at the times of the killings. However, the thought prevalent in many people's minds was that there was a great deal of hostility between Emma Borden and Lizzie Borden and the stepmother. Actually, about 6 years before the killings, the sisters stopped calling her "mother" and started calling her "Mrs. Borden."

This split in the relationship developed from Mr. Borden buying a home for a relative of his wife's and not giving the daughters the same amount of money. Spiering (1984) offers a theory that Emma Borden was the killer with her sister as an accomplice. He further offers the "false alibi" that Emma was 15 miles away at the time of the murders but was really hiding in the upstairs of the Borden home, committing the murders and then driving back to Fairhaven to await the telegram. The author further offers a thought that while both sisters were involved in the murders, they protected each other at the trial. However, years later there developed a rift between the two over Lizzie's possible lesbianism, and Emma Borden left her sister and moved into her own private home.

Regardless, Emma Borden was never charged with the murders.

Unknown Laborer

The same afternoon immediately following the discovery of Mr. and Mrs. Borden, police arrested a laborer in downtown Fall River. He was considered a suspect in the case but was released after questioning.

William Borden

William was the slightly mentally challenged illegitimate son of Andrew Borden. He and Mr. Borden had a violent argument several days before the killings. The content of the argument concerned itself with Mr. Borden not giving William any money from Borden's estate. There was no resolution to the argument, and both men were angry with each other at the time of the killing. No one seems to think of William as a viable suspect, principally because of his mental disability. Brown (1992) offers the theory that the sisters, John Morse, the defense attorney for Lizzie Borden, and Dr. Bowen all knew of the crime committed by William and decided to keep the killer protected, letting Lizzie stand trial because they all knew she would be found not guilty.

There were no other viable suspects in this case.

❖ CONCLUSION

To the time of her death Lizzie Borden denied killing her father and stepmother. Despite the efforts of the commonwealth of Massachusetts and the commonwealth attorney's office, they were never able to prove she did do it. Truly she had the means and opportunity, and perhaps even a motive, but there was never enough proven in court to convince the jury that she was guilty of parricide. Maybe it was because she actually did not do the crime, maybe because there was no physical evidence to convince the jury that she indeed did do the crime, and maybe because the prevailing thought of the time was that women were incapable of committing such heinous crimes. Whatever the reason(s), Lizzie Borden was found not guilty.

So if Lizzie Borden did not commit the crime, who did? What do you think? Bridget Sullivan had the opportunity and was personally upset with Abby Borden at the time of the killing because Abby was not sympathetic to her health at the time, but was that enough? Someone could have come into the Borden home unseen and left undetected. John Morse had the opportunity to come back to the house before, during, or after his visit with his relative in town, only a short walk from the home.

As we look at the wounds received by Mr. and Mrs. Borden we can draw some conclusions about the relationship, if any, between the

Figure 14.7   The House Where Lizzie Lived After the Murders

Bordens and the killer. Since many were personally violent and directed toward the head, one would believe that there was a close relationship between the killer and the victim; however, that is mere conjecture at this point. Also, we know that the upstairs guest bedroom was accessible only by the front stairway, and the bedroom of the parents was accessible only by the rear stairway. Did the killer know this and was just fortunate to pick the right stairway and come upon Mrs. Borden cleaning up the bedroom after Mr. Morse had slept in it the night before? Did the previous burglary of the house have any connection with the murders?

These and other questions are important to consider in developing a psychological profile. What do you think?

❖ REFERENCES

Brown, A. (1992). *Lizzie Borden*. New York: Dell.

Gross, G. (1963). The Pearson-Radin controversy over the guilt of Lizzie Borden. In G. Gross (Ed.), *Masterpieces of murder: An Edmund Pearson true crime reader*. New York: Little Brown and Company.

15

The Victim in Criminal Profiling

❖ ❖ ❖

Perhaps no single element in the profiling process has been neglected more than the victim. The Behavioral Science Unit (BSU) of the FBI has been active in securing data regarding the social and behavioral characteristics, as well as the reputations, of victims. These are crucial in the profiling enterprise, although it has been noted that the victim profile and victim activity have been frequently neglected, for whatever reason, as reported elements.

The victim is usually the only person to witness the crime, and if alive, the victim can tell a great deal about what happened. If the victim is deceased, however, the crime scene must tell the story. In either instance, therefore, the profiler should be as much interested in the activities of the victim as in any element of the submitted package of information accompanying the request for a profile.

❖   ELEMENTS IN THE VICTIM PROFILING PROCESS

To appraise a crime without some knowledge of the victim is certainly remiss. Unfortunately, however, victim information is frequently lacking in substance. The usual report received from an agency contains varying degrees of information about the type of weapon used, the position of the victim's body, the amount and type of physical evidence, the autopsy, and other important items of the case. It is equally important to include certain cognitive elements concerning the lifestyles, habits, oddities, friends, and so on of the victim. Table 15.1 lists the elements important to victim profiling.

Physical Traits

Perhaps the most obvious element in the profiling process is a physical description of the victim. Much care must be taken in gathering an accurate description of the victim's basic physical characteristics. Age, for example, could be a critical victim selection factor. Jerry Brudos, a serial killer and serial rapist from Oregon, selected young women from 19 to 23 years of age.

The sex of the victim is often the overarching element in the selection process. Because the young and women are typically considered to be more vulnerable, they are recurrently victimized. More than one serial rapist and murderer related a conscious effort to select a victim predicated on perceived vulnerability.

The type of dress may be of some significance for selection. For example, one serial murderer designated his victims because they

Table 15.1   Important Elements in Victim Profiling

- Physical traits
- Marital status
- Personal lifestyle
- Occupation
- Education
- Personal demographics
- Medical history
- Psychosexual history
- Court history
- Last activities

looked like prostitutes. None of the four women he abducted were prostitutes, but they were all selected because in his mental reality they appeared to be prostitutes, so they must be prostitutes. Their style of dress signaled their apparent vocation and, in effect, their death.

Hairstyle and hair color may also be preeminent for the violent personal offender. Recall Ted Bundy's reported fondness for your college-aged women with long hair parted in the middle. One serialist reported his preference to us: "blond hair only" (authors' files).

Marital Status

As much information as possible should be known about the victim's marital status. Too often, the report will simply state "married." Obviously, this is not adequate. In a recent case, the nude body of a woman was found along a rural road. She had not been raped, but she had been shot five times. It was reported that she had been happily married for 15 years. There were no children. The police report mentioned the couple had been regarded as pillars of the community and were civic oriented and involved. Employed, she was athletic and went to an exercise center two evenings a week. All outward appearance indicated a marriage that was committed and happy.

A statement by the homicide detective said the woman, an introvert, had no personal friends and no known enemies. To have an attractive young woman, athletic, a golfer with some promise in her youth but with no close personal friends seemed unusual. Her sole contact with the other sex, beyond her husband, was an exercise class at the local health club. The detective discovered several leads predicated on the result of a determination that regardless of how it appeared, all was not well within the marriage. The profiler noted this inconsistency in his report to the police. Closer investigation found a husband with a very jealous disposition and a wife with an outside love interest. One small, seemingly insignificant statement signaled an inconsistency that led to the successful resolution of the case.

Personal Lifestyle

A victim's daily activities could yield vital information concerning the victim's character. These data may also serve as an index of the type of people who not only make up a circle of friends but also the many others with whom the victim may have come into contact.

Hobbies, sports interests, drug use, frequenting bars, drinking habits, or any recent changes in behavior or personality may also be indicators of consequence. Many victims have significant others who serve as sources of such information. They should be queried regarding any sudden or recent change in the social life or personality of the victim. This information may serve as an index of not only availability but susceptibility.

Occupation

The occupation and employment of a victim expands the network of relationships. The number of people involved in a business relationship with the victim, not only on a professional basis but also on a personal one, can, understandably, be quite large. Nonetheless, a careful examination of the number of persons having frequent contact with the victim may lead not only to a better discernment of the victim's personality but also of the victim's personal organizations.

Special training and education may indicate organizations, associations, conferences, or meetings in which the victim may have been active. Groups of people at these occasions share common interests. Special training also indicates an aggregate of people temporarily together for a common purpose.

The investigator should not ignore the past positions and employment of a victim, because there too has existed a network of friends, enemies, or acquaintances.

A profile was completed recently on a young woman who was repeatedly stabbed in the neck. In the setting where she worked for the last 7 years, one fellow worker remarked that there was a male coworker who had tried unsuccessfully to date the victim. Also the victim had once stated that if anything ever happened to her, "John would probably be the one to kill me." From talking with fellow workers, two viable leads were developed. This is obviously nothing new to experienced homicide investigators; it does help, however, in painting a picture of the victim with an eye toward understanding both the victim's personality and the type of person who would commit such an act.

Education

It is important to realize not only the extent of the victim's education but also the various schools and programs attended. As with occupation, education widens the network of acquaintances. Ted Bundy, for example, was thought to be in the same psychology class as Lynda Ann Healy. Although not verified by school officials at the University of Washington, this connection was reported in several different sources, including in an interview with Ann Rule (author of *The Stranger Beside Me* and friend of Ted Bundy) in 1987. Rule also related that Healy had shopped at the same grocery store where Bundy had worked as a stock boy, which was two blocks away from where Healy lived and was subsequently murdered. As a law student living on a college campus, Ted Bundy was able to associate with young women who would be vulnerable and easy to kill.

The intelligence of the victim may serve as an indicator of the type of people with whom she or he associated: People often associate with those of like intelligence. This may be especially important when the attack occurs in a process-focused orientation and away from the home. Also remember that many times victims are victims of opportunity and therefore little stalking may occur. As more stalking of the victim is evident, certain elements are more viable and helpful than others.

Personal Demographics

The location of the victim's home may play an important role in the manner in which the victim was attacked. It may be undeniably true that many crimes of a violent nature occur in lower-class areas with high crime rates. If the victim resides in such a neighborhood, then this becomes valuable information.

Past residences are also valid indicators of the victim's housing pattern, selected because of preference or necessity. Useful information may be obtained from a thorough canvassing of the neighborhoods of previous areas of residence. Past neighbors and friends can lend an appraisal of the victim's lifestyle and circle of friends. The same names may appear, connoting a continued relationship.

The investigator must be aware of the neighborhood's complexity. Racial composition is one item that should be carefully taken into account. Although it is true that most rapes and murders occur within the perpetrator's race, if the racial composition of the victim's neighborhood is radically different from the victim's own race, several possibilities may immediately arise that may account for the victim's living in a particular area.

Medical History

The obvious benefit from a victim's medical history is that it could yield presence of communicative illnesses, such as venereal disease. It was stated in one interview that one of Bundy's early victims had gonorrhea; he did not test positive for this sexual disease. The dental records of a deceased victim could lead to the identification of a corpse, especially if there is an advanced state of decomposition. The dental records proved invaluable in the identification of Susan Rancourt, an alleged Bundy victim, when she was found a year after she was reported missing.

The mental health history of a victim should be carefully investigated. This record could supply valuable information regarding the victim's psychological background as well as other persons with whom the victim could have come into contact. It may also serve as an indicator of the behavior exhibited by the victim consistent with daily life and activities. Some behavior may be commonplace with some people but quite inappropriate with others.

Psychosocial History

All people have some fears. Some people have more than others, but all of us have some irrational fears. Some people may feel quite fearful of high places, elevators, restaurants located on top floors, and so on. A list of such fears gathered from friends, relatives, and acquaintances might supply a personality profile that will give the profiler and the police a better understanding of the victim's personality.

Psychosexual History

The victim's sexual history might also provide a clue to the crime. For example, a young woman dated several men, took showers with them, involved herself in mutual oral sex and masturbation activities, but she would not have vaginal sex with the men. She was "saving" herself for her husband. The victim was found dead in her bedroom, raped and repeatedly stabbed. The information developed in this case was important because it opened the case for another avenue of analysis. It was determined that the original suspect was not guilty of the crime; another suspect was developed and the case was later resolved.

A firm understanding of the personality assessment of the victim is also significant. The personality, as stated earlier, is the sum total of what the person is. It is not static. The personality of any individual, male or female, victim or not, will change subtly over time. The essence of the personality will remain the same over time, but there may be some minor changes. For this reason, a personality profile should be obtained not only from current sources but also from sources outside the present time frame.

From an examination of the personality of the victim, a picture may be drawn of the type of associates with whom a murdered victim may have been involved or to whom she or he had been exposed. The importance of a full understanding of the personality cannot be stressed too strongly.

Court History

As vital as it is to understand the type of person the victim was, equally important is to realize the experiences the victim may have had with the criminal justice system. For this reason, the investigator should be aware of any past arrest records, court appearances (as offender, victim, or witness), and any pending cases. In acquiring this information, the profiler will have a more complete portrait of the victim.

Victim's Last Activities

In the development of any psychological profiling, special attention should be directed to the victim's activities, phone calls, meetings made or missed, or anything that appears to be out of the ordinary from the victim's usual pattern of daily activities. In other words, did the victim do something unique today that alerted someone to the victims' vulnerability and availability?

❖ CONCLUSION

This chapter offers insight into the role of the victim as it relates to the crime itself. It must be borne in mind that regardless of daily activities, lifestyle, interaction with the criminal justice system, or sociological or psychological aspects that conflict with the lifestyle or personal preferences of the profiler, the victim must be considered an integral component in the profiling process—he or she has an integral part in the crime that has been committed. Just as the crime scene, a disposal site in a murder case, special words spoken during the crime, and so on all have import to the profiling process, for a full and complete understanding of the crime, the victim must be added to the picture.

16

The Future of Criminal Profiling

❖ ❖ ❖

Additional Uses for Profiling

Education and Training for Profiling

Computerized Monitoring

Computerized Profiling

Online Graduate Programs, Seminars, and Degrees

Conclusion

Τhe future of psychological profiling is becoming more and more promising as the "art" of profiling becomes better. By utilizing the sciences of psychology, sociology, psychiatry, and criminology, profilers are getting better at their work. Also, the number of cases that are being submitted for profiling appears to be increasing. Once viewed with some skepticism, many law enforcement professionals are becoming more confident in the information submitted on their cases. They view it as one additional tool in the criminal investigation process. We must always stress that psychological profiling by itself has never solved a crime; it is only one tool.

Of course, many are still reluctant to accept profiling as a reliable and valued tool. Godwin (1978) stated that psychological profiling served little purpose in the investigation of crime and offered:

> Nine out of ten of the profiles ... are vapid. They play at blind man's bluff; groping in all directions in the hope of touching a sleeve. . . . Those [the police] require hard data: names, faces, fingerprints, locations, and times. None of which they [profilers] can offer. (p. 276)

He went on to describe how profiles themselves are of little use in the identification of murderers: "Unfortunately, this tool, no matter how expertly implemented, is inherently limited in its ability to help solve crime" (p. 175).

As we have noted, profiling is best considered a starting point for the investigation of particular crimes; we make no claim that it should stand on its own as the sole forensic tool in criminal cases.

❖ ADDITIONAL USES FOR PROFILING

Historically, the preponderance of requests submitted to the FBI have sought information regarding homicides and rapes. Other crimes include child molestation, bank robberies, kidnapping, and other forms of violent crimes.

Many profiles have been developed by the FBI as well as other profilers concerning different forms of violent predators. Certain criminals such as Westley Dodd, a mysoped or sadistic child offender, or Edmund Kemper, a serial killer, have cooperated with law enforcement and profilers to develop profiles of like offenders. Dr. Al Carlisle, the former prison psychologist for Gary Gilmore and Ted Bundy in Utah State Prison, spent many hours with Dodd, interviewing this killer of three small children, to attempt to understand the mind and mentality of the child killer. Dodd would share with Carlisle his many violent and sadistic fantasies. It was from these interviews with a real expert in the field of child murder that information was gleaned that would be of invaluable help to the investigator.

Other researchers have developed a generic profile for the obscene phone caller and the obscene letter writer (Casey-Owens, 1984), the suicidal personality (Holmes & Holmes, 2005), and many others.

Thus through the uses of profiles for cases other than murder and rape, perhaps the role of the psychological profiler will gain more acceptance in the field of criminal justice investigation. And the more acceptance gained, the more the use of profiling will become more widely accepted and used more routinely to help investigators deal with other types of offenders.

❖ EDUCATION AND TRAINING FOR PROFILING

There is nothing mysterious or magical about the art of psychological profiling. It is based on paying attention to details and looking for nonphysical evidence. Just as the main character in the TV show *Psych* pays attention to details, the profiler does the same thing. The "artist" enters the scene and starts with the big picture, realizing that the offender is doing the best he can do under the circumstances and is, in a manner, offering the alert investigator clues to the resolution to the case.

We will be the first to agree that psychological profiling is an art, not simply a science. By that we mean that two plus two in a crime scene does not always equal four. It may equal five or five hundred. That is where the art comes into play.

But there must be some education offered to make sense of the art and to offer clues to understanding the mind and mentality of the seriously violent offender. Both authors have experience in the academic classroom, and we have heard many times a student say when we present crime scenes, "The professor really knows his stuff. He must be really smart—but I can't understand how the clues presented provide evidence to reach their conclusions about the killer or fantasy/motive behind the violence." On the contrary, we believe that a truly intelligent professor is careful to teach in a comprehensive manner to students. Academicians and other professionals are infamous for creating jargon that protects their knowledge—as well as their status—from close examination. This is true of many fields and disciplines, including medicine, psychiatry, psychology, law enforcement, and it has recently emerged in profiling. Some would like others to believe that profiling can be done only by a select few who have special and unique education and training somehow gained through osmosis as a result of close association with the "masters."

Our message here is that profiling can be done by many different people. Touted "authorities," many of whom sit behind desks hundreds of miles from the crime investigations and scenes on which they consult, may lend insight into certain crimes, but no preponderance of empirical evidence exists to support the position that police investigators with some knowledge of the social and behavioral sciences cannot just as reliably profile their own cases. Many have done so on a small scale for years. In seminars across the nation, we always stress that profiling can and should be done by those who are closest to the crimes, the police. Again, we emphasize: There is nothing magical or mysterious about the profiling process.

To develop a profile of the perpetrator of a violent crime, one needs to have knowledge of sociology, psychology, psychiatry, and criminology and the ability to blend the theories of these disciplines. No one has a monopoly on such knowledge. Common sense combined with sound social and behavioral concepts can yield valuable and reliable results. Unfortunately, sometimes law enforcement turf issues hinder the profiling process, and sometimes the successful resolution of a case is impeded by the individuals refusing to accept the opinions of others, especially those outside of their agency or jurisdiction.

❖ COMPUTERIZED MONITORING

The computer revolution has arrived in our world. It controls our world. The Internet provides instant information for us, information that tells us how to build bombs or get a date for the next weekend.

Law enforcement and the criminal justice system are now intimately involved with the computer. Federal agencies use computers for tracking offenders and exchanging information at the touch of the Enter button on the computer keyboard. For example, in Kentucky, one can easily access the Kentucky State Police homepage and see how many sex offenders live in one's zip code, or even on one's street. The Drug Enforcement Administration (DEA) uses a tracking system called the Drug Abuse Warning Network (DAWN), and there are many other examples of such systems operating within the United States today.

❖ COMPUTERIZED PROFILING

Although the profiling process is in part an art that can be practiced only by humans, in the near future a computerized profiling program might help law enforcement personnel to define quickly and efficiently the types of personalities associated with such violent crimes as lust murder, rape, and serial murder. Certainly, the examination of a crime scene requires a human element, but computers can be used to analyze the data accumulated by humans and to summarize the analysis in a series of statements that can provide some basic information about an unknown subject or suspect. A profiler makes calculated and educated guesses—these are more than wild guesses, but they are guesses nonetheless. A computer can be used to collate information and even to notify other police agencies participating in similar cases and offer them the same personality profiles.

The design of any computer program developed to create offender profiles must take into account all of the information outlined in this volume. The crime scene elements, personality characteristics, deviant behaviors, everyday activities, and other factors associated with violent criminals will be vital components of any such program. The authors of such a program must be aware of and theoretically fluent in the concepts of the academic disciplines already mentioned. Indeed, the authorship of such a program would be best achieved through the joint endeavor of investigators, theoreticians, and information technology professionals.

❖ ONLINE GRADUATE PROGRAMS, SEMINARS, AND DEGREES

There has been tremendous growth in online courses and degrees in the last 10 years. There have been offerings on campus or in off-campus locations. For example, the Southern Police Institute at the University of Louisville has offered homicide investigation seminars both on and off campus. They have had special and qualified instructors lecturing on psychological profiling for students, including former FBI profiler Roy Hazelwood. Many universities, including the University of Louisville and the University of Central Florida, offer psychological profiling courses and certificates for a collection of coursework both online and in the classroom.

Government agencies and police departments sometimes offer seminars on psychological profiling. For example, the Australian Institute of Criminology offers a seminar on the introduction to psychological profiling and an assessment of its accuracy in assisting violent crime investigations. There are also private companies that will teach the principles of psychological profiling. Forensic Solutions, LLC, advertises on the Internet a criminal profiling offering for students interested in pursuing a career in psychological profiling. The site also advertises that investigative and court consultations are available with the initial consultation free.

Of course the FBI's Behavioral Science Unit (BSU) appears to be held in the highest regard not only as the practitioners but as instructors. On the homepage of the FBI, the BSU is featured. The site states, "The Behavioral Science Unit focuses on developing new and innovative investigative approaches and techniques to the solution of crime by studying the offender, and his/her behavior and motivation" (www.fbi.gov/hq/td/academy/bsu/bsu.htm). It continues, saying that the BSU "conducts specialized and applied training . . . as they pertain to law enforcement for New Agents, FBI in-services and symposia, as well as for the FBI National Academy Program. . . ."

Our search of the Internet for online programs turned up many that offer a master's degree. There are few that offer a PhD in psychological profiling with all classes taken online, but we have an opinion that this too will change as time passes. It will be up to the market to decide whether the academic rigor and the success of such graduates will assist the resolutions of violent crimes in the future. Despite any such debate, the more students and law enforcement professionals have in this field, the more likely they will be able to investigate and bring to a resolution many of the unsolved violent crimes and cold cases that each agency and jurisdiction has become accustomed to.

❖ CONCLUSION

The computer revolution is having a dramatic influence on the criminal justice system. Computers have been in use for some time now by law enforcement for storage of records, personnel files, and criminal files; for case management; and for management of fiscal matters. Computers are also now used to track crimes and criminals. Psychological profiling would seem to be the next logical task for the computer. The human art of profiling can benefit from the speed and accuracy of analysis that computer technology represents.

Profiling is finally coming of age in the battle against violent crime. We have stressed in this volume not only the components of profiling but the need for profiling itself. As we noted in Chapter 1, a profile can narrow the range of effort, identify suitable interrogation techniques, and help with the evaluation of the unknown suspect's personal belongings. Profilers should make use of all available legitimate resources, including sociological, psychiatric, psychological, and crim-inological theory; the experiences and expertise of law enforcement officials; and computer technology. The computer may be the next major advance in our arsenal of weapons against crime.

❖ REFERENCES

Casey-Owens, M. (1984). Anonymous letter writer. A psychological profile? *Journal of Forensic Sciences, 29*(3), 816–819.

Godwin, J. (1978). *Murder USA: The ways we kill each other.* New York: Ballantine.

Holmes, R., & Holmes, S. (2005). *Suicide: Theory, practice and investigation.* Thousand Oaks, CA: Sage.

Credits

Chapter 1

Table 1.1 SOURCE: Adapted from "Psychological Profiling," by V. Geberth, 1981, *Law and Order, 29*, 46–49; and *Murder in America* (2nd ed.), by R. Holmes & S. Holmes, 2000, Thousand Oaks, CA: Sage.

Steven Kazmierczak SOURCE: © Getty Pictures.

Cho Seung-Hui SOURCE: © Getty Pictures.

Chapter 2

Case Profile SOURCE: Author's files.

Chapter 4

Figure 4.1 SOURCE: © Sigmund Freud Museum/Writer Pictures / drr.net.

Table 4.1 SOURCE: From *Criminal Man, According to the Classification of Cesare Lombroso,* by G. Lombroso-Ferrero, 1911, New York: G. P. Putnam's Sons.

Table 4.2 SOURCE: From "Men and Their Bodies: The Relationship Between Body Types and Behavior," by R. Montemayor, 1978, *Journal of Social Issues, 34*(1), p. 56.

Chapter 5

Table 5.1 SOURCE: From "Scene and Profile Characteristics of Organized and Disorganized Murders," 1985, *FBI Law Enforcement Bulletin, 54*, pp. 18–25.

Table 5.2 SOURCE: From "Scene and Profile Characteristics of Organized and Disorganized Murders," 1985, *FBI Law Enforcement Bulletin, 54*, pp. 18–25.

Table 5.3 SOURCE: From "Crime Scene and Profile Characteristics of Organized and Disorganized Murders," 1985, *FBI Law Enforcement Bulletin, 54*, pp. 18–25.

Chapter 6

Table 6.1 SOURCE: From "Arson Fire Statistics," by the U.S. Fire Association, 2007. Retrieved April 1, 2008, from: www.usfa.dhs.gov/statistics/arson/index.shtm.

Table 6.2 SOURCE: From "Crime in the United States, 2006," by the U.S. Department of Justice, 2007, in *SOURCEbook of Criminal Justice Statistics,* Washington, DC: U.S. Government Printing Office.

Table 6.3 SOURCE: From "One Man, More Than 100 Fires: Seattle Area's Wave of Terror," by L. Sharn and D. Glamser, 1994, *USA Today,* p. 9A.

Table 6.4 SOURCE: From "A Report of Essential Findings From a Study of Serial Arsonists," by A. Sapp, T. Huff, G. Gary, D. Icove, and P. Horbert, 1994, unpublished manuscript.

Table 6.6 SOURCE: Adapted from *Crime Classification Manual* (2nd ed.), by J. Douglas, A. W. Burgess, A. G. Burgess, and R. Ressler, 2006, San Francisco: John Wiley & Sons.

Table 6.7 SOURCE: From *Crime Classification Manual* (2nd ed.), by J. Douglas, A. W. Burgess, A. G. Burgess, and R. Ressler, 2006, San Francisco: John Wiley & Sons.

Chapter 9

Box on p. 173 SOURCE: APBnews.com, July 11, 2001.

Table 9.1 SOURCE: Adapted from *Child Molesters: A Behavioral Analysis for Law Enforcement Officers Investigating the Sexual Exploitation of Children by Acquaintance Molesters,* by K. Lanning, 2001, Washington, DC: National Center for Missing and Exploited Children, pp. 25–26.

Chapter 11

Figure 11.1 SOURCE: From *The Satanic Bible,* by A. Lavey, 1969, New York: Avon, p. 25.

Chapter 12

Table 12.1 SOURCE: From "The Measurement of Mental Rape: An Experimental Model for Studying Conceptual Spaces," by D. Stea, 1969, in K. Cox and R. Golledge (Eds.), *Behavioral Problems in Geography,* Evanston, IL: Northwestern University Press.

Table 12.2 SOURCE: Adapted from *The Image of the City,* by K. Lynch, 1960, Cambridge, MA: MIT Press, and "Place, Space and Police Investigations: Hunting Serial Violent Offenders," by D. Rossmo, 1995(a), in J. Eck and D. Weisburd (Eds.), *Crime and Place* (Vol. 4), Monsey, NY: Criminal Justice Press.

Table 12.3 SOURCE: From "Place, Space, and Police Investigations: Hunting Serial Violent Killers," by D. Rossmo, 1995(a), in J. Eck and D. Wesiburd (Eds.), *Crime Prevention Studies* (Vol. 4), Monsey, NY: Criminal Justice Press.

Chapter 14

Figure 14.1 SOURCE: © Bettmann/CORBIS.

Index

About the Authors

Ronald M. Holmes is the coroner in Louisville, Kentucky, a post he has held since 2003. Before he was elected to this position he was a professor of justice administration at the University of Louisville for 28 years. He has written numerous books on serial murder, mass murder, suicide, homicide, sex crimes, psychological profiling, and the criminal justice system. He is also the author of scores of articles in professional journals on related criminal justice topics.

Stephen T. Holmes is associate dean and associate professor of criminal justice at the University of Central Florida. Prior to this position, he was a social science analyst for the National Institute of Justice in Washington, DC. He has written 8 books and more than 15 scholarly articles dealing with policing, drug testing, probation and parole issues, and violent crime. He received his doctorate from the University of Cincinnati.